Ethics as First Philosophy

Ethics as First Philosophy

*The Significance of
Emmanuel Levinas for Philosophy,
Literature and Religion*

Edited by

Adriaan T. Peperzak

ROUTLEDGE   NEW YORK AND LONDON

Published in 1995 by

Routledge
29 West 35th Street
New York, NY 10001

Published in Great Britain in 1995 by

Routledge
11 New Fetter Lane
London EC4P 4EE

Copyright © 1995 by Routledge

Printed in the United States of America

All rights reserved. No part of this book may be reprinted or reproduced or utilized in any form or by any electronic, mechanical, or other means, now known or hereafter invented, including photocopying and recording, or in any information storage or retrieval system without permission in writing from the publishers.

Library of Congress Cataloging-in-Publication Data

Ethics as first philosophy / edited by Adriaan T. Peperzak.
      p.   cm.
  Includes bibliographical references and index.
    ISBN 0–415–91142–7. — ISBN 0–415–91143–5 (pbk.)
  1. Levinas, Emmanuel. 2. Levinas, Emmanuel—Ethics.
  I. Peperzak, Adriaan Theodoor, 1929– .
  B2430.L484E78 1995
  194—dc20
                                                           95–8032
                                                              CIP

Table of Contents

Key to Abbreviations — VII
Preface — IX

Part One: Characterizations

1. Catherine Chalier: *The Philosophy of Emmanuel Levinas and the Hebraic Tradition* — 3
2. Robert Gibbs: *Height and Nearness: Jewish Dimensions of Radical Ethics* — 13
3. Charles E. Scott: *A People's Witness beyond Politics* — 25

Part Two: Ethics as First Philosophy

4. Bernhard Waldenfels: *Response and Responsibility in Levinas* — 39
5. Hugh Miller: *Reply to Bernhard Waldenfels, "Response and Responsibility in Levinas"* — 53
6. Patricia H. Werhane: *Levinas's Ethics: A Normative Perspective without Metaethical Constraints* — 59
7. Elisabeth Weber: *The Notion of Persecution in Levinas's Otherwise Than Being or Beyond Essence* — 69
8. Robert Bernasconi: *"Only the Persecuted...": Language of the Oppressor, Language of the Oppressed* — 77
9. Fabio Ciaramelli: *The Riddle of the Pre-original* — 87
10. Paul Davies: *On Resorting to an Ethical Language* — 95

Part Three: Psychism

11. Andrew Tallon: *Nonintentional Affectivity, Affective Intentionality, and the Ethical in Levinas's Philosophy* — 107
12. William J. Richardson: *The Irresponsible Subject* — 123

Part Four: Art

13. Edith Wyschogrod: *The Art in Ethics: Aesthetics, Objectivity, and Alterity in the Philosophy of Emmanuel Levinas* — 137

Part Five: Religion

14. Merold Westphal: *Levinas's Teleological Suspension of the Religious* — 151
15. Theo de Boer: *Theology and the Philosophy of Religion according to Levinas* — 161
16. Jill Robbins: *Tracing Responsibility in Levinas's Ethical Thought* — 173
17. Adriaan T. Peperzak: *Transcendence* — 185
18. David Tracy: *Response to Adriaan Peperzak on Transcendence* — 193
19. John Llewelyn: *Amen* — 199
20. Hent de Vries: *Adieu, à dieu, a-Dieu* — 211

Part Six: Levinas and Benjamin

21. Rebecca Comay: *Facies Hippocratica* — 223

Contributors — 235
Index — 239

Key to Abbreviations

Levinas's Works

ADV	*L'au-delà du verset.* Paris, Minuit 1982.
AE	*Autrement qu'être ou au-delà de l'essence.* The Hague, Martinus Nijhoff 1974.
CP	*Collected Philosophical Papers.* Trans. Alphonso Lingis. The Hague, Martinus Nijhoff 1987.
DE	*De l'existence à l'existant.* Paris, Vrin 1947.
DEHH	*En découvrant l'existence avec Husserl et Heidegger.* 3rd ed. Paris, Vrin 1974.
DF	*Difficult Freedom.* Trans. Seàn Hand. Baltimore, Johns Hopkins University Press 1990.
DL	*Difficile liberté.* 2nd ed. Paris, Albin Michel 1976.
DMT	*Dieu, la mort et le temps.* Paris, Grasset 1993.
DVI	*De Dieu qui vient à l'idée.* Paris, Vrin 1982.
EE	*Existence and Existents.* Trans. Alphonso Lingis. The Hague, Martinus Nijhoff 1978.
EeI	*Éthique et infini.* Paris, Librairie Arthème Fayard 1982.
EaI	*Ethics and Infinity.* Trans. Richard Cohen. Pittsburgh, Duquesne University Press 1985.
EN	*Entre nous: Essais sur le penser-à-l'autre.* Paris, Grasset 1991.
HAH	*Humanisme de l'autre homme.* Montpellier, Fata Morgana 1976.
HS	*Hors sujet.* Montpellier, Fata Morgana 1987.
IOF	"Is Ontology Fundamental?" *Philosophy Today*, Summer 1989, 121–29.
LR	*The Levinas Reader.* Ed. Seàn Hand. Oxford, Blackwell 1989.
MT	*La mort et le temps.* Paris, Éditions de l'Herne 1991.
NP	*Noms propres.* Montpellier, Fata Morgana 1976.
NTR	*Nine Talmudic Readings.* Trans. Annette Aronowicz. Bloomington, Indiana University Press 1990.

OB	*Otherwise Than Being, or Beyond Essence.* Trans. Alphonso Lingis. The Hague, Martinus Nijhoff 1981.
OS	*Outside the Subject.* Trans. Michael Smith. Stanford, Stanford University Press 1993.
S	"La substitution," *Revue Philosophique de Louvain* 66 (1968), 487-508.
Si	"Signature." Ed. A. Peperzak. *Research in Phenomenology* 8 (1978), 175-89.
SS	*Du sacré au saint.* Paris, Minuit 1977.
TA	*Le temps et l'autre.* Montpellier, Fata Morgana 1979.
TaI	*Totality and Infinity.* Trans. Alphonso Lingis. The Hague, Martinus Nijhoff 1969.
TeI	*Totalité et infini.* The Hague, Martinus Nijhoff 1961.
TO	*Time and the Other.* Trans. Richard Cohen. Pittsburgh, Duquesne University Press 1985.
TrI	*Transcendance et intelligibilité.* Geneva, Labor et Fides 1984.
TTO	"The Trace of the Other." Trans. Alphonso Lingis. In *Deconstruction in Context*, ed. Mark Taylor. Chicago, University of Chicago Press 1986, 345-59.

Other Works

BT	Martin Heidegger, *Being and Time.* Trans. John Macquarrie and Edward Robinson. San Francisco, Harper, 1962.
ED	Jacques Derrida, *L'écriture et la différence.* Paris, Seuil 1967.
EL	*Emmanuel Levinas.* Ed. Catherine Chalier and Miguel Abensour. Paris, Éditions de l'Herne 1991.
FFL	*Face to Face with Levinas.* Ed. Richard Cohen. Albany, SUNY Press 1986.
PL	*The Provocation of Levinas.* Ed. Robert Bernasconi and David Wood. New York, Routledge 1988.
RL	*Re-Reading Levinas.* Ed. Robert Bernasconi and Simon Critchley. Bloomington, Indiana University Press 1991.
SL	Maurice Blanchot, *The Space of Literature.* Trans. Ann Smock. Lincoln, University of Nebraska Press 1982.
WaD	Jacques Derrida, *Writing and Difference.* Trans. Alan Bass. Chicago, University of Chicago Press 1978.
WoD	Maurice Blanchot, *The Writing of the Disaster.* Trans. Ann Smock. Lincoln, University of Nebraska Press 1980.

Preface

Before 1961 Emmanuel Levinas was hardly known outside a small group of French philosophers working mainly in the field of phenomenology and existentialism, such as Jean-Paul Sartre, Gabriel Marcel, Jean Wahl, Maurice Merleau-Ponty, Maurice Blanchot, and Simone de Beauvoir. These philosophers respected him as the man who had introduced Husserl and Heidegger into France through an extensive review of Husserl's *Ideen* (1929), an excellent dissertation on Husserl's theory of intuition (1930), a translation, together with Gabrielle Peiffer, of the *Cartesian Meditations* (1931), and several essays on Husserl's and Heidegger's phenomenology. His little book *De l'existence à l'existant* (*From Existence to Existents*), published in 1947, had attracted little attention, although Jean Wahl invited him in the same year to give a course for his students, the text of which was published soon after under the title *Le temps et l'autre* (*Time and the Other*). This situation changed, however, when, in 1961, Levinas published *Totalité et infini* (*Totality and Infinity*). Suddenly a master of thought was revealed who not only renewed twentieth-century phenomenology but also combined a radical critique of Western philosophy with a Platonizing retrieval of the pre-Platonic tradition of Israel. Translations into many languages spread his fame; the author was invited to give lectures in many countries, and he received honorary doctorates from several universities. Levinas then became astonishingly prolific (in 1989 his publications included more than five hundred books, essays, and interviews, including their translations), and the growth of secondary literature related to his work was overwhelming.

The difficulty of Levinas's language and revolutionary thought was such that widely held agreement among scholars with regard to its interpretation and evaluation was not immediately possible. Many readers did not recognize the rigorously philosophical character of Levinas's investigations; others suspected him of trying to update an old form of metaphysics in a quasi-phenomenological language of our time; still others accused him of promoting a pre-Nietzschean moralism and saw a confirmation of their judgment in the enthusiasm with which not only philosophers but also theologians, psychologists, and social workers hailed his work; finally some dismissed his thought because of Levinas's obvious interest in religion, the Infinite, and even God.

Levinas's publications after 1961 clarified certain questions, but they also posed new ones since his thinking had continued to evolve. His second major book, *Autrement qu'être, ou au-delà de l'essence* (*Otherwise Than Being or Beyond Essence*), which appeared in 1974, and the essays published shortly before and after it represent a new stage in his thinking, one even more original than the former. The language in which they are written is surprising, and the philosophical method practiced within them imposes high demands on the reader, even on those who are familiar with post-Heideggerian phenomenology. Much interpretative work has already been done, but still more is necessary for an adequate and thorough understanding of Levinas's oeuvre as a whole.

The philosophical work of Levinas became known in America through the early translation of his main texts by Alphonso Lingis (*Totality and Infinity*, 1969; *Otherwise Than Being or Beyond Essence*, 1981; *Collected Philosophical Papers*, 1987) and, since the early seventies, through a growing number of explanatory studies, most of which show sympathy for Levinas's attempt to renew the perspective and the methods of philosophy. The mixture of Heideggerian and sharply anti-Heideggerian features characteristic of his work made him a controversial figure among phenomenologists. Among deconstructionists, too, he became recognized as a key figure of contemporary philosophy, mainly through the English translation of Jacques Derrida's critical essay *Violence et métaphysique: Essai sur la pensée d'Emmanuel Levinas* (1964; the English translation appeared in 1978). Since this essay showed a deep respect for Levinas's work but criticized it for remaining caught in the intricacies of Western metaphysics, some Derrideans have spread the rumor that Levinas's thought is outdated by Nietzsche, Heidegger, and Derrida. The controversies generated by these differences in reception are far from resolved, but few philosophers outside of the so-called analytic philosophy deny Levinas's prominence as one of the two or three most important European philosophers alive.

The brief overview given here suggests the need for a judicious assessment of Levinas's significance for philosophy. The time has come to gather the results of thirty years of Levinas scholarship, at least to determine where we stand in the critical understanding of his oeuvre. This was the consideration that led to the organization of the International Levinas Conference, "Ethics as First Philosophy? The Significance of Emmanuel Levinas for Philosophy, Literature and Religion," which was held at Loyola University Chicago on May 20-23, 1993. Thanks to the generous support of the National Endowment for the Humanities and Loyola University Chicago, this conference brought together a large number of well-known scholars from America and Europe for a critical discussion of Levinas's work. All the speakers were asked to focus on key questions of his philosophy, leaving the application of his position to other disciplines and concrete problems within ethics, psychology, literary theory, and the study of religion for another occasion. From the papers given at the conference, twenty-one were selected for this volume, which presents their revised versions. The papers can be grouped roughly according to four general perspectives, though these perspectives overlap, while several papers combine more than one perspective. Some situate Levinas within specific philosophical or religious traditions of the past and the present; others concentrate on an accurate interpretation of difficult texts and their relevance for our time; some discuss key concepts and theses of Levinas's work in a more thematic way, while still others explain the affinities and differences between Levinas and other writers of the last two centuries, including Kierkegaard, Benjamin, Blanchot, and Derrida.

Before indicating the topics and theses of the singular contributions to this volume, I owe the reader a succinct justification for gathering them under the title *Ethics as First Philosophy*, a title given by Levinas himself to one of his programmatic essays (*Éthique comme philosophie première*, 1984) and used as subtitle for a French conference volume that was published after our conference: *Emmanuel Lévinas. L'éthique comme philosophie première* (1993).[1]

Levinas has declared several times over the years that he never wrote an ethics, and this is obvious from the ensemble of his texts if we understand "ethics" as a doctrine about the moral principles, norms, obligations, and interdictions that rule human behavior. The word "ethics" in "ethics as first philosophy" points to something more radical and originary: it indicates a "point" where the ethical and the theoretical cannot yet be opposed—or even distinguished—a "point" where the opposition between "is" and "ought" is neither valid nor even possible. If "ethics" is the thoughtful consideration (or theory) of the ethical—and primarily of its root or origin—while "first philosophy" is the most "originary" or "radical" dimension of theory—a dimension that, as originary, must precede all other dimensions—then ethics and first philosophy coincide. This is the position of which Levinas's entire oeuvre is the demonstration. In this he agrees with the basic intention of the great classics from Parmenides and Plato to Hegel and Heidegger, but his argument is different. Instead of seeing *theoria* as the ultimate level of human perfection, he maintains that good practice—the practice of the good—transcends contemplation, and his proof consists in refined analyses of an undeniable, central but trivial fact: the fact of everybody's being faced by other humans. The face-to-face reveals my being-for-the-Other and the inexhaustible responsibility contained in this structure. This "being-for" is not merely an ethical principle, however; it also is the "pre-original" or "an-archical" birthplace of all theoretical relationships. Responsibility generates *and* relativizes the autonomy of thematic thought. Philosophy is discovered to be the wisdom of an exhausting *philia*, rather than the long-standing devotion to the contemplative *sophia* of Western history.

The core of Levinas's philosophy can be approached from many perspectives and can be formulated in various ways, but all these ways and perspectives converge in their reference to the relation between the Other and me; or—in more abstract and Platonic terminology—they elaborate the basic heteronomy (which is also a heterology) that relates—without uniting—the Other to the Same. The contributions to this volume display a great variety of approaches, but the hermeneutical loyalty of their interpretations guarantees that convergence.

The three first papers presented here situate Levinas's work in its Jewish context. Catherine Chalier and Robert Gibbs approach Levinas's thought from his religious background and their own Jewish perspective, but they also show why and how Levinas is a philosopher, not a preacher or prophet. Charles Scott reflects on the same background as understood by a postmodern, non-Jewish philosopher.

The following four texts concentrate on two central concepts of the Levinasian oeuvre. Bernhard Waldenfels and his commentator, Hugh Miller, discuss Levinas's central concept of responsibility from a phenomenological perspective, and Patricia Werhane critically reflects on the basic principles of Levinas's ethics from an analytic point of view.

Elisabeth Weber offers a thematic study of persecution from the perspective of Levinas, while Robert Bernasconi analyzes the paradoxical structure of responsibility for one's own persecutor.

The next two papers focus on Levinas's language in order to understand the peculiarity of his thought. Fabio Ciaramelli explains why Levinas avoids the terms *origine* and *original* or *originaire*, but instead uses *pré-originaire* (pre-originary) or *an-archique* (an-archical) to indicate the a priori that precedes all freedom and ontology. Taking up discussions inaugurated by Blanchot and Derrida, Paul Davies investigates the problems involved in Levinas's "ethical language."

Andrew Tallon and William Richardson challenge Levinas's work from a psychological and psychoanalytical perspective, respectively. While Tallon discusses his phenomenology of affectivity, Richardson confronts his analyses of consciousness and preconscious substitution with Lacan's theory of the unconscious.

Little has thus far been written on Levinas's philosophy of art. Edith Wyschogrod fulfills this need with her study on aesthetics and ethics according to Levinas.

The next seven studies investigate different aspects of Levinas's analysis of religion and its unbreakable tie to the ethical. All the authors are concerned with the relations between religion, ethics, and philosophy and with the philosophical character of Levinas's treatment of them. Merold Westphal's discussion stresses some parallels between Levinas and Kierkegaard. Theo de Boer investigates the methodical aspects of Levinas's philosophy and its relations to ontology and theology. Jill Robbins concentrates on Levinas's analysis of "the trace" and Adriaan Peperzak explains how Levinas understands "transcendence," while David Tracy responds to that understanding from the perspective of a Christian theologian. Taking as his point of departure Nietzsche and Rosenzweig, John Llewelyn analyzes what Levinas, after the death of (a certain) God, evokes in the word "God," while Hent de Vries meditates on the expression "A-dieu" as a summary of Levinas's position between Kierkegaard and Derrida.

The last paper, by Rebecca Comay, focuses on a certain proximity between Levinas and another Jewish thinker of our century, Walter Benjamin.

Obviously, these brief sentences cannot do justice to the real content of all these elaborate studies; they only serve to highlight one striking aspect of each.

Many people and institutions have made this book possible, too many to mention them all. I want to especially thank, however, the National Endowment for the Humanities and Loyola University Chicago for the financial support that made the Levinas conference and this volume possible. During its preparation I was helped by David Coder's good advice and by the secretarial assistance of Debbie LoPresti and Kate Barrett. Without the dedication of Beth Spina, who before, during, and after the conference took care of all administrative and many managerial concerns, the conference could not have become a success and this book would not have seen the light. I want to express my deep gratitude to all of them. My colleague at Loyola, Hugh Miller, did all of the editing and composed the index of this volume. For this time-consuming and demanding, humble but most necessary work, I owe him special thanks.

Notes

1. Jean Greisch et Jacques Rolland, eds., *Emmanuel Lévinas. L'éthique comme philosophie première*. Actes du colloque de Cerisy-la-Salle, 23 août–2 septembre 1986. Paris: Du Cerf, 1993.

Part One: Characterizations

1
The Philosophy of Emmanuel Levinas and the Hebraic Tradition

Catherine Chalier

Emmanuel Levinas started learning the Bible while he was a child in Lithuania, yet he discovered the rabbinic commentaries later on, after the Second World War, after the Catastrophe, while living in Paris. His master was named Chouchani, a mysterious master but also a very renowned one. To this day Levinas does not neglect to quote and praise him. In this paper I shall explain why both the Bible and the rabbinic commentaries—which are absolutely indissociable for a Jew—are essential in order to understand Levinas's philosophy.

My first aim will be to articulate the significance of the tension between philosophy and Judaism in Levinas's thinking. In the second part of this paper I shall refer to the ideas of responsibility and freedom in order to elucidate better this significance.

Philosophy and Judaism

One of Levinas's philosophical aims is to refer to the Greek language of philosophy—a language he asserts to be of universal import—in order to elucidate ideas that come from the Hebrew worldview, from the prophets and from the sages. He wants to give a new insight into Greek categories and concepts, but he refuses to abnegate the philosophical requirements for accuracy. That is why when he refers to biblical verses or to talmudic apologies, or when he makes mention of one sage's name or another's, he does not want to prove anything: "The verses of the Bible do not here have as their function to serve as proofs; but they do bear witness to a tradition and an experience" (HAH 96; CP 148).

They bear witness to a tradition of thinking—and not to a faith. According to Levinas, this tradition of thinking is essential to human thought as such. Yet Levinas's philosophical writings are indeed philosophical because their author does not yield to the temptation of substituting the authority of a certain verse or a certain name for the philosophical requirement of argumentation.

Levinas explains that "the split within the spirit between Jewish wisdom and Greek wisdom," "the rift in a world which is both attached to its philosophers and to its prophets" (TaI 24), puts its mark on the spiritual and intellectual history of Western culture.

Of course, philosophers have been thinking about Judaism—thus Hegel assigned it a place in his system—but they have not really been anxious to learn something from it since, according to most of them, Judaism has been surpassed by Christianity. None of them could really admit Judaism as a living reality. Philosophers have borrowed some important ideas from the Bible—such as the ideas of transcendence or of creation—but Judaism cannot be reduced to a philosophy. This knowledge remains far away indeed from the lively tradition of reading the Torah, which is what counts in Judaism.

It is also true that Judaism has always been suspicious of philosophy. The rabbis have always looked askance at the ideal of a conceptual mastery of reality and of the autonomy of a reason that does not care to obey Revelation. It is true that Philo of Alexandria and Maimonides, for instance, tried to join together philosophy and Judaism. Philo tried to give an allegorical interpretation of the Bible by using Plato's philosophy; Maimonides tried to do the same by using Aristotle's main concepts. But their endeavor is not widespread among Jewish thinkers and it has been, and still is, much criticized. At any rate, Levinas's project is very different from these earlier ones.

Levinas lives and thinks in a world that is wounded. After the Shoah, how is it possible to think the way people were thinking before this disaster? He thinks he has to explain to the Jews—and, of course, to every one else—that Judaism can give us back the meaning we have lost in this disaster, a meaning that philosophy and Christian culture were unable to protect. He thinks his task—which is very urgent—is impossible, however, without referring to the philosophical way of thinking. One has to use a universal means of communicating, which for Levinas is the *logos*.

An alliance of Judaism with philosophy is necessary for the Jews who have been living in a Christian world for years without knowing anything about Judaism. It is necessary if we want Judaism to be something besides a mere memory, since a memory does not replace a civilization.

It is also necessary for philosophers to understand better why when a man agrees to be inspired by a prophetic book, it does not mean that he praises irrationality but that he tries to explain why human thinking may not be content with discursive reasoning. According to Levinas the appeal to prophetic inspiration means, instead, that the first word of all language, the Saying—the word to which all the others, the Said, answer—is greater than being and transcends it. The rational way of thinking tries to master such an "extravagance," such a "delirium," and to rebel against an original transcendence that breaks the *logos*. The rational way of thinking requires a consistent discursive reasoning. Yet it recognizes the extravagance against which it fights. In Levinas's philosophy, such an extravagance is the extravagance of the Infinite or of God, the extravagance of a transcendence that directs all thoughts and all words toward meaning.

After the collapse of Western culture, Levinas wants to explain to his contemporaries what is unique in Judaism, but he wants to remain faithful to the language of philosophy. He thinks that the conflict between, on the one hand, the upholders of inspiration by a prophetic book and, on the other, those who deny that such a book has any value from a philosophical point of view must not be settled by the victory of one camp and the disappearance of the other. We must not avoid the conflict, as it may be, according to Leo Strauss, "the secret of the Occidental vitality." Now if we try to oppose these two ways of thinking, and deny to one of them the right to exist, we shall see how this vitality—which is first of all the vitality of thinking—will decrease. It is certainly a good thing to condemn the obscurantism of all those who preach a total submission to the Bible and who use it as a means to prevent men from thinking, but do we have to agree that a prophetic book necessarily leads to superstition and fear? Is it indeed antiphilosophical to open the Bible and the rabbinic commentaries as Levinas does?

If we try to bring back in favor, in the philosophical field, the idea of inspiration, and if we want to explain that this has nothing to do with an archaic urge that prevents us from thinking clearly and distinctly, we have to be humble when thinking, which means that we have to look for the essence of thinking in our dedication to the Infinite and in our vow to answer it. Reading Levinas may help us to go forward on that way.

From this point of view I shall try now to explain the importance of freedom and responsibility in Levinas's philosophy and to point out the links between such ideas and the Hebraic tradition.

Responsibility and Freedom

According to Levinas the terrible suffering of the persecutions must not lead to despair but must rouse one to make new demands of oneself. When suffering, one may yield to the temptation of thinking only of oneself, forgetting the other man's distress. Yet Levinas argues that the memory of the persecutions and the guilty feeling that is a specific characteristic of the survivors—he says he experiences the latter feeling—must not lead us to despair but, on the contrary, to place new demands on ourselves. He wants to pass on how "the cruelty and the burning sensation of my suffering and the anguish of my death were converted into dread and concern for the life and death of my neighbor" (ADV 18).

Levinas remembers that the Nazi was yelling to the Jew, "You have no right to be." Yet, according to him, the Jew who remains alive must not try to protect himself by maintaining that he is an innocent being but by asking himself, when facing the weak and the oppressed, whether his life is indeed a just life.

Have I the right to be when facing the other man's suffering? Such is the human question par excellence in Levinas's philosophy. This question conveys a meaning of *holiness*. Levinas prefers this word to the Greek word 'ethics' for describing the highest human destiny, holiness meaning a life wholly for the other.

Let us now try to understand how he argues this idea and let us underline the tension between Judaism and philosophy in his argumentation.

The Critics of Autonomy

Most philosophers think freedom is equivalent to autonomy. Man is free when he listens to the voice of reason in himself and when he imposes his own will on himself. According to Kant, for instance, freedom means obedience to the moral law of reason. Consequently, if one man obeys the will of another, he loses his freedom. Heteronomy means alienation and prevents man from being an adult. By contrast, according to Rousseau, "to obey a law one has stipulated for oneself is an act of freedom."[1] A people that stipulates a law for itself is a free people, a people full of self-command and sovereignty. A people that surrenders to a law that is not its own is not free and does not even deserve the title of a people.

From both a moral and a political point of view, therefore, freedom seems to be the highest value. Nevertheless, Levinas does not agree with the traditional argumentation that I have here summed up very concisely. He criticizes this kind of freedom in a chapter of *Totality and Infinity* entitled "Freedom Called into Question." Levinas writes that according to this philosophical tradition, "the spontaneity of freedom is not called in question; its limitation alone is held to be tragic and to constitute a scandal. Freedom is called in question only as much as it somehow finds itself imposed upon itself: if I could have freely chosen my own existence everything would be justified" (TaI 83).

It is only because freedom fails that man criticizes it. Man knows it is impossible to live peacefully with another man if both of them do not agree to limit their freedom; he knows laws are necessary to protect himself from the other man's spontaneity of freedom. To this consciousness of failure, Levinas opposes the consciousness of guilt:

> This self-criticism [of freedom] can be understood as a discovery of one's weakness or a discovery of one's unworthiness—either as a consciousness of failure or as a consciousness of guilt. In the latter case to justify freedom is not to prove it but to render it just (TaI 83).

Thus, according to him, freedom is not called into question because it fails but because it is neither just nor moral. Morality does not start with freedom: it is aroused in man's consciousness when he becomes aware of the guilt of such a freedom. The neighbor does not oppose his freedom to my freedom, he does not challenge it and does not compel me to enter into a contract with him so that we shall not destroy each other, but he "calls in question the naïve right of my powers, my glorious spontaneity as a living being." Levinas concludes: "Morality begins when freedom, instead of being justified by itself, feels itself to be arbitrary and violent" (TaI 84). Contrary to the traditional view of freedom, Levinas thinks morality is rooted in *heteronomy*; the neighbor is the origin of this heteronomy. Morality does not take root in a reasonable will or a reasonable freedom but in my aptitude to welcome the neighbor in such a way that his life will be more important to me than my own life.

This idea of freedom being subject to an exteriority—the exteriority of God and the exteriority of the neighbor—is also one of the main ideas of the Hebraic tradition. According to that tradition, "the free man is pledged to his neighbor" (HAH 97; CP 149). Such an assertion is a paradoxical one, since, usually, freedom means that I choose to act in a certain way while when I am pledged, I am bound to do something. (The French word is *voué*, "called to," here "called to look after one's neighbor even if one does not want to.") If we assume that freedom is equivalent to autonomy, this paradox is indeed a complete contradiction.

Yet Levinas does not think that freedom is autonomy. According to him, moral freedom must be constantly oriented by the exteriority of the other. Nevertheless such a heteronomy does not mean alienation or tyranny for two reasons:

1. It helps the self to be conscious of the other man and to be aware of the true meaning of the word "human." This heteronomy leads to the "difficult freedom" of one who agrees to be a creature, a creature whose existence answers a calling that is prior to it, a calling which is waiting for its answer. We find a similar idea in Franz Rosenzweig's *Star of Redemption*, a book that was of extreme importance for Levinas's thought. According to Rosenzweig, creation is the miracle that enables man to listen to the calling of God asking, "where are you?" (Genesis 3:9). The significance of the self lies in its answering this calling. The uniqueness of the self—which is a prerequisite of freedom—does not rest in its self-asserting but in its answering the calling that appoints it as unique.

2. Heteronomy as defended by Rosenzweig and Levinas is a loving one: "The law is the very badgering of love. Judaism, woven from commandments, attests the renewal of the instants of God's love for man, without which the commanded love could not have been commanded. The mitzvah, the commandment that holds the Jew in suspense, is not a mere formalism, but the living presence of love" (OS 57).

For these two reasons, heteronomy does not lead to slavery but to goodness, and the paradox I mentioned—that "the free man is pledged to his neighbor"—is not a contradiction. But it also means that the difficult freedom described by Levinas is the freedom of a religious election.

Now, what is the significance of such an election? It entails the obligation to serve the other, the awareness of a responsibility that is prior to freedom, that comes first. Let us try to understand it better.

Freedom as an Answer to a Calling

Generally speaking, to be responsible means to answer for one's acts and words before other men. Such a responsibility is a limited one. It is founded on freedom and has no value beyond a free choice. From this viewpoint no one can be held responsible for what is beyond his or her freedom.

Levinas's thought is very different indeed. Levinas disagrees with the priority of freedom over responsibility and asserts responsibility to be infinite. He wants to explain how it is indeed possible "to be responsible over and beyond one's freedom" (OB 122). He argues that man is invested with responsibility even when he does not want to be. He belongs to responsibility rather than chooses to be responsible. "In spite of his wishes," he is responsible. In order to describe this responsibility beyond freedom, Levinas quotes Ezekiel 8:3: "And he put forth the form of a hand and took me by a lock of mine head." It is as if responsibility were a fate rather than a free choice. Passivity lies at the core of it; yet passivity does not mean inertia or apathy but man's ability to be moved by what happens to his neighbor, to be called by him.

Responsibility is an obsession that comes from a past that man does not remember. It describes the situation of a man facing another man: "Responsibility in obsession is a responsibility of the ego for what the ego has not wished, that is for the others" (OB 114). Man is not only responsible for himself and for his acts before others, he is responsible for others in such a way that he loses his innocence when he looks at them. He becomes really human when he is ready to answer, "Here I am" ("*Hinneni*") to the call of the other.

Philosophers who stand up for freedom criticize Levinas's ideas. They underline their excessive consequences: Do I really have to think that I am responsible for all the sufferings that occur in the world? For all the atrocities? Is it not enough for me to be responsible for the wrong I have done? Levinas's idea of responsibility seems to them extravagant, and they assert that it leads to a pathological feeling of guilt.

Yet Levinas does not surrender to such criticism. He does not want to be more moderate, even when philosophers say his ideas are not sensible. The Hebraic tradition is not moderate either. Let us understand now the link between Levinas and this tradition as regards this idea of responsibility.

I do not intend to find in an etymological investigation the secret of a strange idea, but it is worth mentioning that in Hebrew, "responsibility" *(ahariout)* and "other" *(aher)* are closely linked. Both words share the same root. While this does not prove anything, nevertheless in Hebrew words that share the same root also share a certain kind of meaning. "Responsibility" in Hebrew is also linked to "time" and "faithfulness," since the Hebrew word for "after" *(aharei)* shares the same root as well.

Now what does the Torah say about responsibility? When we read the story of Cain and Abel we understand that responsibility does not mean freedom. God asks Cain: "Where is Abel thy brother?" (Genesis 4:8). If God thinks this question is a relevant one, it means that according to him Cain is responsible for his brother's fate, even if he does not want to be. Levinas quotes this verse and writes, "One is his brother's keeper, one is in charge of his neighbor" (HAH 14). It is true that the story of Cain and Abel is a story of a real and terrible guilt, but the Torah emphasizes man's responsibility for the other. The question "Where is Abel thy brother?" is asked of everyone as if each were responsible for all the Abels who are suffering and dying in the world even if he or she personally has not actually killed them or made them suffer.

In the Talmud the Sages also argue in favor of a responsibility beyond freedom. In their commentary on the biblical verse "And they shall fall one upon another" (Leviticus 26:37), they explain: "It means they shall fall because of their brother's guilt, it teaches us that we all are responsible for one another" (Babylonian Talmud, Tractate Sanhedrin 27b). If a man is not opposed to his brother's guilt, he is responsible for this guilt. He will have to answer to this charge. According to Rav Papa, "The Princes of the world have to answer to all charges" (Babylonian Talmud, Tractate Shabbat 55a). And it is also worth quoting the famous sentence: "All Jews are responsible one for the other" (Babylonian Talmud, Tractate Shavuoth 39b).

This sentence means no one of the Jewish people may care only for himself. The Jews have an essential solidarity among them and this solidarity is so deep as to include the *Shekhinah*, the invisible presence of God among them, since, according to the Sages, the *Shekhinah* does not hesitate to go with them into exile. And it is worth remembering here that, again according to the Sages, hatred and a lack of responsibility brought about this exile.

The Sages teach that it is impossible to manage on one's own without taking care of the other. On the contrary, they think that the fate of the just depends on the iniquity of the people: "The just man perishes and no one cares: good men die and no one realizes that it is because of the surrounding perversity that they die" (Ibid.). It is as if the weight of evil were so heavy on man's shoulders that he could not remain alive and even less take refuge in an easy conscience. No one may thus try to save his or her life when humanity is in distress and unable to find those true values that would help it to recover. It is impossible for someone who is part of "the Covenant of responsibility," the *Brit LaHariout*, to desert and to choose the easy way of a proud and selfish freedom.

Even the non-Jews are bound to the Covenant of responsibility since, according to the Tradition, they all belong to the Covenant of Noah. In a beautiful comment on the verse "And they went unto Noah into the ark ... and the Lord shut him in" (Genesis 7:16), Levinas explains that it was impossible for Noah to shut the door and be safe with his family and the animals while all the other peoples were doomed to die. "A human soul does not retreat into itself.... How would it be able to retreat when humanity is perishing? Here lies the impossibility of interiority.... No one may remain in one's self: man's humanity, subjectivity, is a responsibility for the other, an extreme vulnerability" (HAH 97; CP 149).

The Jewish tradition constantly underlines the importance of this responsibility for the other and the feeling that one has to be liable for what one does or does not do. It stresses the impossibility of forsaking one's neighbor. Even Moses had to suffer with his people. According to the Talmud, he used to say, "Seeing that the people of Israel suffer, I suffer with them" (Babylonian Talmud, Tractate Taanith 11a)—and we know he did not enter the promised land.

But the responsibility and feeling in question here are not born from free choice. Man does not want to be responsible instead of selfish. He is called to responsibility because he belongs to the Covenant of Noah or to the Covenant of Abraham. Responsibility does not result from a free choice but from the consciousness of this Covenant, which has elected man before he could utter a word. And of course it does not mean man is happy to be responsible for the other; he will most likely try to forget it.

In the Torah, election does not give man special rights of superiority or priority. On the contrary, it stresses man's duties and man's responsibility, a responsibility that is incumbent on him and him alone. Man may not be released from it. He may not pass his responsibilities on to someone else. Election is also linked to the feeling of strangeness in the world and to the necessity of a teaching which is not a natural one: "I am a stranger in the earth: hide not thy commandments from me" (Psalm 119:19). These commandments must help us to live according to values that are different from what we find in nature. Election means obedience to these commandments. Instead of being proud and eager to dominate, instead of thinking his conscience is the true measure of all values and meanings, a man who obeys election knows he has to submit to a teaching that requires a lot from him, most of all humility, *anava*.

Humility is indeed a high value in the Bible. Abraham, in his prayer for Sodom, says, "Behold now, I have taken upon me to speak unto the Lord, which am but dust and ashes" (Genesis 18:27). Moses is said to have been the humblest man of his generation, yet the best example of humility lies in Abraham's answer to God when he calls him and orders him to leave his country: "Here I am." It is indeed not an easy answer when this calling prevents one from remaining serene in one's own country and forces one to go into exile. But this answer, "Here I am," is also the beginning of humanity, since humanity begins in the alertness of mind that helps man understand that the calling is indeed for the benefit of humanity. Thus when one hears the calling, one has to leave one's native country if one wants to be human.

Consequently we may argue that the significance of responsibility in the Torah is linked to a very special idea of a truly human man. For this man, election prevails over freedom, solidarity prevails over peace of mind, and humility and alertness of mind prevail over concern for oneself. Yet in the Judaic tradition such ideas are not explained in a philosophical way. As we have noted, the rabbis were not concerned with philosophy; they were even suspicious of it, except for some great philosophers in the Middle Ages, such as Maimonides. Now when Levinas writes: "The responsibility for another is precisely a saying prior to anything said. The surprising saying which is a responsibility for another is against 'the winds and tides' of being, is an interruption of essence, a disinterestedness imposed with a good violence" (OB 43), or when he explains how one must "show in saying, qua approach, the very de-posing or desituating of the subject, which nonetheless remains an irreplaceable uniqueness, and is thus the subjectivity of the subject" (OB 48), he argues, in a philosophical way, the significance of the idea of election. He gives a new insight into the philosophical ideas about responsibility, freedom, and subjectivity thanks to his faithfulness to his Jewish heritage.

After its dedication "to the memory of those who were closest among the six million assassinated by the National Socialists and the millions on millions of all confessions and all nations, victims of the same hatred of the other man, the same antisemitism," *Otherwise than Being* bears in its first epigraph a quotation from Ezekiel: "Or if a righteous man turn from his righteousness and do what is wrong, and I make that the occasion for bringing about his downfall, he shall die; because you did not warn him, he shall die for his sin, and the righteous deeds which he has done shall not be remembered, but his blood will I require at your hand" (3:20). This epigraph is significant. It is linked to Levinas's main idea of election as an infinite responsibility. The calling is indeed a calling to a responsibility for the other, without explanation and without justification. "The surprising saying" is inscribed in man's subjectivity even if he is not well aware of it.

When Levinas explains how responsibility is indeed infinite and prior to freedom, when he analyzes how this responsibility is above all explanation and justification and how man's subjectivity is structured as a "for-the-other," he does not only try to philosophize "otherwise." I think that he is trying to use the philosophical medium, the *logos*, in order to help us understand the significance of ideas that come from the Torah, and above all the significance of election. The "break" in man's desire to be, the interruption of being that occurs when God calls and man answers—"Here I am"—are the source of his new way of understanding responsibility. Levinas uses a philosophical language that in spite of all its greatness was compromised by the terrible calamities of this century. The language of philosophy has been distorted by those philosophers who were faithful to the idea that responsibility must be limited by freedom. These philosophers also thought that what happens to one's neighbor is less important than the fate of being (Heidegger). But for Levinas, the ontological question is not the first question in philosophy. According to him the main question is indeed the question of the Good beyond being.

The Tables of the Law

Man's responsibility is not only a private behavior: it has to become the core of an entire civilization, it has to become the common behavior of a people.

Yet political institutions do not always secure freedom and justice. When they fail, the only protection against barbarity is man's inner life, man's election, or man's assignment to responsibility. During their long history, the Jews often have had to live without the protection of political institutions: they have had to watch over a "morality without institutions" (NP 181). Nevertheless, such a morality is not enough, the inner life is not sufficient: "An existence that is free, and not a velleity for freedom, presupposes a certain organization of nature and society; the sufferings of torture, stronger than death, can extinguish inward freedom. Even he who has accepted death is not free. The insecurity of the morrow, hunger and thirst scoff at freedom" (TaI 241). Thus it is necessary to have laws and political institutions. Levinas explains that this necessity means that a people has "to fight for the Republic" (DL 198). Let us here point out a difficulty in his philosophy.

On the one hand, Levinas says that a people has to fight for the Republic, and he seems, uncharacteristically, to stand up for autonomy rather than heteronomy since, in a republic, the laws are the laws of the people. On the other hand, he writes: "Hence freedom would cut into the real only by virtue of institutions. Freedom is engraved on the stone of the tables on which laws are inscribed—it exists by virtue of this incrustation of an institutional existence. Freedom depends on a written text, destructible to be sure, but durable, on which freedom is conserved for man outside of man" (TaI 241), while adding that freedom may lead to a possible tyranny of what remains impersonal. Even in a republic whose institutions stand up for freedom and justice, tyranny arises when man forgets the necessity of the inner life, when he thinks written laws are sufficient to look after morality.

In the passage I have just cited, the sentence "Freedom is engraved on the stone of the tables" is a clear allusion to the Bible. Nevertheless, in the Bible, this freedom is inseparable from heteronomy, as I have already pointed out. I shall quote here a famous sentence from *Sayings of the Fathers*: "And Scripture [Exodus 32:16] says, 'And the tables were the work of God, and the writing of God graven on the tables,' read not *haruth*, that is to say, 'graven,' but *heruth*, that is to say, 'freedom,' for none is your freeman but he who is occupied in the study of the Torah."[2] Is there thus a real contradiction in Levinas's thought? How can he claim that a people has to fight for the Republic and, at the same time, argue in favor of heteronomy?

I do not think there is such a contradiction in his thought because according to him, all laws—be they the laws given to men by God or the laws created by men in order to live better together—call for man's inner life. Man must listen to this calling as if it were a personal commandment—"Thou shalt"—that compels him to obey.

It means that even in a republic, even when laws are the expression of the free will of a people (autonomy) and not the expression of the will of God (heteronomy), one has to obey the laws as if they were a personal requirement. Therefore Levinas thinks that even in a republic, man has to welcome the laws as if they were mandates, as if they were addressed to him personally, since without the inner life, even the laws of a republic will turn into tyranny. Thus receptivity to laws is always bound to heteronomy, since all laws are in need of man's inner life—which does not mean spontaneity but obedience to a calling. And, according to Levinas, the ultimate meaning of such a calling is *holiness*, life for the other.

Notes

1. Jean-Jacques Rousseau, *Le contrat social* (Paris: Garnier-Flammarion, 1965), 56.
2. *Sayings of the Fathers*, trans. R. Travers Herford (New York: Schocken Books, 1962), chapter 6, n. 2, p. 151.

2
Height and Nearness: Jewish Dimensions of Radical Ethics

Robert Gibbs

Injustice is suffered in this world, not in the next. And ethics seeks justice here and now, not in the world to come. But ethics does not conform to this world, it does not affirm this place. Instead, it makes a demand on us, a demand that obliges even before it is comprehended. Ethics demands a transcendence in the material world, a gap or shadow, an aura, a flashing, that orients us toward others and toward the transcendent responsibility for others. My responsibility demands more of me than I want or know, more than I can think or choose—but it does not ask me to exist as an angel, in some eternal mode without a body. Transcendence cannot transport me to some other kind of place and time but must disrupt me here and now, commanding me to transcend myself and remain here and now.

We are most familiar with Levinas's exploration of the ethical dimensions of time. Our normal perceptions of time are disrupted as the now becomes an urgent present, the past a deep past that was never present, and the future a not-yet that lies beyond the horizon of expectation. But consider the correlate change in understanding space. If my now has become a moment in which to respond to the other person's needs, then my here must also change under the force of ethics. While it is always true that I am here (and not somewhere else), the transcendent demand of ethics is not that I go somewhere else, to some there. Rather, the nature of here itself is changed. Here is not the place I occupy on my own, my little kingdom of control. The here of totality is the here of my consciousness, of my body, as my own space. In the place of such a here, the here must be seen in relation to an other person, to someone who is not connected to me. But that is not the face-off between two people who are each their own heres. Rather, the relation is a directedness toward the other person. A point becomes a vector, or even better a field. Transcendence occurs in this world not by ecstatically pulling me out to some other world but by changing what it means to be in this world. In response to the relativity of frames of reference in a mathematical model, I propose we orient ourselves in space by relating to others. Spatiality will become charged with ethical force, and my own place, my here, will become a place of response, a place oriented by the other person's demand.

I must add that this paper attempts something a bit more complicated than merely turning the space of ethics into the ethics of space, because my claim is that the two dimensions Levinas interprets (height and nearness) are developed through Jewish tradition. To explore the radical transcendence disrupting my here will require a relation to theology, to a discussion about the spatiality of God. But, as we know fairly well, in Jewish thought God's spatiality is not like that of a chair, or even a partner, and certainly not like that of a Greek god, reigning in his temple. The way to interpret spatiality in Jewish theology is to insist on ethical commandment in place of ontological description. Clearly then, Levinas's ethics, and our own concern for ethics, may be suitable for Jewish theological reflection, but it is not clear why we must make the detour from ethics to Jewish theology only to interpret that as ethics again. The detour, aside from offering us genealogical insight into Levinas, points out the radicality of the transcendence in ethics.

There is one further question that guides my thought: Why should there be two dimensions, both height and nearness? Why does ethical space need more than one dimension? The two dimensions work together, coordinating space. This paper views the two dimensions as establishing a rhythm, an unresolvable doubling of transcendence, a doubling that will reflect not only the two dimensions but also the relation of Jewish thought and philosophy.

Levinas's Treatment of Height and Nearness

The reorientation of space by ethics is a constant concern in Levinas's works. I will sketch the place of height and nearness in only a few works, among them *Totality and Infinity* and *Otherwise than Being*. There is a shift of focus from the first of these two works to the second: height is more important in the former, nearness (or proximity) in the latter. I will begin, then, by limiting myself to each work's main tendency and then noticing striking passages in both where the two dimensions intersect.

The subtitle of *Totality and Infinity* is *An Essay on Exteriority*, and that leads to Levinas's generally positive interpretation of separation. Ethics requires separation for the sake of the other person. The other person is free if he is separate from me, beyond my physical and mental control. So long as the other person is not separate, my here dominates the other person, permitting no ethical relations, no generosity, no relation to what cannot be made to be here, within my grasp, my mind's grasp. Levinas identifies the separation in question here, the fundamental condition of ethics, as height. The other person appears higher than I. Separation becomes height in order to indicate the lack of reciprocity between us: we do not constitute each other in a moment of encounter (TeI 77; TaI 103). Rather, the other regards me, while I am incapable of looking back in the same way. His height is the transcendence beyond my here, my grasp—but the asymmetry is that I cannot say that his here is similarly displaced. His looking down at me, therefore, is not my looking up at him. We have a disparity, an asymmetry in the spatial field that happens vertically and not horizontally.

This separation is the physicality of the human body, particularly of the other person's body. At one point, Levinas refers to "the human body raised from under towards the top (*vers le haut*), committed in the direction of height" (TeI 89; TaI 117). This sense of standing up, of raising oneself up, is the material referent of height. What transcends my here is another person's body—not the stars, the sky, and so forth. Indeed, the context for the physiological reference is not contemplation but labor, which in *Totality and Infinity* is always after ethics, after an encounter with another person. The face is at the top of the person, but, more important, the raising of the body, the standing up to meet the other person, displays the core meaning of height.

Paradoxically, height is not socially constructed by power; rather, Levinas insists, that height is encountered as the other person's poverty, destitution, and, most important, humility (TeI 175; TaI 200). This paradox of height and lowliness only shows further what sort of height Levinas is describing: neither the stars and the heavens nor the high and mighty (the rich and famous) but the one who, in standing up, rises above me, with an ethical demand. The demands of the other person transcend my here, my own sense of being in this place, of being at home. Neither the physicists' wonder nor the intimidating power of violence can so transcend my here.

The social image of height Levinas prefers is that of a teacher (TeI 146; TaI 171). The encounter with another person is one in which I am taught, not from some outside but from above. The powerless force of ethics, the command not to lay hold of the other with my hands or my eyes but to learn from the other, is height. Height signals this resistance without power, a command that can compel only pacifically. Levinas calls this teaching. And the other speaks from this height, constituted merely by the moral authority of an other person, a person who, facing me, questions and criticizes me.

This moment of encounter, where another person higher than me questions me, describes a curvature of space itself (TeI 267; TaI 291). Space is not linear, or simply continuous, but is curved up from me—and beyond. For height is the gradient of transcendence (TeI 59; TaI 86). Space moves up, disrupting my immanent vision of here. The primary dimension of ethics is one-way transcendence, a going beyond here, which changes the here, by opening it up. Face to face with another person, I witness the hole in my world, the gap or fissure in the totality of my making. Before the other, my here gains height.

Such transcendence in the here is bound up with metaphysics, and ultimately with God. Levinas links height with desire in *Totality and Infinity*, with that insatiable need for what is other, but other to such an extent that it can never be grasped, never be seen. Levinas uses the phrase The Most High, a name of God from Hebrew Scriptures, El Alyon, as the name for this superlative height of the infinite of desire in *Totality and Infinity* (TeI 4; TaI 34). Ethics requires a metaphysics of invisible goodness, of a beyond being here, but Levinas is not simply changing genres, ethics for theology. He resists the claim that the other person is simply an incarnation of God—which would make his discourse exclusively theological. Instead, Levinas writes:

"The other person is not the incarnation of God, but precisely by his face, where he is disincarnated, the other person is the manifestation of the height where God reveals himself" (TeI 51; TaI 79).

Levinas insists that in our relations with other people we find the only meaning that theological concepts can bear. Height, as found in the magisterial authority of the other, before whom I stand, is where God is revealed. And that height is bound to the other metaphysical term: the infinite. For Levinas, the infinite is not a negative judgment but a perfection. Height stands as the dimension of perfection, largely because of the asymmetry and the general sense of the escape of the other from my horizon. Thus "the idea of the infinite designates a height and a nobility, a transascendence" (TeI 12; TaI 41).

Levinas himself changes the emphasis from height to nearness (or proximity), and explains some of his difficulty with height, in the essay "God and Philosophy." He criticizes rational theology for limiting transcendence to being by its use of height, particularly in the *via eminentia* where God's being was higher than all height (DVI 95; CP 154).

The qualification of the verb "to be" by height, however, points beyond being. Levinas criticizes the cosmic sense of height, of the reference to the heavens over our heads, as too much bound to the realm of being. Height, at least in its theological use, seems to fail to evoke ethical transcendence.

To introduce the second dimension, nearness, I turn to *Otherwise than Being*. The family of Levinas's terms that are relevant includes "proximity," "neighbor," and "the approach." Levinas writes that the saying itself (as opposed to the said) is an approach to a neighbor, a coming near the other person (AE 61; OB 48). Ethics transpires between me and another whom I approach. I do not merge with the other person, nor need I make contact, but I come closer, opening myself to the other, offering myself by moving nearer. My here reaches out toward the other but does not include that other.

Levinas rejects the ontological view of nearness as a distance diminished, as though two entities were in motion or were found in a certain placement (AE 19; OB 16). Nearness is not simply the spatial contiguity (AE 127; OB 101) of two things that touch or border each other. Rather, nearness itself is the ethically charged approach to another person, a spatial relation from which continuity is derivative. Because we experience our responsibility when we are near another person, we reflect and represent space as continuous, as a medium in which two can meet (AE 103; OB 81). But the reflection on this meeting is a step back from the responsibility and the asymmetry of coming close to another person. The discontinuity of people who approach is the origin of our sense of space—and that sense is at first one of responsibility for the other person.

In this act of drawing near to the other person, responsibility magnifies, with the result that I do not reach the place in space where the other stands; rather, I must keep coming close. Nearness, then, is an infinite judgment, a kind of infinitesimal distance, which draws me in, both breaking up my here with something that cannot be included in my here and stretching my here toward what lies near it. The approach is one in which I have always taken one more step toward my neighbor, whom I am responsible to approach, ever nearer (AE 106; OB 84). This, says Levinas, is not an asymptotic *sollen*, in the mode of Hermann Cohen's ethics. Perhaps we can imagine it as not parabolic but hyperbolic: the other is not a term, fixed in space, to which I draw near, but is the one for whom I am responsible. Ethics notes that the more I draw near the further away I am. The more I see the other as the one for whom I must answer, the greater my responsibility will become. As I step closer, my obligations grow, the task of approaching becomes more arduous, and responsibility increases. This hyperbolic infinity of responsibility is not resolved by making contact with the neighbor. The contact itself expresses the vulnerability of my relationship to the other person, the vulnerability of being in my skin, but the closer I come, which means the more I answer for the other, the more I have to answer for (AE 177; OB 139). This infinition of my responsibility occurs in nearness to the other.

But it is also a trace of God, who, as the infinite, orders me to draw near the other person: to come closer to my neighbor (AE 191; OB 150). The theological term here becomes a way of naming the ethical force that I respond to in approaching the neighbor. One responds for the neighbor, but one responds to a command to approach. Here is a force that cannot compel but commands nearness. This shift into a theological gear is difficult for Levinas, because the nearness itself must carry the weight of the analysis. The other person's face is not the sign of a hidden God, of a being now secreted who could become revealed. Rather, the face is a trace of itself, a lingering of something that never appears. The neighbor is near but never present, and the infinite it traces is never present either. The infinite is the impossibility of presence, the nearness without continuity of the neighbor, of the one whom I approach (AE 119; OB 94).

The infinite gains ethical import by making the distance between us immeasurable, to mark between me and the other person a gap that I experience as drawing me near without ever getting me to the other person as orienting me toward the other, for whom I become responsible. Responsibility, with its traces and enigmas, requires a spatiality of incomprehensibility, of discontinuity. Nearness expresses the irresistible pull toward an other person such that, as I experience the impossibility of grasping the other person, I become available for the other. The theological significance of infinity is translated into this ethics of approaching.

Despite my own separation of the terms, there are texts in the works I am examining in which they overlap, or better, intersect. In *Otherwise Than Being*, on the penultimate page, Levinas refers back to height in opposition to Heidegger. He refuses the privilege of the court of being, that things must appear in reality in order to count. In its place, he refers to hyperbole, the superlative, the use of eminent terms to break out of the horizons of phenomenality and ontology. I am called by something that falls up and out of phenomenality. Here, in the context of breaking a hole in the horizons of reality, Levinas will say, "Height, Heaven: the kingdom of heaven is ethics" (AE 230; OB 183). Height becomes the hyperbole par excellence, the hyperbola of excellence.

Finally, in *Totality and Infinity*, there is one text concerning fraternity where height and nearness intersect. The fundamental equality and connection of each of us to one another centers on the individuality of each and not on "family resemblance." "Society must be a fraternal community for it to be the measure of rectitude—of the nearness par excellence—in which the face presents itself to my welcome. Monotheism means that human kinship, that idea of a human race which refers back to the access of the other person in the face, in a dimension of height, in the responsibility for the self and for the other person" (AE 190; OB 214).

The intersection of the two dimensions refers directly to theology, but only as theology refers me to every other person. The insistence on One God is an insistence that no one can be excluded from fraternity, and that no one is someone for whom I am not responsible.

Jewish Dimensions

This one God, the infinite, is recognizably the Jewish God. This becomes clearest in Levinas's essay "Revelation in the Jewish Tradition." The God who leaves a trace in Levinas's philosophical texts is named the Most High (El Alyon), a name that appears occasionally in the Bible and later Jewish texts. My task is briefly to rehearse how height and nearness emerge as important dimensions of ethics prior to Levinas. I will first address Levinas's immediate precursors and then jump backward quickly.

The first step back is to Rosenzweig, and particularly to *The Star of Redemption*. Levinas explicitly recognizes his debt to this work, and it is easy to find the ethical dimensions in it. Rosenzweig often refers to his work as orienting in space. He finds that speech, particularly of an I and a you, orients us. Indeed, not only does it locate a here and a there, but for Rosenzweig it also situates me in relation to the world and to God—who is now above. The mathematically relative relations between elements are converted into an absolute location and an absolute direction by the act of speaking with one another—a speaking that will also appear to be an approach to the other person. The theological relations in *The Star of Redemption*, moreover, lead directly to the ethics of relations with another person. Hence, as in Levinas, we have an ethical reading of theological concerns.

This is clearest when God's love toward us commands us to love our neighbor.[1] The responsibility we have to the infinite commits us to approach the one nearest us, the neighbor. Rosenzweig's play on this family of terms—"approach," "nearest," and "neighbor"—allows him to circumvent an ethics of rules or principles. The specificity of the nearest one determines the duty I have, and thus the spatial quality of nearness replaces the formalism of traditional philosophical ethics. But nearness is not merely physical in this case. Rather, the near one represents all others, represents the eventual diffusion of love and community to all others. The neighbor is the other person, who is not recognized by subordination to a genus but from whose specificity my responsibilities increase. His nearness, thus, represents the ever-expanding circle of responsibility that emanates from his unique speaking.

To take one more step back, I move to Hermann Cohen. His ethics does not condone the use of spatiality in orienting responsibilities. Moreover, Cohen is critical of the use of nearness to one's neighbor as a criterion of ethics because it is often used to justify preferentially helping your friends (who are near to you). But the structure of nearness to God is of great interest to Cohen, and when we follow Cohen's interpretation of the correlation of theology and ethics, we find again an important antecedent of Levinas's thought. In Cohen's *Religion of Reason out of the Sources of Judaism*, Cohen discusses nearness to God several times. It appears most prominently as the climax of the discussion of the love for God. First of all, we must note that nearness, for Cohen, preserves separation. The Jewish desire for nearness with God, as expressed in the Psalms and elsewhere, is not the mystical union, or any sort of ascent into the godhead but a recognition that God will always be otherwise than a human, and that drawing near to God is the highest possibility for us.[2]

Cohen argues that nearness is a process that people pursue. The act of loving God is a drawing near, not a being near.[3] The discrepancy between God's being and human becoming cannot be reconciled by establishing a neutral space in which two things stand in relation. Rather, the human party must approach, must always be engaged in a coming near and not a being near. I am never here, with respect to God, but coming here. While Cohen's system requires an ontology that Levinas will reject, it does preserve a difference between the two parties in question: and the nearness becomes a drawing near, an approach, precisely because those two parties can never appear in a common place. That difference is a here dislocated and stretched, or replaced by a field polarized toward God.

But the key move in Cohen's thinking is the claim that nearness to God is grounded in statutes.[4] That is, the significance of the approach to the infinite is found in the commandments. This notion follows the general thrust of Cohen's *Religion*, that relations with God are to be interpreted through an ethics of interaction between human beings. The drawing near to God then becomes a drawing near to the other person. The same absence of union, the same sense of fundamental difference and of the responsibility incumbent on me, directly correlates into an ethics. This correlation involves a solidarity and a suffering with others, but the approach to them, the drawing near, and the orientation of my here are at issue in this paper. Nearness is displaced in Cohen by drawing near, and so ethics does not happen in space but is the production of a space, of the possibility of nearness.

Let me now turn quickly to the Bible. The term for God that Levinas prefers, the Most High (El Alyon), has limited use there. It occurs often in the Psalms but otherwise appears in what historians would identify as the earliest strata of the texts: for instance, when the Canaanite priest Melchizedek makes peace with Abraham, Melchizedek uses this term to refer to God. Bilam, another Canaanite, uses it to praise God. And David and Moses use it in some of the most obscure and antique texts in the Bible.

When we advance to the era of the Sages (from approximately 70 C.E. to 500 C.E.) the term "the Most High" refers solely to buildings and generally represents the structure of height. The exceptions are remarkable, however. In the prayer instituted by the Sages, the Amidah (literally, "the standing," a prayer recited while standing up), the very first benediction contains this name of God in the midst of the list of God's names. However, in other texts, the term is seldom used and almost never refers to God. In the mystical texts of the Middle Ages, it usually refers to the highest sphere of heaven or the upper world, but not to God.

This term, El Alyon, the Most High, thus appears to be a term that since earliest times has not been used by the Jewish tradition, except in prayer. There is some discussion of people, especially sages, being higher than others, and a general association of height with teaching, but the ethical dimensions of height, and of the superlative reference to God, are undeveloped in the Jewish tradition.

The case is utterly different with the term for nearness, *kirvah* (or *karuv*), based on the root *kuf, resh, bet*. This root abounds throughout the different strata of Jewish texts in a wide family of meanings. The meanings share a sense of what is near, and even more of what approaches. But not only do we have the various senses of bringing, being made to approach, the ones who are near—called relatives—but strikingly, most sacrifices offered in the tabernacle and in the Temple were called *korban*: that is, near-things, or even better, things made near. The Sages use this wide variety of terms regularly, because of the multitude of references to them in the Bible, in relation to sacrifices, but also in referring to the various social and interpersonal dimensions of nearness. One of the strongest ethical meanings is to befriend, to become close with someone (see Babylonian Talmud, Tractate Shabbat 31a).

Why have I called both height and nearness Jewish dimensions, since height seems to be much better understood as a pre-Jewish dimension, one that Jewish thought preserved but did not employ? I would note to begin with that the obligatory sense of nearness comes not from any social context—there is no obligation to draw near a person, per se—but from the obligation to offer animals and food, sacrifices, to God. Levinas and Rosenzweig (and others at other times) have addressed the ethically charged field of nearness, but the source of that field's ethical import for Jewish traditional thought resides in the use of the same words for the goods that were brought near to God. Though the divine economy of those near-bringings is of interest in itself, the issue for us is what sacrifice has to do with ethics: the correlation between bringing goods near and approaching the other person. In neither case is there continuity; there is never a "getting there." As Cohen noticed, one cannot be near God because God is not there the way a human being is. There is a hole in the horizon; space is ethically charged and does not actually provide continuity between the two parties.

But when continuity is impossible, height does seem important, even for Jewish thought. In its best light, height directs us to the transcendent, absent, discontinuous shape of space. Looking up toward the other, one discovers that the immanent realm, even in its totality, is somehow punctured. As a hypothesis, I would like to suggest that the earlier tradition of seeing God not as high or as one of the High Ones but as the supreme one, as the Most High, was a way of attempting to push God beyond the ontotheology of the pre-Jewish community. That excessive supremacy is never lost in the tradition. But the localization of it becomes embarrassing. God's transcendence is not to be higher than the heavens. (Plato makes a similar move in the *Republic*, reproaching Glaucon for assuming that the visible stars were the mathematicals—and that very Platonic deconstruction or despatialization of transcendence is cited by both Cohen and Levinas.[5]) As radical as the transcendence of superlative height is, some alternative relation to transcendence is needed, one that will not invite what Hegel would call a bad infinite of "higher's."

The altar is the first solution, the place where goods are brought near. The near-bringing makes the absence of the Most High spatial, but it also disturbs space, making a place in space that does not fit in the normal geography of space. The argument from Jewish sources, in fact, would treat this one place, the altar stone, as the very point for orienting all space, both holy and secular. And we could oppose the movable altar of the years before the Temple with the fixed point of the altar in the Temple. That very spot, moreover, is identified by the Sages as the place where Melchizedek pronounces the name of God as Most High. The place for bringing near, thus, is the spot where the two dimensions intersect, and in so doing, orient all of space, a space charged with obligations to God.

But the Temple lies in ruins, and the Jewish tradition relocates the orienting spot to the home of the Sanhedrin, the higher court (see Levinas's talmudic reading "As Old as the World?"). The attempt to relate to the radically transcendent requires a more radically conceived relation of nearness—the nearness to other people. The space of study and judgment, a space oriented by the nearness of people, becomes the place where the Most High is approached. And the same puncture of space occurs because the place of intersection becomes a spot that transcends a merely immanent interpretation of space.

The theological problem is how to mark off God's transcendence, while the human problem is how to make ethics vigorous and irrefusible. In his interpretative essay for *The Star of Redemption*, "The New Thinking," Rosenzweig wrote, "Theological problems want to be translated into human ones, and the human propelled into the theological."[6] The dimension of height does not work well enough as a theological solution, and already in the Bible one can sense the inadequacy of it, but the dimension of height does indicate just where the problem lies in theology. The attempt to find a place on a continuum, even a place that is most noble and honored, fails to recognize the impossibility of locating transcendence. The search for a "there" for transcendence does not change the "here" enough, does not bind me to respond to an other. But, as Levinas noted, when I look up to another's face, there is a way I can begin to recognize transcendence in human posture in the uprightness even of a lowly person. By the use of hyperbole we can break out beyond being, for this dimension of height is a dynamic and a hyperbole directing us beyond being and beyond the immanent.

Only after thrusting us toward an outside and a beyond (which can never be found as such) can the truer sense of approach and of bringing near emerge. For the very excess of height now violates the continuum of space between two people. The separation between God and the human now appears as a separation between two people, as an unbridgeable gap, but one that is polarized by an ethical charge, a field of ethical force, directing me not to destroy the gap but; in accepting it, to transform my relation to the other person. Nearness becomes the basis of spatial relations but interrupts our normal views of space. The ethical significance of approaching another person lies, therefore, in the polarized gap. Height serves as a hyperbolic sign of that gap; it serves well because it denotes superiority, but it cannot fully serve to mark our relation with an other person because it leaves us imagining either an attainable distance or a sublime judgment vulnerable to a transcendental reduction in the mode of Kant's *Third Critique*.

To assess the Jewish dimensions in Levinas's ethics requires a rhythmic sequence of height and nearness. Levinas's use of the term "the Most High" reflects most likely the Torah passages by Melchizedek and Bilam and the first blessing of the traditional prayer. His rhetorical reasons for using it have much to do with a philosophical tradition that saw transcendence largely as height. In Levinas's terms, height secures an atheism, but only when taken so hyperbolically that we would not think height theologically. In Levinas's move toward proximity we sense a repetition of the earlier Jewish movement. The difference, however, is that Levinas does not abandon height and can use it, in fact, especially in *Totality and Infinity*, because the need to focus ethics away from the immanent is more pressing than the parallel risk of paganism was for the earlier Jews. But once we make allowances for this difference, we see a Jewish hesitation with height emerge in Levinas's writings.

That hesitation should not confuse us, because without the radical transcendence that height provides for Levinas, nearness could not possibly serve as radically ethical. But here I must make one more jump, because I wish to argue that the move from height to nearness, both within Levinas and within Jewish tradition, is parallel to the move from Jewish tradition to radical ethics. What makes Levinas's ethics Jewish is not the use of Jewish sources (generally rare in his philosophical writings) or the evocation of a Jewish revelation. No, the key point of identification is the insistence on a radical transcendence of God made concrete in a radical ethics—that height becomes nearness. Hence I would argue that Jewish tradition is particularly well suited to a correlation with ethics, because it deconstructs its own ontological theology in favor of an ethics of separate people, bound in an ethically charged field, not itself reified. That such a tradition needs to become an ethics is developed by the Sages, interpreting the insertion of the near-bringings to the altar in the Bible and further humanizing the radical claims of this nonontological God.

But does this mean that, conversely, radical ethics needs Judaism? Yes. Not in an absolute sense, and certainly not in a dogmatic sense. Jews have no monopoly either on this God or on the struggle for this ethics. But Judaism is of value in the sense of Hermann Cohen's great work *Religion of Reason out of the Sources of Judaism*. Ethics needs Jewish thought in the sense that it requires a true infinite, a radically transcendent God who can make the dimension of height turn into hyperbole. Without that infinite, that nonontological God, the relations between me and another person will always risk collapsing back into some sort of mediated identity, however richly dialectically constructed, and the demand of a Good beyond being will be impossible. Only where such height intersects nearness is space rendered ethical, is a saying possible, my saying, as I utter the words "Me voici," "Here am I," "*Hinneni.*"

Notes

1. Franz Rosenzweig, *Der Stern der Erlösung*, vol. 2 of *Franz Rosenzweig: Der Mensch und sein Werk: Gesammelte Schriften* (The Hague: Martinus Nijhoff, 1976), 239; *The Star of Redemption*, trans. William W. Hallo (Boston: Beacon Press, 1971), 215.
2. Hermann Cohen, *Religion der Vernunft aus den Quellen des Judentums*, reprint of 2d ed. (1928, Wiesbaden: Fourier Verlag, 1988), 248; *Religion of Reason out of the Sources of Judaism*, trans. Simon Kaplan (New York: Frederick Ungar, 1971), 225.
3. *Ibid.*, 189-90, 160.
4. *Ibid.*, 91, 78.
5. Plato, *Republic*, 529b.
6. Rosenzweig, "Das Neue Denken," in *Zweistromland*, vol. 3 of *Franz Rosenzweig: Der Mensch und sein Werk*, 153.

3

A People's Witness beyond Politics

Charles E. Scott

> But to hear a God not contaminated by Being is a human possibility.
>
> —*Otherwise Than Being*

"Oh hear, Israel, the Lord our God, one God." This prayer and affirmation without a copula permeates Levinas's writing. It is not a statement about pervasive sameness in reality or immediate presence. It is not a statement about a divine nature in which all people are participant. It recalls that God is the One who called a people, gave them to be Israel in a covenant that preceded their identity, freed them from slavery by a bonding they could not choose, and gave them in their lives a law of life. It is a prayerful saying by a people of God who do not have God before them. It is an affirmation by a people who came to be a people in the call, who were not before the call, who found themselves in a call that was there when they knew who they were. In it God is not a being but is nonetheless God, so other that nothing they say or know grasps or conceives this one God, this Other who gave them to be. As a people they are witness to this Other who is never an object, not even in prayer, and who gave them to be in a call beyond consciousness, to be hearers of God's word before all people, to be God's testament to the entire world. This awful responsibility, which is at once a gift of persecution, "a deafening trauma" (OB 111), and a destiny, which is alien, beyond Western identity, and yet something to which a people of the West belongs and to which European civilization belongs, this awful responsibility is the call to which Levinas gives answer in his writing. He thinks in response to an Other-beyond-presence, to an Other-beyond-consciousness, to an Other-beyond-human-origination as he calls into question the lineage of Logos, Theos, the Hellenistic Christ, the lineage of *Geist*, the self-presenting intentional subject, the divine condition for the possibility of rational truth, and human nature as the seat of responsibility. Levinas's thought and the ethics that he discovers answer the Singular Other of Israel who, One beyond Oneness, (is) the Only One who called this people and gave its individuals to know that what God gives is beyond conscious value. Levinas's writing knows that individual life in its flesh may not be taken by humans without violating the Singular One. He knows that God gives singular lives beyond understanding, and our hope is not in understanding but in obedience to the covenant. It is a people's hope. It is a covenant that requires an embodiment of responsibility to the flesh of others, to that flesh that is struck by death but, being able always to die, does not age as flesh and blood (OB 106). His writing is permeated by this affirmation, which has its bearing in impossible situations of death, persecution, exile, and suffering when a people knows that before God Theos and immediate presence are lost, that God—the Singular One—is heard as Israel remembers its name.

"In the form of an ego, anachronously *delayed*," Levinas says, "behind its present moment, and unable to recuperate this delay—that is, in the form of an ego unable to conceive what is 'touching' it, the ascendancy of the other is exercised upon the same to the point of interrupting it, leaving it speechless" (OB 101). We are turned by him to the other, not to a divine presence, as he turns to hear God beyond the contamination of human responsibility. The other beyond contamination commands our first attention. The movement begins in a people who, as a people, have already heard God, and in this beginning our attention is turned not to divine presence but to the other who is proximal to us in our having been already called. That this "us" is in some sense Israel is an issue that will recur. For the moment, I note that instead of invoking a category of universality, Levinas suggests—always indirectly and subtly—that we Westerners, we Europeans, are already of Israel and that Israel is of us. It is not a question of human universality. It is a question of a people already covenanted by God without choosing the commission or necessarily knowing about it. In this condition, we have an opportunity to discover ourselves as a people in confronting a responsibility that precedes our intentions and theories. We who are of the Greeks are more of the Hebrews than we may know.

In our thinking we must assume a contour of consciousness as described in broad idealistic and Husserlian terms: consciousness as a structure and movement that is a priori and before the presented object. The neighbor's coming, however, is not described by consciousness. "He" or "she" is not, in this coming, consciously ordered. The neighbor's proximity is neither spatial nor temporal nor present in a conscious presentation. The neighbor does not originate in any intentional synthesis. The neighbor's coming is not part of a social history. He or she does not occur first with a social definition as poor or powerful or strong or deprived or victim or gendered or child or attractive or authoritative or curly-headed. The neighbor does not come temporally as young or passing away or finite or changeless. The neighbor does not come spatially as here or there or present or absent. He or she is not contextualized by any conscious order. The neighbor comes singularly but anarchically, not as part of a stated whole. The neighbor is not part of a nation or race or culture.

His or her proximal but unpresent touch obsesses and persecutes consciousness in refusing the interrogation that the neighbor incites and in escaping the reach for which the neighbor calls. An act of consciousness is delayed in its self-enactment before the neighbor who, being without a who or consciousness, is timelessly before the act of consciousness that unavoidably bestows time and presence on the neighbor. The neighbor is before the before, unlost before being lost, utterly unpolitical before its political beginning and consciousness. The neighbor renders us speechless in giving us to speech. It denies consciousness the identity of its self-enactment in giving its identity. It breaks the truth of consciousness, its self-disclosure. Foundering in its struggle for recuperation, consciousness, which is always political, finds itself without the authority necessary to found an order for the neighbor and loses the neighbor in recognizing the neighbor. Whatever consciousness does regarding the neighbor, it contaminates by ordering the neighbor's coming: by orders of respect and benevolence, by orders of generosity, greeting, concern, protection, and nurturance. No politics will reinstate the neighbor's touch. No grammar will move the neighbor to renewed life. No gesture will designate the neighbor without contamination. No thought of excess will restore the neighbor to the integrity of its ownness. In this persecution of consciousness, this ceaseless cutting into the texture of consciousness's body, we must turn without authority to oppression and suffering to find the vacuum of our words and values. We are lost before we began. Our community is severed. *Homo politicus* finds its home in the neighbor's loss.

This incommensurability of the other and consciousness resonates with the incommensurability of God and Israel. Proximal and yet absent in presence, bespoken and yet unbridgeably different, the other is lost to its naming and placement. "A responsibility stranger than death," Levinas says (OB 194).

I wish to emphasize the importance of the notion that social history does not constitute ipseity. One might be tempted to hear the echo of transcendental thought in this anarchy. With ipseity we are not transcendental consciousness. Rather we face the transcendence of an unreachable Other whose call or covenant is already in effect in our recognition of ourselves, a call or covenant that does not constitute an a priori element in our identity but rather interrupts our identity in giving identity, a proximity that obsesses us in holding us to something impossible for us, one that sets us apart from ourselves and from *our* history and gives another impossible history in which we are without initiative and in which we are always beginning in loss before proximity. We face not transcendental identity but transcendent loss of our identity in the bestowal of our identity. Levinas chooses well the word "exile" in this thought. We are already—i.e., transcendently—exiled.

This thought is so very nongenealogical, so very non-Nietzschean. We might give genealogies of our limits and possibilities as a people. But even here Levinas appears to be willing to give the idealists the day in their accounts of consciousness. The problem is that the language of Levinas, its *abusive* quality, in his terms, is an abuse that is not inclined to find its capacity to signify in its lineage. Something proximate and other to its lineage is so privileged as to escape the history of abuse and exile. We could say that proximity is historical *before* any history or that it is political before any politics. And yet Levinas pits a Hebrew lineage against a Greek lineage, even as he joins them, pits a midrashic thinking against a thinking of *logos*, a lineage of persecution against one of aesthetic satisfaction and self-contemplation. He speaks as though the neighbor were there before determinant time and history, as though being were broken before being, as though responsibility were always unsaid, as though passivity has always already interrupted spontaneity, as though we were already called to the abuse of language before the instated orders of *logos* and self-relation.

This context of Levinas's thought is one of departure from the priority of consciousness and subjectivity in transcendental idealism, particularly its nineteenth-century legacy in Hegelian thought and classical phenomenology. He sees—accurately, I believe—that when the other is found in movements of self-presenting consciousness, the other is dying; that when God is the object of belief because of subjective necessity, God is dead; that when consciousness is founded in its own self-positing and self-recuperating movements, alterity is lost in the sameness of this reflexive movement. Through Levinas I hear in transcendental philosophy a certain blind cleansing of the other's otherness, a reduction of the other to the sameness of consciousness, a subtle and demonic attack on whatever takes consciousness from itself. And Levinas hears as well in transcendental thought an atheism in its theism that is far more severe than his own atheism in the name of God's otherness. The transcendental placement of God, the demand that God be for the sake of world order, loses God's continual misplacement, God's infinity, and God's specificity, which displace all conscious acts that would find God, name God, or know that God *is*. The other, rather, comes in a specific proximity and call, not hidden as a thing behind or beyond the phenomenon but as a proximity so real that I have no choice but to respond, so real that I am responding as I find myself to be. And I—I am in response to the other before the other is a phenomenon, before I intend the other in any way, before I am conscious of the other.

This context is not only one of departure from mainstream Western thought and experience. It is also one of hearing *in* Western consciousness an obsession that interrupts it. I shall return to this interruption, but I note now that we are not leaving Western thought in this departure. We are finding in Western thought a departure that it has ignored. This departure from consciousness occurs in Western consciousness. In Levinas's work we hear something of our lives that has been lost to our dominant values and theories.

The moment of maximum interest for us is not found in the theoretical sparring with transcendental thought in which Levinas engages with skill and subtlety. One *could* become dazzled by the ways in which Levinas uses the language of condition for the possibility of consciousness in order to overturn the transcendental conditions for alterity. Or one could develop and extend Levinas's thought of consciousness as assassination, language as abuse, and the other as persecutor. But *the* moment of interest occurs when thought comes to an end and one, in the silencing of reflection, hears and responds to an other—hears and responds not as a philosopher or priest or rabbi but as only this one who belongs to the other's proximity and who responds out of a passivity and a covenant that originates in the other's call or cry. I then do something in the interruption of originary spontaneity. I might do my best to redress the killing appropriation of my recognition of other, hear the other in a call that escapes my intentionality, and *take* responsibility in the responsibility that the other has already bestowed on me. I would then respond in my responsiveness.

This nodal point is beyond undecidability. Up to this moment nothing is decisive. Whether there is a God, whether the other is really there and outside of conscious appropriation, whether I am constituted by responsibility beyond spontaneity and the freedom of autonomy: all that is undecidable. Although Levinas makes his descriptive claims with the intention of accuracy, and although he means that his account is more accurate than other accounts, he has already required undecidability by his claim, which he thinks is accurate, that language and consciousness, in their meanings and syntax, are murderous distortions of the other. We know, in this discourse, that the other is before meaning and before the stated ethics that befall the other. We know that we must use language abusively in order to break its sense of essence and the dominance of its requirements. We know that the other is beyond the "is" that identifies and places the other. Hence what we know and recognize in Levinas's language is undecidable even if it is by the canons of descriptive discipline accurate and convincing. Only in the contortions of Levinas's language, contortions that give it its poetic effect, does the trace of something other to subject and object and beyond description cut the reminder that our covenant with the other is not produced, posited, or formed by anything that can be meant or signified. In its meaning and by its own account, Levinas's thought requires suspicion of *what* it says.

But this undecidability is broken when I respond to the other in a division from consciousness as I answer the other. I may answer in hatred or love or concern. But the answer in its language and recognition is also before language and before recognition of the other by name and status. Then it is the other and I before we are ranked in our positions of designation. I may pull the trigger, offer solace, turn my back, give food, or say yes in sorrow over my inability to be fully one for the other. In such "words" before there is language I am this one for this one, and life is real, concrete, decided. Nothing is derived from nature or rights. That moment is derived from proximity in call before there is selfhood and otherness.

I want to concentrate on this moment. It appears to me to be constituted by values that Levinas does not fully account for. It appears to me to be the appearance of a tradition that is before the other. And the bearing of this tradition, as it disappears in Levinas's account, is what I find most telling, most important, and what I shall call the crisis, the turning, and the before-politics of the other.

I shall turn for a moment from this most interesting point of movement from thought and theory to the other in order to raise an issue that will bring us back to this point. The singularity of our values and traditions usually defines our local practices. We know from long experience that when a locale or a people universalize their peculiar values and turn the tribal into an encompassing, universal expectation for all people, justification for conquest, colonialism, and oppression is a small step away. German tribalism and German National Socialism, for example, are not separable. Claims to racial superiority and claims to cultural superiority are often mutually dependent. Such experience gives us caution before any elevation of spontaneity and appropriative assertion over reticence, reserve, and kindness regarding the differences that separate us. We are well aware today of the dangers of local and tribal formations as we face the fragmentation, nationalism, and war that arise as various peoples reassert their ancient tribal and national identities. Such assertiveness is, I believe, among the dangers that Levinas's thought invokes as he turns the priority of consciousness and subjectivity in our lineage toward its inevitable assassination of the other.

Although I cannot here fully engage the question of universalization in Levinas's thought, I note that in his language there is—perhaps in spite of himself—a turning from universalization in the very claims to which he seems to give universal meaning. His descriptive claim, for example, that consciousness has as its necessary condition a radical passivity that is other to consciousness, so other that the possibility of dialectical relation between consciousness and other is impossible—this claim finds its crisis in a movement of response to the other that is not reflective or syntactic. This most interesting point of contact is both the meaning and the destruction of the meaning of Levinas's thought. His claims about possibility and proximity become in the retrospect of hearing and answering the other more like a proclamatory language that is closer to prophecy or a kind of prose poetry than it is to a systematic and descriptive account of essence and other to essence. The obsession that accompanies the ego's exile and persecution returns us always to something lost in every "said," returns us to the unsaid word of the oneself, returns us to the utter and fleshly other-beyond-consciousness. Our thoughtful, universalizing language dies at this turning point, a point to which Levinas's thoughtful and universalizing language brings us.

But this crisis point marks the space where the local and tribal are most in effect, and something like an unspoken universalization is the greatest danger in this turning. The unspoken universalization can happen in the radicalization of particularity as feeling becomes predominant in the other's proximity.

We might call this crucial point of enactment a tribal universalization that occurs when a people's sense of common identity falls out of question in their rituals, in their practices of returning into themselves, in their reinvocation of the common ways of dwelling which give them to know who they are *and* when in this movement they find not only themselves but also a feeling of specialness and ascendancy regarding others. This feeling of ascendancy is veiled in Levinas's thought. It takes the form of radical responsibility for the other in which one answers God and confirms the singularity of God's call in a people's most fundamental identity. "Oh hear, Israel, the Lord our God, one God."

Surely Levinas is guarded against such a predominance. Surely passivity beyond passivity and the one for the other are far removed from the control of feeling. And surely the very idea of the priority of feeling is an aspect of the privileging of consciousness that Levinas overturns with remarkable originality. But we are at the point where thoughtful precaution fails, where the overturning of universalizing syntax lapses. We are at the point of concretion and radical singularity of the other with me. We are at the point of my answer before the other, an other who is outside of discourse and the precautions of philosophy. This is the area where identity is most likely to function as a practical absolute, where I am most simply this Jew, this Gentile, the one who belongs to this language, these practices, and, above all, to these values. As I turn and find my neighbor in proximity—*in the turning*—who I am most particularly becomes definitive in the proximity as well as in my word of response. In this turning and finding my neighbor to whom I belong, feelings beyond which there seems to be nothing feel the place of my existence. Here is where I will be with God or without God, where I will feel bereft or liberated in a fleeting absence of God. Here is where values feel their value, where the important things of life stand out, where rituals speak in silent, life-giving meaning, where one knows nonreflectively how to live and die.

This concrete turning point is, in a word, the space of greatest ethnic determination. It is where all living things belong to a world, where meanings give syntax far in excess of our grammars and logics. It is the space of relatedness and disrelation, where one feels connected or dispossessed, where one feels one's life to be alive or lost. The determinations of one's life, in their full arbitrariness, are *already* intimate with the world and its things. These determinations give the world order. These determinations give the world in its apparent universality. The concreteness of things, of *their* lives, of *their* coalescence, is in their determination, and when things are determined in a call of other, when they exist already in external exposure to the word of God, they, in *this* determination, belong already in their existence to an ethnic God. Far from determination by consciousness, the other, determined by this God, is sedimented outside of the reach of consciousness. The other is identified from the outside, from an outside so removed from conscious origin as to be hidden and revealed by constant interruptions of removal from human intentionality and self-conscious identity. In this Hebraic determination, one *must* depart from the ethics of other Western peoples, depart from all that is foreign to the foreign proximity of "a God," depart from any theology that emerges from human familiarity in order to return to the recurrence of the other in its outsideness vis-à-vis human creation and bestowal.

This point of greatest interest, this contact with that which is other before ego-identity, is far removed from consciousness and subjectivity, but it is not on that account removed from determination and meaning, from the flow of practices, from the formations of lives, or from the meanings that let a world cohere. Although the other cannot be constituted by conscious intentionality or by the self-positing reflections of subjectivity, the other nonetheless gives passivity to the self. The other withdraws as other from the sameness of consciousness. The other exposes the I and renders naked what is covered by being. The other requires response. The other, that is, is determined as other in its interruptive determination of meaning, and in that interruptive determination an entire history plays, a history of covenant, call, guilt, mission to all people, separation from God, exile by failure before call, persecution by deafness to call, sorrow for lostness before God, and the joy of response to God in which, in the failure of the response ever to capture or see God, one knows obliquely the unspeakable Otherness of the One who does not cease to call because he has promised to be there, utter and apart, but proximate and life-giving.

We can see that 'what' is otherwise than being and beyond essence carries with it, in the language of its lost recognition and the power of its meaning beyond meaning, a tribal tradition, the heritage of a people in exile. And we can also see that what is beyond universalization suggests something more than a universal. It suggests a faith founded in a sense of call beyond consciousness and meaning.

But this is not news to Levinas. Of course the interruptive determinations of the other carry with them a tradition, and of course Levinas's own language is determined by faith and culture. Why else would he be writing in the face of the erosion of this faith in the idealism and empiricism of the nineteenth and twentieth centuries? Although I believe that Levinas's work is moved by the persona of the rabbi who is also a philosopher, the neighbor is not dependent on the rabbi. The rabbi is dependent on the neighbor. More than dependent, the rabbi stands in unceasing indebtedness before the other and, as rabbi, kills what is not to be killed as surely as the nonrabbi kills. And kills in his or her effort to free the other as other. The value of this discourse is not found in its successes or its vitality or its syntax. Its value is found in its abusive turn on its success, vitality, and syntax, in its losses and failures before the other that gives it to be. The value of this discourse is in the other's recurrence—a recurrence before value—and not in the persistence of the discourse. Only the other's loss, not the other's presence, is to be found in Levinas's discourse.

At this most interesting point of contact with the other, both ontological claims and a tribal faith are interrupted by the other's cut. The other does not happen as it is *said* to happen. But we *can* bear witness to a determination beyond conscious events. We can see that crisis accompanies conscious determination. We can hold clear the obsession that accompanies the other's determinations. And in this we turn toward an ethic beyond the ethics of essentialist persuasion.

I believe that we have come to a still point, a point without ontological or pistic validity. Even the meaning of showing the loss of the other and the priority of the neighbor is in question, because such meaning is saturated by ontological values and the meanings of a tribal faith. The other is valuable in Levinas's discourse by virtue of a series of affirmations: the other withdraws "from the game that being plays in consciousness" (OB 107); "this withdrawal excludes all spontaneity" (OB 107). The one for the other is "incommensurable" with consciousness (OB 100). "Anarchy troubles being." The "Infinite" comes to pass in "an extreme proximity of the neighbor" (OB 156). The other is the neighbor. "God" is "the apex of vocabulary, admission of the stranger than me in me" (OB 156). Our most interesting point demands doubt and yet leaves no room for doubt of the infinite importance of the other, whose importance cuts through the determinations that both make it important and foreshorten its importance. "Proximity can remain the signification of the very knowing in which it shows itself" (OB 157).

So there could *be* no other as Levinas finds it were there no ontological language and tribal faith. Even the other to the other of this language bespeaks a midrashic faith of the other's loss in its determination. And the infinite value of the other speaks in Levinas's recognition of other-beyond-value. A faith turns through itself and rediscovers itself in the withdrawal of what it posits. In this turning an exilic faith loses itself and returns to itself as it marks the other-beyond-determination. This faith finds itself articulated in the proximity and withdrawal of the Other-in-Infinity it recognizes and before which it gives its fealty. Far from withdrawing us from the tribal, this discourse reestablishes the tribal in an unending movement of removal and rediscovery. Beyond universality, it bears witness to the Infinite in its Infinity.

This return to the tribal out of a contestation of what the tribal establishes takes place in an affirmation of the proximity of the other, in an ethics that vastly exceeds any normative ethics. The movement to note is that of return. Levinas, as we have said, makes many descriptive claims as part of this movement. In such descriptive statements Levinas bears witness to something that is to be "seen." His purpose in *Otherwise than Being* is "*to see* in subjectivity an exaggeration putting out of order the conjunction of essence, entities, and the 'difference'; *to catch sight*, in the substantiality of the subject, in the hard core of the 'unique' in me, in my unparalleled identity, of a substitution for the other; *to conceive* of this abnegation prior to the will" (OB xli-xlii, emphasis added). Levinas writes as a witness who sees more than can be said and who remains faithful to this knowledge of excess. As a witness, in being a witness, he returns to the tribal but now in a way which suggests that the tribal has opened something so determinate and pervasive as to exceed the parochial universality of consciousness. It is a return not unlike that described by Nietzsche in Book III of *The Genealogy of Morals*, in which the ascetic priest brings self-sacrifice full circle to the full meaning of self-sacrifice and to the authority of the one who knows self-sacrificially this meaning most intimately. In this book Nietzsche, in the role of the ascetic priest, sacrifices both the meaning and the self-sacrifice and gives way to a self-overcoming of the moral tribe. Without such self-overcoming, the meaning of tribal prophecy, self-contestation, and cultural identity recur at the tribe's point of contact with what it knows it had lost in the beginning. In the loss it regains what is lost and rediscovers itself full and clear in its impairment.

This movement of departure and return is not entirely dissimilar to that of consciousness as Levinas describes it. Our consciousness is an unending process of self-loss and self-recovery, a process that establishes a sameness for all aspects of consciousness. We might call it an obsession with identity in which conscious identity finds itself through an endless process of contamination and conversion. The other obsession that interrupts this conscious obsessive process—the other obsession that Levinas describes—turns us beyond consciousness, crosses all conscious order and quietly gives witness to freedom and responsibility outside of conscious spontaneity, commitment, and normativity. The return that we are tracing in this other obsession, however, is one which directs us by a tribal language, a language which is remarkably sophisticated and well versed in the languages and practices of adjacent tribes, to what is described as one-for-the-other, proximity beyond conscious constitution, and an ethics of responsibility that is constitutive of our "unparalleled identity" (OB xli). In this witness we are given to see something that is beyond our common syntax and intention which already identifies us and which is more deeply composed of the syntax of covenant, call, and radical monotheism than any language in the syntax of *logos* and conscious subjectivity can properly say. It appears like a deep and covered-over alertness in our heritage that has accompanied the dominant and dominating discourse of Western awareness and selfhood. It appears as a recovery of the Hebraic experience and meaning that have been submerged in our Greek and modern lineage, as something other to the dominating and complex subjectivity that constitutes an anti-Hebraic force which depends on its Hebraic aspects. In this witness on the part of Levinas many people should find a surprising expansion of their own sense of identity, undergo a discovery of themselves in their Hebraic lineage, and, surprised to find themselves also Jews, experience fearful relief in a rediscovered ethics of God's call. The tribes mixed long before our births, and that mixture has surely given us to desire, deep within ourselves, the dark clarity of God's call in the values which allow us to know ourselves and all others.

In Levinas's writing we may experience a return not to transcendental consciousness but to the transcendent meaning of a covenant with God that calls us preconsciously to be in God's hearing as we name what is good and bad. It is a tribal call, and we probably prefer, like all tribes, to universalize by fundamental values and rights a particularity that gives us our names and values, even when we are otherwise exiled and homeless. As we return to our Jewishness with a renewed sense of rootedness and identity, we make the ancient movement that holds a tribe together: we return to founding meanings, no matter how elusive and terrible, and to a sense of rightness, no matter how interrupted and fragile. This movement of return, which Nietzsche found definitive of the ascetic ideal in our lineage, while it interrupts a language of essence, nonetheless restores an identity in its loss. The tribe makes metaphysicians of us all.

This movement of return in Levinas's thought is before politics when by politics we mean a complex conscious structure for actions among peoples. At the beginning of these remarks I recalled that the "Oh hear" affirmation is a prayer that arises from Israel and is addressed to Israel. It is a people's prayer by which they know themselves in a covenant with a Singular One. It is not addressed directly to God. But it arises from a people who belong to this Singular One, and it gives expression to Levinas's interruptive thought in the context of Western experience and theory. This belonging is before politics, but it is political in the sense that it gives a people to be *this* people. The "Oh hear" affirmation recalls for a person that he or she belongs to a people called by God when in the greatest of life's extremities as well as in the normal everyday. While this belonging is pretheoretical and prior to any stated value or course of action, it is ethnic in that it both bestows and expresses identity as well as constitutes a direction of destiny in that identity. This belonging is a political dimension in Levinas's thought. It is not theological. But it is constituted as a movement of return in a people's "God-given" identity, a movement and identity of which Levinas's thought is a part. The saying of this identity begins as a prayer and finds its expression in witness—the witness of responsibility of the one for the other in writing as well as in attitudes and other actions. We have located the danger of this political witness in its return to itself, in the "Oh hear, Israel" by which return we as Jew Greeks find ourselves confirmed before all thought and value in our loss of God's presence as we hear God, who is not contaminated by being and who calls us in Goodness beyond value to be obedient in his call.

ns as First Philosophy
Part Two: Ethics as First Philosophy

4
Response and Responsibility in Levinas

Bernhard Waldenfels

> Répondre de ce qui échappe à la responsabilité...
>
> —Maurice Blauchot, *Le pas au-delà*

Responsibility has to be taken as a key concept, from which the reorientation achieved by Levinas's ethics can be clearly understood, right up to the problems that this reorientation leaves behind. The implications of this central concept are immense. I shall restrict myself to showing how a thematic thread arises in the traditional form of self-responsibility, ending in the weavings of a new kind of responsibility for and to the other, exploring these concepts especially as they are developed in and around *Autrement qu'être*. The turning point from the traditional to the new conception is the *retraduction* of "responsibility" into a kind of responding, into a "response of responsibility" (AE 180; OB 142). In the so-called philosophy of dialogue we encounter the effects of this retraduction at every turn, but more decisively than the dialogists, Levinas tries to dislodge this idea from the routes of communication and the latter's symmetrical arrangements. One may object that responsibility for the other, in its radicality, precedes even my responding. But I hope that in the course of my reflections it will become clear why we should be warned against skipping the step of responding. In the background of my own reflections we find the contrast between a communicative ethics moving in advance on the common ground of community and another form of ethics born from the spirit of responding, so that it might be called a responsive ethics.

Self-Responsibility

The traditional idea of responsibility means that wherever something is said and done, everybody speaks with his own voice and that in one's own voice the universal voice of reason also finds expression. The dialogical idea of giving account (λο'γον διδο'ναι), inherited from the Greeks, meets with the juridical idea of imputation (*imputatio*) invented by the Romans. Thus somebody is responsible for something to somebody, three instances taking part in the process of giving account.

First, something is said or done *for which* one is responsible. Here we are dealing with what results from saying or doing. The process of saying or doing coagulates into a state of affairs, into the facts of the case. The issue of justification consists in what Levinas calls work (*oeuvre*) or what he—referring to speech—calls the said. The consequence of this approach is that, in the act of calling to account and rendering accountable, everything is put in the perspective of the past, and not merely coincidentally. As Aristotle's *Rhetoric* already showed, the genre of court speech prefers the past tense. Here, every time something is made good, it is remade good, repaired, and it makes no great difference whether we are responsible to a secular court of law, to the tribunal of reason, or to the last judgment.[1]

Moreover, we are responsible *to somebody*, to a forum or a tribunal, which is more or less personal or anonymous. The crucial point is that words and deeds are regarded and treated from the perspective of a neutral Third, with the effect that only reasons count and not opinions and wishes. Only from the transsubjective standpoint of the Third is what is said and done transformed into an objective state of affairs subjected to objective standards.

Finally, somebody, being responsible, has to justify *himself*. The state of affairs would be a mere fact and not a deed if it could not be causally attributed to a certain or to several speakers. This attribution or imputation does not happen to the subject of speech and action *après coup*. On the contrary, someone constitutes him- or herself as "subject" by assuming responsibility, by being responsible. Hence responsibility in the sense of "imputability" becomes the criterion of deciding whether somebody has to be treated as a "subject" of "sound mind," as the bearer of duties and rights.

Responsibility in its traditional sense is related to responding, but this relation is a rather restricted one. Somebody behaves responsibly if he or she—like the Platonic dialectician—is able to give an account of or answer for what he or she has said or done as often as interrogations, charges, or accusations arise. Because the Third to whom someone has to respond accepts only general or universal reasons, we see that the same reason speaks in the voice of the judge as in the voice of the perpetrator. The process of increasing moralization changes the heteronomy of a law according to which I am called to account into the autonomy of a law that I give to myself. The "responsibility to others" and the "holding others responsible" is grounded in a last, radical and universal "self-responsibility."[2] Just as the Platonic dialogue tends to turn into a "dialogue of the soul with itself," giving account tends to become a "negotiation of the soul with itself," where the soul gives account to itself.

On the ground of self-responsibility a communicative ethics flourishes that absorbs every form of being responsible to others and for others. It makes little difference whether the instance of unification consists in a universal subject of reason, in an intersubjective community of monads, in a more or less anonymous tradition, or in a transsubjective discourse. What matters is the assumption that responsibility is centered in the monologue, in a singular *logos*. "Reason, being unique, cannot speak to another reason" (TeI 182; TaI 207). Where, after all, one and the same instance will decide, the net of intrigue draws together to one and the same nodal point, and the drama begins to resemble the epos. Thus even the Platonic dialogue is for Levinas "the reminiscence of a drama rather than the drama itself" (AE 25; OB 20).

Responding

The great vision of a responsibility culminating in self-responsibility finds its limits in the fact that it subjects the exigencies of speaking and doing to an order that does not originate from speaking and doing itself. What has to be said and done here and now appears from the very start as a means to a goal, as a case in point of a law, or as a solution to a problem, that is, as part of a pregiven order wherein the difference between the proper and the alien is subjected to a dialectical negation (*Aufhebung*) or leveled off. We speak and act under the auspices of a Third or in the medium of an all-encompassing whole. This interpretation of the world of words and things, however, presupposes that there is only one order to which our saying and doing can be coordinated or in which it can be incorporated, and it presupposes that our saying and doing can be attributed to so-called subjects in a nonambiguous way. If these presuppositions fail because the order that arises in space and time can change, an abyss of irresponsibility opens up behind every form of responsibility whatsoever. There may be reasons for what someone says or does, but not sufficient reasons; and someone may be calculable in what he says or does, but never totally calculable, in spite of the possibility of imputation. Our saying and doing is no longer reduced to what is said and done, and no longer explained by a pregiven order. Responsibility that arises only *après coup* is turned back into a process of responding, so that behind the justifications in the sense of giving reasons (λο'γον διδο'ναι), the gesture of giving reappears. Levinas also calls this kind of responding "responsibility."[3] But this new kind of responsibility is not restricted to giving reasons; rather, it increases the gift of speech to a "gift of the self," and as a "superabundance of responsibility," it does not come to rest in any result (TeI 184, 222; TaI 208, 244). It thus gives rise, as Blanchot remarks, to another kind of philosophy.[4]

In consequence of this analysis, the three aspects of responsibility mentioned before are transformed into corresponding aspects of responding. This means first that the response does not primarily refer to something which has been said and done but rather to something which has to be said and done. The gerundive precedes the indicative, which names something, and it also precedes the optative, which refers to what is to be wished. It depends on an imperative, audible only when I listen to it in agreement or disagreement. The gerundive opens up a future, but a future that exceeds my own possibilities and creates a "passage to the time of the other" (DEHH 192). As saying that cannot be absorbed by what is said, responding is a sort of doing by which the respondent gives what he does not have. If responsibility goes together with the power of disposition over what is said and done, responding appears to some extent as irresponsible, even if I stand behind what I have said.[5]

In the process of responding the Other does not appear initially as the Third before whom I have to justify myself; he first appears in terms of the dative, the case of giving, as somebody to whom saying and doing are addressed. To that extent, responding eludes the perspective of the comparing Third. As the respondent, I do not relate to the other as he or she does to me; I am standing on this side of the chasm, not on both sides at once or above them.

Finally, behind somebody who "gives himself" when giving an answer, there is no person in the form of the nominative. There is neither a sovereign speaker or actor preceding[6] the responding nor a judge considering both sides; the respondent who does not merely transfer existing sense becomes what he is by and in the very process of responding. He or she is not a subject in the traditional sense, "underlying" certain acts but a respondent through and through, who in a certain sense remains unknown to him- or herself. If we want to continue calling him a "subject," then we do so in the sense of his "subjection" to the demands of the Other (AE 17, 161; OB 14, 125). For Levinas this subjection, which, with different accents, plays an important role in Lacan and Foucault too, constitutes subjectivity, excluding the possibility that the subject represents itself in another way than by the traces it leaves behind (AE 142; OB 112). I do not get an answer to the question, Who am I? by regarding myself but by responding to somebody and by distinguishing myself from the Other in responding to him. I do not proceed from myself, but rather I return to myself by a retrograde movement that Levinas calls recurrence (AE 130-39; OB 102-9).

A responsive form of ethics capable of preserving the spirit of response presupposes that not only the self but also the common ground between ourselves and the Other is contested. That contestation occurs in terms of a demand (*Anspruch*) which arises simultaneously as a claim to (*Anspruch auf*) something and as an appeal to (*Anspruch an*) someone. This kind of demand in its double sense does not fall under the usual distinctions between "is" and "ought," because it can neither be reduced to an empirical fact nor sublimated to a general law. The demand to which I am to respond breaks up the symmetrical and recurrent relation of communicative ethics, that is, of a kind of ethics founded on the participation in a common reason or on an implicit contract of reason. The demand of the Other cannot be fulfilled like a wish or an order; it breaks through every sort of intentional or regulative circularity. It also breaks through the hermeneutic circularity, for a demand coming from the Other is no longer open to the precomprehension of a communicative community. We dwell on a premoral and prejudicial level at which one always does the Other wrong according to distributive or corrective justice. The demand of the Other can be fulfilled only insofar as it is inserted into a teleological or deontic order as a step toward a goal or as a case covered by a law, that is, insofar as it has been stripped of its alienness or alterity and rendered commensurable to my own demand. If this is the case, every kind of fulfillment turns out to be a partial or indirect form of self-fulfillment, be it in the sense of a good that fulfills, after all, my own needs, or be it in the sense of a law that I fulfill myself. In contrast, responding to the demand of the Other is an "empty response," and not only in the sense of Husserl's "empty intention" (*Leermeinung*) that is awaiting fulfillment but also in the sense of an irrevocable void, a "corporeal absence" (*leibhaftige Abwesenheit*): "the neighbor does not satisfy the approach" (AE 114; OB 90).

Responsibility for and to the Other

The response that does not converge with any question and does not stimulate any expectation of consent refers to a double-sided asymmetry and irreciprocity which—as Levinas shows again and again—cannot be compensated and balanced out by a Golden Rule. But Levinas goes one step further, delivering responsibility itself up to a preceding and immemorial responsibility for the Other. The attempt to explore this new landscape of ethical thinking would present an enormous task.

If we look back once more to the traditional concept of responsibility, we have to distinguish between responsibility *for* the Other and responsibility *to* the Other. Being responsible for the Other would thus mean giving account for what others have said and done, no matter if these Others operate inside or outside of myself.[7] The whole project of self-responsibility would break down if the words or deeds of Others could be substitutes for my own. There would be no "subject" at all who was responsible for him- or herself. Within this traditional framework, responsibility for the Other can only be taken as an enlarged form of self-responsibility, as *responsabilité élargie* rooted in a *raison élargie*. This enlarged form of responsibility would be an originally limited form of responsibility, measured by my liberty and by what is possible for me (AE 129, 164; OB 102, 128), in contrast to an unlimited responsibility that becomes limited only afterward (AE 165; OB 128). According to Heidegger's concept of care (*Fürsorge*), I am able to substitute myself for the Other or to precede him in his own possibilities. The guardian (*Vormund*) does the latter, anticipating the responsibility of the Other—temporarily, if the Other has not yet awakened to his own reason, as in the case of a minor; permanently, if the Other has lost his own responsibility, as in the case of the insane person. Furthermore, I can assume responsibility for those consequences of my action which cannot be foreseen or planned, and are in any case not to be undone. But the core of self-responsibility is not affected by these preliminary, substitutive, or supplementary extensions of my own responsibility. Much the same can be said about the responsibility to Others. Insofar as universal laws are represented by the Third, I am responsible to him. But as long as these laws are not arbitrary ones, to which I owe at most external obedience and not consent, these laws are ultimately based on autonomy, where I am responsible to myself.

But Levinas pleads for a responsibility for Others (*responsabilité pour les autres*) that is anything but preliminary and secondary. The responsibility to Others that

Levinas takes into consideration in terms of the Third may be left aside in this context; it is obvious that it is derived completely from the first form of responsibility. We thus have to ask how to understand the primary responsibility for Others. Levinas takes this kind of responsibility as original substitution. Through this substitution, I become a corporeal hostage of the Other and have to substitute myself for him with life and limb, and that in a radical form. The responsibility for Others that originates at this point does not mean a pure co-responsibility, which would presuppose self-responsibility and which would be grounded in compassion, benevolence, and empathy. On the contrary, I am responsible by substituting myself for the Other. Using Husserl's terms, we could put it this way: originally I am not here but there where the Other stands. And modifying Kant's terms we could say, responsibility is not the faculty to begin by oneself but the compulsion to begin by the Other. Ecstasy, mostly interpreted as centrifugal movement, turns into exposure: I am outside, *au dehors*.

Response of Responsibility

Such a responsibility from the outside, which Levinas introduces in order to put in question the nearly proverbial "inner responsibility," confronts us, as may be expected, with a lot of puzzles and enigmas.
1. The problem begins with the responsibility *for* the Other. What does it mean to be responsible "for" the Other? The previously mentioned "for" in the sense of *"in favor of"* must be eliminated as conceding to the responsible person an advantage, so that he is or has what the Other is not or does not have. The "for" in the sense of a perfect "gratuity" (AE 123; OB 96) does not correspond to the *prod-esse* that goes beyond the interest in being. It corresponds rather to a form of *stare pro*, a standing and answering for. The responsible person speaks and acts *instead of*, and this has to be understood as substitution, as the title term in the central chapter of *Otherwise than Being* reads. The "for" of the substitution does not place terms in relation *to* each other, it *is* the relation. "My responsibility for the other is the *for* of the relationship, the very signifyingness of signification, which signifies in saying before showing itself in the said" (AE 126; OB 100). "One-for-the-other" (*l'un-pour-l'autre*), as is said again and again, can be neither broken down into elements nor welded to a whole, originating as it does, as an interruptive, intermediary event (*Zwischenereignis*),[8] from the responding saying and substituting saying, interrupted by the "for" as if by an insurmountable barrier.

For the self, substitution does not mean a mere change of place, for the place where it is exposed to the Other proves to be itself a "nonplace" (*non-lieu*) that does not fit into any ontological cartography. Neither does substitution stand for alienation, because this would imply that there is already a self that becomes alien to itself. "Paradoxically it is qua *alienus*—foreigner and other—that man is not alienated" (AE 76; OB 59). Nor, finally, does substitution perform a reversal, which would result in the Other taking my own place in a way similar to the movement by which altruism turns egoism into its opposite. Mere reversal, about which Derrida warns us unceasingly, remains attached to what it reverses. Those passages in which Levinas (by the way, not without hesitation) speaks of inversion—for example, of the "inversion" of intentionality (AE 60, 142; OB 47, 111)—have to be regarded with caution. If there is something like "conversion," then it leads to a "concave without a convex" (*envers sans endroit*) (AE 63; OB 49).[9] Alienation is further excluded because "the Other in the self" (*l'autre dans le même*), as the refrainlike formula reads, means "my substitution," and does so with respect to a responsibility in which I am irreplaceable, in which I cannot let myself be replaced, and in which, consequently, I am not another (AE 146, 163; OB 114, 127). Paradoxically spoken, I am irreplaceable as a substitute.[10] Levinas's reference to the "substitutive one in the other," to an "intrigue of the other in the same" (AE 31; OB 25), corresponds to Husserl's remark, made in *The Crisis of European Sciences and Transcendental Phenomenology*, to the effect that everyone's "intentionality reaches into that of the other and vice versa"[11] and that there is an "inward being-for-one-another and [a] mutual interpenetration."[12] This responsibility for the Other, which is far from amounting to a common sense, creates a drama that leaves every form of intentional teleology behind.

2. A second question concerns the self of the process of being (one)self responsible for the Other *(sich verantworten)*. As Levinas stresses, this self *(se, soi)* is so far away from the identification place of Being that it bears his name only "as a borrowed name, as a pseudonym, as pronoun," and even this pronoun is put into the accusative, not to be derived from any nominative (AE 134-35, 143; OB 106, 112). The expression "me voici," literally, "here see me," is introduced as a primordial form of "response of responsibility" (AE 180; OB 142). I do not begin as "I," let alone as "the" or "an I."

From this insight, Levinas draws the unusual conclusion that responsibility for the other precedes not only the dialogical exchange of question and answer (AE 142; OB 111) but also every free initiative or involvement of myself. The response of responsibility is a response that "answers, before any understanding, for a debt (*dette*) contracted before any freedom and before any consciousness and any present" (AE 14; OB 12). This responsibility, beyond any initiative, refers to an "anarchist" prebeginning, more beginning than any beginning I make; it refers to a prepast, more past than any past I remember; to an original passivity, more passive than any passion I can assume; ultimately, it refers to an original corporeality in whose skin I do not feel at home (AE 137; OB 108). These all are figures of the Other in me which rule out speaking of the Other without speaking of myself but which exclude even more the possibility that I speak of myself before speaking for the Other. I always come too late to assume my responsibility; so the response of my responsibility precedes every answer given by myself.

But this "inversion of Me into the Self—the deposition or dismissal of the ego" (AE 65; OB 50)—reaches a critical limit when it approaches the point where self-responsibility gets absorbed into the responsibility for the Other. Certainly, there is no residual ego that could be preserved from being contested by the Other; we can only stake everything on what appears within the contestation itself.

In this context we should take into consideration the following points. If the prebeginning of my saying did not permanently refer to initiatives coming from myself, the prebeginning would fall back onto a pure beginning, and the "anarchist" would yield to the original power of an *arché*.[13] As for the self (*se, soi*), we should distinguish more clearly than Levinas does between the accusative which points to the provocative action of the Other and the reflexivity which points to a relation to myself, and which Levinas emphasizes much more in the domain of feeling and enjoyment than in the field of speaking. When Levinas suggests that *se dire* and *être dit* amount to nearly the same thing (AE 55; OB 43), he follows a trace of the French grammar that seems to belong to the surface structures of language. When Levinas assumes that responsibility for the Others proves to be a sort of "saying prior to anything said" (AE 56; OB 43), this event of saying should appear not only as diachronically but also as dia-lectically refracted. We want to think of dialectic in a new way, that is, by making the assumption that our own saying and that of the Other defer to each other in terms of words and counterwords which do not follow from each other as a result, or simply follow each other as a sequence, but interfere in the process of speaking and hearing. The differentiation into proper and alien, which does not count on the instance of a Third, cannot occur unless the self in its recurrence opens up a fissure, allowing for mirroring and echo. Only in this way does the ego appear "in itself like a sound that would resound in its own echo" (AE 130; OB 103), audible *only* in its own echo (AE 134; OB 106). The "saying itself" (*se dire*) within the saying (*dire*; see AE 55; OB 43) that responds to the other generates the minimal difference which prevents self-responsibility, the response of the responsibility, from becoming absorbed in the responsibility for the Other. Even if we admit that our speaking and doing has to be characterized as responding through and through, we cannot conclude that responding is completely determined by the demand it has to respond to. In this context, the question arises of whether we do not deprive the act of responding of its indispensable scope of free play when we confront the ego with the alternative between "responsibility beyond freedom" and "freedom without responsibility, a freedom of play" (AE 148, 154 n. 24; OB 116, 197 n. 24), as if play could be restricted to a pure play of Being and a pure play of consciousness in which one possibility passes into the other (AE 134; OB 106). Can we say that a "true response" without alternatives, arising from a "saying in which there is no play" (AE 58; OB 46), is still a response? Shouldn't we distinguish between the unavoidable of the situation we have to respond to, that is, the *necessary* in its literal sense—and the range of possible responses? If Levinas assumes a certain "ambiguity" of the said that, by saying, is alternatively affirmed and retracted (AE 56; OB 44), doesn't this ambiguity, too, require a certain free play within the responsibility of saying?[14]

3. If the recurrent "self" (*se*) of responding to oneself (*se répondre*) is underdetermined, the weight shifts to responsibility insofar as it is for the Other. Thus I no longer substitute myself for the Other, I am unavoidably occupied by him or her. Provided that we give to each other and take from each other words as well as bread and caresses, one could assume that the Other to whom the gesture of giving is

addressed originally appears in terms of the dative. But this relation already seems to presuppose a giving subject put into the nominative, that is, a giver who has him- or herself and something to give, to give away, or to retain. Responsibility would once more be left to my own initiative. On the contrary, when responsibility expands to substitution, where one substitutes him- or herself for the Other, the self becomes dispossessed, denuded, and evacuated (see AE 139-141; OB 109-111). Nothing is left to the self except the "nonplace" of the hostage where it is the Other who rises to speak within the Self. If we pose the question of what one is responsible for when summoned and accused as responsible for the Other, we must say, the self is responsible for what Others do and endure or suffer (AE 143; OB 112), including the liberty *and the responsibility* of Others (AE 139, 150; OB 109, 117). The responsibility that falls on me is a debt that "goes beyond having, but makes *giving* possible" (AE 139; OB 109). Consequently, I even owe the Other the answer I give. My selfhood, also the selfhood of the giver, arises from the "recurrence" by which I return to myself from the Other, and from an incarnation which inscribes the giving in the corporeal gesture of giving (AE 139; OB 109).

At this point it becomes clear what Levinas means when he tries to find his way back to "the center of gravitation of a being outside of that being" (TeI 158; TaI 183). Responsibility for the Other operates in the field of gravity of the Other's demand. In the course of this displacement of weight, certain ambiguities we have attributed to the self seem to come up again in the reverse direction, that is, in relation to the role of the Other. The substitution *for the Other* (*pour autrui*) which continues to suggest a stand and a step of my own is linked to a suffering *from the Other* (*par autrui*) which chains us to the Other as to a persecutor (AE 141, 150, 161; OB 111, 118, 125). How does the one aspect fit the other?

The responsibility would not be *my* responsibility, the substitution would not be *my* substitution if totally achieved or enforced by the Other. The substitution for ... would lapse into the suffering by ... as into a sea of suffering where my own and the Other's doing become blurred. Nothing would be more alien to Levinas than such a philosophy of suffering life. In his view, the substitutive responsibility consists in the fact that I take upon myself the "suffering *by* the fault of the other" in the form of "suffering *for* the fault of others." The passive changes into passion, whereby the difference between "being accused" and "accusing oneself" fades, because bearing responsibility means bearing one's own guilt under the accusation of the Other (AE 161; OB 125). "In the incomparable relationship of responsibility the other no longer limits the same, it is supported by what it limits" (AE 146; OB 115). We may speak of a certain interpassion in this respect. Here responsibility reaches its highest degree. Responsibility for the Other means responsibility not only for the Other's deeds and suffering but also for what he does to me. The self precedes its own initiative, with the effect that every form of assumption of oneself is in delay (AE 161; OB 125), turns back to oneself in the course of one's endurance, in the patience that includes one's own being as victim of the Other, as "patience of undergoing imposed by the other" (AE 161; OB 125). Without the transformation of what I suffer from the Other into what I am for the Other, the responsibility for the Other would, after all, be nothing but an imposed destiny. For one moment, if only for one moment, the text recalls the Stoic wisdom (AE 222; OB 176) or Nietzsche's *amor fati*; it recalls the consent to destiny that cannot be derived from destiny itself—otherwise ethics would be a pure phantasm. Responding for oneself (*se répondre*) presupposes a taking-upon-oneself; without this "less than nothing" (AE 118; OB 93) there would be no substitution at all. There would be no substitution that could interrupt the course of things.

4. We could be inclined to remove this ethic in the spirit of substitution into a mythic or religious sphere, deeming it an "expiation" which reminds us of the scapegoat or the sacrificial lamb in the Bible and which would subsume ready-made answers under the "religiosity of self" (AE 150; OB 117). However, even if we avoid such premature "substructions," a lot of questions arise.

The situation of responsibility for the Other is depicted by Levinas in expressions that not only respire hatred and violence but pass over into criminal and clinical phenomena. Responsibility is combined with persecution, the accusative is taken literally as the case of accusation, the passive turns into passion in the case of suffering from the Other. The focus of description thereby shades away from "normal" phenomena such as fatigue and growing old toward excesses of hatred and violence, but the change of focus is not sufficiently reflected. Two examples will illustrate this point. First we read, "Obsession is irreducible to consciousness even if it overwhelms it. In consciousness it is betrayed but thematized by a said in which it is manifested. Obsession traverses consciousness countercurrentwise, is inscribed in consciousness as something foreign, a disequilibrium, a delirium. It undoes thematization" (AE 128; OB 101). This "an-archist moment" is contrasted with Fichte's consciousness thesis, according to which everything that is posed *in* consciousness, is posed *by* consciousness. In contrast to this, consider another passage: "The face of the neighbor in its persecuting hatred can by this very malice obsess as something pitiful" (AE 141; OB 111). The excess of the Other's demand increases again and again; it abruptly jumps to the excess of the Other's violence. Levinas once speaks of an "overdetermination of ontological categories...which transforms them into ethical terms" (AE 146; OB 115). In a similar way, we could speak of a further overdetermination of the ethical concepts, which again and again explode, thus approaching the limits of the supportable. Why is this so?

We find a first answer to this question in the bilingual motto placed at the head of *Otherwise Than Being*: Levinas is certainly "thinking after Auschwitz."[15] But this answer will not do. Levinas's thinking often reminds us of certain ways of thinking in Plato. In the second book of the *Republic*, Socrates connects the praise of justice with the extreme situation in which the just man is tortured to death whereas the unjust man is blessed with every sort of good, including the benevolence of the gods purchased by offerings (to be substituted today by the benevolence of the world public). So in the view of Levinas, responsibility that excludes the extreme case would be worthless. "It is the passivity of a trauma.... This passivity deserves the epithet of complete or absolute only if the persecuted one is liable to answer for the persecutor" (AE 141; OB 111). Were something or somebody excluded from responsibility by a kind of *reservatio moralis*, the circle of calculation and exchange, of misdeed and revenge, of reproach and counterreproach would still retain its force. The restriction of responsibility to responsibility for *certain* Others would have the effect of subduing the otherness of the Other in advance, subjecting it to the order of the Third—before whom the Other has to legitimate his or her demand and prove his or her right; but this restriction presupposes already the response of responsibility—it comes too late (AE 110; OB 87). We can ask, however, if equalizing responsibility for the Other and persecution by the Other does not have the effect of affirming the victimization as such.[16] If one would go a step further and ask, Why responsibility at all? "Why does the other concern me? What is Hecuba to me?" one would beg the question by the mere fact of posing it; for whoever poses such a question has already assumed that the ego's "concern for itself" is the first and last word (AE 150; OB 117). The expectation that responsibility could be legitimated and founded would be out of place; it would be like asking Plato why everything should aspire to the Good or asking Kant why we should follow the categorical imperative.[17] Responsibility that arises from responding is unable to say or know in advance to what it responds and why it does so. "The ethical situation of responsibility is not comprehensible on the basis of ethics" (AE 154; OB 120). To that extent, every moral has its blind spot.[18]

5. The fact that a responsive ethics cannot be founded without presupposing itself does not mean that it is free from further explorations. If we return once more to the traditional scheme of responsibility, the question about responsibility *to Others* remains. First, as Levinas states, in the face of the Other, *responding before* or *to* (*répondre devant* or *à*) and *responding for* (*répondre de*) are linked together in an ambiguous way: he evokes the "enigma or exception of a face which is at once both judge and involved party" (AE 14; OB 12). The situation of the judge is similarly blurred: "The judge is not outside the conflict, but the law is in the midst of proximity" (AE 202; OB 159). If the role of the judge were separated from the emergence of responsibility, we could again move *within* a moral order, a moral "bookkeeping" (AE 161; OB 125); guilt could be forgiven like debts are paid; there could be no incomparable and unsubstitutable responsibility. Nevertheless, we have to ask if there is not at least a minimal difference between the demand of the Other and the concurrent demand *(Mitanspruch)* of the Third. If we assume, following Levinas, that the responsibility for the Other is not subsumed under any a priori (AE 109; OB 86), the possibility remains that the responsibility for the Other lets a response constellation co-originate, wherein the Other appears as *this*, and not *that* Other, that is, by a certain exclusion of other Others. Second, we have to ask how responsibility *for the Other* goes together with responsibility *for Others*, and if responsibility "for everything and everyone," the "support of the universe" (AE 145, 148; OB 114, 116), can really mean more than a "surplus of responsibility" (AE 126; OB 100), which by no means excludes conflicts between responses, and which casts doubt on the assumption that the "violence of choice" may ever be completely changed into the "good violence" of Good itself (see AE 19, 56, 73; OB 15, 43, 57). What can responsibility for everyone and everything signify besides responsibility

not only for this or that Other? This "not only" would include the ethical utopia invoked at the end of *Otherwise than Being:* "The openness of space as an openness of self without a world, without a place, utopia, the not being walled in, inspiration to the end, even to expiration, is proximity of the other which is only possible as responsibility for the other, as substitution for him" (AE 229; OB 182).

Notes

1. God's judgment constitutes an exception for Levinas: it does not silence one's own voice or the "revolt of apology" (TeI 221; TaI 244). On the temporal orientation of responsibility, see Paul Ricoeur, *Soi-même comme un autre* (Paris: Du Seuil, 1990), 341-43. The fact that responsibility, in its substance, extends into the future and the present does not prevent it from remaining faced toward the past on the level of saying. If future risks, such as the consequences of environmental destruction for future generations, are thematized, then this takes place in the *futurum exactum* tense.
2. See, for example, *Husserliana* (Hua) 15:422, and also Hua 6: 271-72, *The Crisis of European Sciences and Transcendental Phenomenology,* trans. David Carr (Evanston: Northwestern University Press, 1970), 337-38, and *Beilage* 10: 423, 425 of the German edition, *Die Krisis der Europäischen Wissenschaften und die Transzendentale Phänomenologie,* ed. Walter Biemel (*Husserliana* 6, The Hague: Nijhoff, 1962). Fittingly, Ricoeur locates accountability and responsibility on one level, which precedes that of the dialectic of self and other (*soi-même*, 343).
3. In French the linguistic proximity of answering and answering for oneself is particularly close: *répondre de* means to answer for something or someone. See also AE 60; OB 47: "dire c'est répondre d'autrui"; the passage quoted below (AE 14; OB 12); and the motto from Blanchot.
4. See Maurice Blanchot, *L'ecriture du désastre* (Paris: Vrin, 1980), 45, where it is said of responsibility: "This banal word that generally qualifies, in prosaic and bourgeois fashion, a man who is mature, lucid, conscious...one must try and understand how Levinas has renewed it, opened it up to the point of making it signify (beyond all sense) the responsibility of another philosophy."
5. For this reason the further question arises of whether the giving of an answer can still be conceived as the deed of a perpetrator or whether there isn't, behind the giving, a possibility of expenditure that precedes every action and passion and thus every imputation. See on this point Blanchot, *L'écriture*, 50.

"Lorsque l'autre se rapporte à moi de telle sorte que l'inconnu en moi lui réponde à ma place, cette réponse est l'amitié immémoriale qui ne se laisse pas choisir, ne se laisse pas vivre dans l'actuel: la part offerte de la passivité sans sujet." In the third part of this paper we will come back to this question.

6. See AE 59, 61; OB 46, 47-48. The sovereign subject, which refers the said to his own saying, occupies the position of the nominative in the manner of the subject of a sentence.

7. Levinas, however, states that we are charged with and responsible for "what the others do or suffer" (AE 143; OB 112). The expansion of responsibility and its shift into the present prevent the self-responsibility and responsibility for the other from replacing one another in a simple quid pro quo.

8. See Bernhard Waldenfels, *Ordnung im Zwielicht* (Frankfurt am Main: Suhrkamp, 1983), 46-60.

9. Levinas plays with the double meaning of *envers* as the side that is turned over and turned to the other. Further passages in which Levinas uses this motif are found at AE 131, 134, 149, 191; OB 103, 106, 117, 149.

10. This "irreplaceability of the substitute" calls to mind Derrida's "original supplement."

11. Husserl, *Crisis*, 254-57.

12. Ibid., 298.

13. Concerning the "archaic" and the "anarchic" Levinas warns against a speech- and consciousnessless an-archy; if there weren't at least a trace of the anarchic, then this would, dominating in its own way, exercise its *arché* (AE 127–30; OB 100-2).

14. See Levinas's remarks concerning the ambiguity of the riddle in the essay "Enigme et phénomène" (DEHH 208, 212; CP 66, 69).

15. For us Germans, as descendants of the National Socialist perpetrators of genocide, there is a danger that the Holocaust overshadows the acts of violence and the victims of the present. "*Vergangenheitsbewältigung*," too, can impair vision, by creating a clean conscience. Let there be no mistake: there can be no question of subjecting incomparable crimes to relativizing comparisons; on the contrary, the point is just the opposite: enduring incomparability. An example from the most recent past: when a political-intellectual opinion leader such as Peter Glotz rejects the designation of genocide (which has, in the meantime, been taken up by the International Court) for what is happening in Bosnia, arguing that one would thereby play down Hitler's attempt to annihilate Jews or Gypsies (see *Der Spiegel*, 3 August 1993), he, too, relativizes, merely with reversed emphasis. We should not forget that Marek Edelmann, the last commander of the Warsaw ghetto, refers to the former Yugoslavia as a "posthumous victory for Hitler," since Europe has not learned anything since the Holocaust and the war.

16. See the critical remarks in Elisabeth Weber, *Verfolgung und Trauma: Zu Emmanuel Levinas's "Autrement qu'être ou au-delà de l'essence"* (Vienna: 1990), 200-3, 240-45.
17. Plato's Good, whose place "beyond being" finds its way into the title *Autrement qu'être*, changes in Levinas from the Good toward which everything strives into a Good that has chosen me before I have chosen it (AE 13; OB 11). On the categorical imperative as an instance that leaves all ontology and theology behind, see AE 166; OB 129.
18. See my study on Nietzsche "Der blinde Fleck der Moral," *Zeitschrift für philosophische Forschung* 47 (1993), 507-20.

5
Reply to Bernhard Waldenfels, "Response and Responsibility in Levinas"

Hugh Miller

Let me begin by saying that I will pass over in the silence of consent most of the first part of Waldenfels's paper, in which he contrasts the traditional account of responsibility with Levinas's own approach and shows how Levinas's account of responsibility as response transforms or disrupts the traditional account. For Waldenfels this means, *inter alia*, that a "communicative ethics moving in advance on the common ground of community" is ruled out by Levinas's "responsive ethics." In this I am in complete agreement with him.

Waldenfels's reservations and hesitations commence with what he calls Levinas's "one step further," the step in which, he says, Levinas delivers the responsible subject up to "a preceding and immemorial responsibility" for the Other. This is the step taken in *Otherwise Than Being* and other recent works, one that culminates in the account of the primary responsibility for the Other as original substitution. I think that Waldenfels is perfectly correct in calling the teaching of original substitution a kind of terra incognita, and its exploration "an enormous task," for ethical thinking. In what follows I hope to tread as lightly and cautiously as Waldenfels.

The first "puzzle" or "enigma" that Waldenfels raises has to do with the status of the (him- or her-) self in the process of being (him- or her-) self-responsible for the *Other (sich verantworten, se répondre)*. For Waldenfels, it is precisely the apparently total absorption of the (him- or her-) self of (him- or her-) self-responsibility into the responsibility for the Other that poses the first constellation of problems. Does not Levinas, he asks, perhaps fail to distinguish clearly enough "the accusative which points to the provocative action of the Other and the reflexivity which points to a relation to myself"? Even if we admit that our words and deeds are a "responding through and through," he asks, must we therefore conclude that responding is *completely* determined by the demand that it has to respond to? Is this not to overdetermine response? Would we not thereby be depriving the act of responding of its "indispensable free play," without which a response could not be genuine, that is, a choice from among real alternatives? Is a response without alternatives, arising from a "saying absolutely without play" still a response? Is not Levinas's dichotomy of "responsibility beyond liberty" and a "liberty of play without responsibility" a false one? "Without the transformation of what I suffer from the other into what I am for the other," he writes, "the responsibility for the other would, after all, be nothing but an imposed destiny.... Responding for oneself (*se répondre*) presupposes a taking-upon-oneself; without this 'less than nothing' there would be no substitution at all."

To address Waldenfels's concerns, we must, I think, look again briefly at Levinas's account of proximity and substitution. In it, the responsibility under which I am placed by the other has the character of obsession. As Levinas writes in "Language and Proximity,"

"Obsession is neither a modification nor a pathological exasperation of consciousness, but the very proximity of beings. Consciousness in all its forms—representational, axiological, practical—has already lost this close presence. The fact that the neighbor does not enter into a theme, that in a certain sense he precedes cognition and commitment, is neither a blinding nor an indifference; it is a rectitude of relationship more tense than intentionality: the neighbor summons me. Obsession is a responsibility without choice, a communication without phrases or words" (CP 120).

In her speech, in the utterance of the "first word," the neighbor or interlocutor makes a contact with "me" prior to my conscious ego's self-constitution. The interlocutor is thus in an important sense not "there," situated within a world-context, a more or less determined object for consciousness. The speech of the interlocutor has arrived before all this. The interlocutor's speech is closer to me than anything could be that was a mere object of my consciousness: in fact, says Levinas, it "skips the stage of consciousness," so that proximity is always "an anachronous presence to consciousness: consciousness is always late for the rendezvous with the neighbor" (DEHH 229; CP 119). The neighbor is nearer to me, so to speak, than I am to myself.

Since the interlocutor's "first word" arrives before any constitutive act of my consciousness, it possesses a meaning *in itself*, in no way constituted by my ego; it is what has a meaning *immediately*. It signifies, therefore, in a way different from that of every other sign. Consider the signification at play in Husserl's passive synthesis. There, signification consists of a reference by the sign, borne by the ego's protention (and retention) toward the double horizon, that is, toward the totality of actual affective presentations, of its significandum, which totality has not yet come to pass, and toward the "infinite (*unendlich*), open, *external horizon of objects cogiven*"[1] with the significandum. But the first word of the interlocutor is not borne by protention or retention and hence does not involve a reference to either an internal or an external horizon. Because the word is not borne by protention or retention, I can never be directly conscious of it, or of its speaker; the interlocutor therefore cannot appear before me by virtue of her word. She remains invisible, never dispersing herself into images, never upsurging into a theme for my intentional consciousness (DEHH 224; CP 116). This invisibility is an invisibility in principle and not merely a "hiddenness" that intentional consciousness might uncover in fulfillment. And since her first word is not constituted in and by my ego's temporality, it does not stand over against me, it is not a *Gegenstand*, a present object: it is, rather, already on the scene before my consciousness arises. Its sense, in fact, summons me to consciousness: "The I is summoned forth and faulty in the consciousness (*conscience*) it has of a neighbor, in its bad conscience (*conscience*)" (DEHH 229; CP 119-20). The prick of conscience precedes the determination of the objects of consciousness. In the first word of the interlocutor the distance between consciousness and its object is obliterated; the word is thus in the most urgent proximity to me, the command to duty imperious, and my ego reverts, in conscience, to obsession with what it cannot place at a distance from itself.

This obsession is excessive: I can never put away the responsibility for the neighbor that her word announces to me; whatever I am able to do is always too little too late. I have no right to myself: in an apt turn of phrase, Levinas says that the ego is first of all "myself," that is, grammatically in the *accus*ative case, as *accusé*, under indictment, before "I" am ever in the nominative (DEHH 233; CP 123). The command is emplaced before my freedom: I am in a position neither freely to accept nor freely to reject responsibility. It is impossible for me to decline to accept responsibility for my neighbor, when the commandment to responsibility has arrived in advance of the arrival of my own freedom, which latter presupposes ego and consciousness. In this extremity of ethical commandment all of the play of liberty, made possible by the distancing of consciousness from its object, is abolished, and existence is transformed into a complete moral seriousness, a perfect gravity.

What is the uttermost extremity of my own response to an infinite obligation? In the first place, it consists of an abandonment of my own claims for what Pascal called "my place in the sun."[2] My "place" is placed at the disposal of the neighbor, to the point that I abandon my claims to entitlement even to the food I eat to sustain my own life, as food stolen from the mouth of the suffering neighbor. But this is not all: to assume infinite responsibility is to assume responsibility not only for my own faults and crimes against my neighbor but for my neighbor's faults as well, of which I had no part in the making. And not just for one but for every possible neighbor's crimes am I responsible. As Alyosha Karamazov cries out in Dostoyevsky's *The Brothers Karamazov*, "We are all guilty of all and for all men before all, and I more than the others."[3] In obsession my being is to be hostage for the other: ethical action is in extremis my expiation for another's sins, for all others'. In substitution for others I empty myself of my being in expiation for them.

But I do not do so to the point of self-annihilation, even of ek-stasis, for it is at this extremity that I can at last realize what "I" am, in the nominative that follows on the accusative: what makes me unique in all the world is not the sovereignty of my "separated" consciousness of myself but rather the fact that no one can take my place in the task of expiation for others. I alone must hold up that weight; no Hercules may assume my Atlas's burden (DEHH 234; CP 124). While I thus am given over as a substitute for others in expiation of their wrongs, no one can substitute for me. The "one-for-the-other" (*l'un pour l'autre*) is "the Other in the self" (*l'autre dans le même*). I do not so much issue from myself—the model of autonomy—as find myself, in Levinas's words, "backed up into myself." The ipseity of the ego—the *se* in *se répondre*—is a recurrence, not an eternal return of the same to itself but an incessant reassignment of the responsible one to her or his post. It is a post that cannot be abandoned, a commission which cannot be resigned. The secret of ipseity is passivity—the passivity of passivity, a passivity more passive than "I" could ever assume for myself. Waldenfels is correct to cite Plato's correlation of the praise of justice with the extreme counterexample of the torture-murder of the just person in the *Republic*. For without the possibility of the extreme case justice is not sufficiently serious. To submit oneself to this possibility is an impossibility; no one would rationally, willingly consent to a principle of justice that might call for his or her own violent death, as Rawls has pointed out. Therefore, for this to be a real possibility in Levinas's responsive ethics, we require precisely a passivity that transcends all passivity which I could gin up from my own "resources." To answer Waldenfels's question, then, means to me to try to see how Levinas explains the possibility of this passivity of passivity.

It is here that I think the notions of trace and illeity might help us somewhat. As Waldenfels has pointed out, the passivity of passivity in recurrence refers to an "'anarchist' pre-beginning," a "pre-past, more past than any past I remember." What does Levinas mean by this?

As we have seen, proximity induces an infinite restlessness in the ego. It is "nonrepose itself" (DEHH 230; CP 120). It is a hunger and thirst, a "contact by love and responsibility" with the proximate neighbor (DEHH 230; CP 120). But if in the first word the neighbor is as proximate as can be, why the restlessness? What is this love, this desire for what cannot be attained or satisfied, if the neighbor is as close as she can be? Why is not proximity complete satiety, the most perfect stillness of contact, more perfect than the repose of the sleeping baby at its mother's breast? Why is proximity not a unity like the condition of the spherical double humans of Aristophanes' speech in Plato's *Symposium*? That it is not indicates that the proximate signifies or refers in the manner or mode of an absence. But the absence is not a lack: it is the infinitely Absent, illeity, absent into an immemorial past. Thus the neighbor is "ordered out of *the absence in which the infinite approaches,* out of its *null site,* ordered *in the trace of [the infinite's] own departure;* it is ordered to my responsibility and my love, beyond consciousness, which it obsesses" (DEHH 230; CP 121).

The infinition of love and responsibility in the provocation afforded my ego by proximity is thus the indirect, discreet signification effected by the divine illeity. The first word refers not to the neighbor as an object of thematizing consciousness but to the neighbor as standing in the trace of illeity out of which she is ordered. But as we have seen, this "standing in the trace" is nothing but an iterated reference to the neighbor who…stands in the trace. And as the divine illeity is infinite, so are the iterations of reference to the neighbor and back to my responsibility and love for her infinite. "The first saying is to be sure but a word. But the word is God" (DEHH 236; CP 126).

In *Otherwise Than Being* Levinas pauses to be quite emphatic on this point: the reference to the trace cannot be read off as a speculative "proof" of God, who is, as illeity, inaccessible:

"The approach [of the neighbor] is a non-synchronizable diachrony, which representation and thematization dissimulate by transforming the trace into the sign of a departure, and then reducing the face either to a play of physiognomy or to the indicating of a signified. But thus opens the dangerous way in which a pious thought, or one concerned with order, hastily deduces the existence of God.... A face does not function in proximity as a sign of a hidden God who would impose the neighbor on me. [The face] is a trace of itself, a trace in the trace of an abandon, where the equivocation is never dissipated" (AE 119; OB 93-94).

By virtue of the "absolute past" of illeity, the face of the neighbor and God can never be brought into a temporal synchrony wherein signification is alone possible. Thus the trace that is the face cannot be a trace of anything but itself. At the same time, however, illeity's mode of signification—departure and absence—disturbs what might otherwise be a straightforward relation between my conscious ego and the face as an object. Thus the face is the trace of a departed "other than the other." This ambiguity is ingredient to the notion of trace: the face of the indigent other is the trace of itself, of illeity. The trace is enigmatic.

Here, then, is what I think is Levinas's response, at least in part, to Waldenfels's concerns. It is divine illeity that ultimately and with infinite discretion founds, without being a transcendental condition, the passivity of passivity. It is the *passé immémorial* of the *Deus absconditissimus* that ceaselessly returns me to my*self* in recurrence and yet never lets me dwell there as in my domicile, my *mi-lieu*, but sends me instantly back out in service. My home, as it turns out, is already occupied, by the homeless, by the Guatemalan refugee, by the Jewish refugee. They are the ones at home; I move about to provide, and return only to bring food, to check on the sanctuary, to find out what is needed. In all of this I do not move as an instrument of destiny or fate; I confront in each instant a welter of possibilities, among which I choose. The possibility even persists, although I override it at all times, of my default, of informing, of giving up. But as the examples of an Oskar Schindler or of the inhabitants of Le Chambon-sur-Lignon, France attest, the words and deeds of "true response" can require the utmost courage, daring, resourcefulness, and conniving cleverness to carry out. If the heroism of the self is to be found anywhere, it is here, in the ultimate audacity to which we are assigned in our acceptance of the enigmatic trace, the at once divine and human assignation that is our infinite service to our neighbor.

Notes

1. Edmund Husserl, *Experience and Judgment*, trans. J. S. Churchill and K. Ameriks, ed. L. Landgrebe (Evanston: Northwestern University Press, 1973), 32-33.
2. See the frontispiece of *Otherwise than Being:* "'That is my place in the sun.' That is how the usurpation of the whole world began." The quote is taken by Levinas from Pascal, *Penseés* no. 112.
3. Fyodor Dostoyevsky, *The Brothers Karamazov*, trans. C. Garnett (New York, New American Library, 1957), 264; quoted by Levinas, EaI 105.

6

Levinas's Ethics: A Normative Perspective without Metaethical Constraints

Patricia H. Werhane

The title of this paper, "Levinas's Ethics: A Normative Perspective without Metaethical Constraints," in some measure belies its content. The paper was originally conceived as a critique of Levinas's approach to moral philosophy from the starting point of confrontation with the Other. It is by and large true that Levinas does not engage in metaethics, that is, the study of morality and the logical status of moral claims, the clarification of meanings and functions of moral discourse, and/or the analysis of the relationship between is and ought. In fact, at times Levinas conflates the descriptive and the normative, about which I shall say more later. It is a gross misreading of Levinas, however, to contend that he merely does normative ethics in the style or tradition, say, of Martin Buber. Levinas's unique contribution is his argument that morality "is not a branch of philosophy, but first philosophy" (TaI 304). With that preoccupation with the normative as first philosophy Levinas overlooks the metaethical perspective from which his analysis is derived. Nevertheless, "morality as first philosophy" is key to resolving some traditional issues in ethics and social philosophy that have plagued thinkers since Plato. So rather than merely analyze Levinas's normative perspective, in what follows I shall sketch out some of the problems in contemporary Anglo-American ethics and social philosophy (some of which have their roots in European thought). Then I shall show how Levinas's thesis that "morality is first philosophy" plays or should play a central role in resolving what have appeared to be some recalcitrant issues in normative philosophy. At the end of the essay I shall return to the question of the role of metaethics in Levinas's work.

One of the most difficult issues in ethics, and, according to Levinas, a difficulty in philosophy since Plato, is the problem of egoism. This issue, exacerbated by Thomas Hobbes, takes at least four forms. First, the thesis of psychological egoism makes the universal descriptive claim that each of us is always motivated by our own self-interests such that I am both the subject and object of my self-interests. A second, less stringent form of egocentrism claims that one is always the subject of and motivated by one's own interests, although the objects of those interests may lie, say, in saving the world, helping others, enforcing justice, and so on. Third, ethical egoism contends that one ought, always, to act in one's own self-interest. Fourth, the rational egoist, agreeing with the egocentric contention that all one's interests are interests *of* the self, argues that minimally it is always wrong to harm oneself.[1]

Crude forms of psychological and ethical egoism have been successfully attacked, since the positions in question cannot hold as universal claims. It simply is not true that one is always the object of one's own interests, and the statement that one ought always act in one's own self-interest is contradictory. The third view, that I am always the subject of *my* interests whether or not the object is myself seems to be a truism from which it follows that I ought not harm myself. But these conclusions leave us in an egocentric loop from which it is difficult or perhaps impossible to escape. If all interests originate and ultimately derive from oneself, philosophy, and thus epistemology and moral philosophy too, are to be grounded from and in an egocentric position.

"Egology" as Adriaan Peperzak calls it,[2] the focus of the subject as the center of being and source of philosophy, ethics, and moral judgments, has influenced social philosophy as well as, in different ways, the philosophies of John Rawls and Jürgen Habermas, particularly in the debate between alleged individualists and so-called communitarians. A central issue in the debate, simply put, is this: what is the relationship between the individual and the community? No one disputes the fact that one is born within and initially influenced by one's community, culture, and society. But is the self merely a product of and determined by community, "radically situated" such that what it does is merely an outcome of the complex interrelationships in which it is continually engaged?[3] If so, it is not easy to explain how it is that we are self-reflective, self-critical, creative, makers of history, and authors of change. Indeed, it is at best difficult to derive a substantive notion of the self from this point of view. If the self develops or can exert itself in a form of disengagement from community, by contrast, does it become so radically disembodied as to become merely a Sartrian *pour-soi*? If so, individuals, as disembodied selves, cannot make choices that are more than merely spontaneous acts rather than rational decisions based on knowledge, context, and past experience. It is not merely Sartre that holds this view. For example, John Rawls argues that rational persons behind a hypothetical veil of ignorance where they are "disembodied" from their history, race, ethnic origin, religion, gender, and social class, can develop principles of justice that apply to real people embedded in social situations. But can a mere subject self actually engage in thinking about such concrete notions as theories of justice? Underlying

Rawls's project is the presupposition that society does not contribute to selfhood, although a collection of selves creates society. But then, how does community develop at all from this collection of radically disembodied subjects?[4]

Jürgen Habermas tries to respond to Rawls's problem with the notion of a "progressively decentered understanding of the world" through which one aims at a more universal moral discourse from an "ideal speech situation." The process of decentering develops from one's initial preconventional stage of self-interest and individuation that originates from socialization.[5] This view, which I have grossly oversimplified, comes closer to Levinas's perspective, yet it does not fully resolve the dichotomy between the self and community.

Moreover, it is not clear that either Habermas or Rawls establishes Levinas's argument that the essence of morality (and thus of justice as well) is "first philosophy." Rawls, for example, begins *A Theory of Justice* with the statement that "[justice] is the first virtue of social institutions, as truth is of systems of thought."[6] But this is an intuitive assumption, not a ground.

The egocentric and communitarian predicaments spill over into (or are derived from) problems in the philosophy of science. Since Werner Heisenberg elaborated the indeterminacy thesis (but really since Kant), we have realized that the observer affects what is observed, so that one cannot get at "pure objective reality." In fact, the expression "objective reality" makes no sense, except as it is defined by the eye, position, perception, or point of view of the observer. The fact that all one can know is observer-biased leads to the temptation to "egolize" the notion of the observer (and Kant may be guilty of this), or to move to a radical conventionalism where reality is not merely constituted by a community of observers but is constructed or created by their conventions as well.

One masterful attempt to resolve some of these issues is exemplified in the later philosophy of Ludwig Wittgenstein, and this attempt links well with Levinas. Wittgenstein argued, in brief, that human beings are intrinsically linguistic. Language is not merely the means of communication; it is constitutive of all human experience and is the way in which we deal with whatever it is we call "reality." Wittgenstein does not go so far as to argue that "essence [and thus reality] is created by grammar" but he does comply with the Kantian-Heisenberg view that "essence is expressed by grammar" and only expressed through grammar. Meanings are linguistically constituted, although reality is not merely linguistically constructed. Wittgenstein escapes radical conventionalism with his neo-Kantian, indeed Chomskyan notion of a rule that is constitutive of the ways in which language, and thus human thought, functions or operates.

Further, Wittgenstein's position on language avoids egocentrism, because he argues that language is rule-governed, such that words and expressions are repeatable, reproducible, and thus at least in principle understandable to the broad community of human beings. Language is inherently social so that the notion of a private language, an egocentric language created by and understood in principle only by its speaker, is impossible, indeed, a contradiction. Thus egocentricism makes sense only in the context of community and language.[7]

Wittgenstein's contributions, however, are incomplete, which is why Levinas's analysis is crucial. While Wittgenstein may have made inroads into egocentricism (and I think he did), he did not go far enough either in developing the thesis that language is constitutive of human experience or in making sense out of the notion of the self. Wittgenstein's fear of dualism, egoism, egocentricism, and solipsism blocked his ability to get at the ground of human experience except through the notion of a rule. Wittgenstein questions the notion of the first person, the self, or the ego in such a way as often to be labeled a behaviorist. The latter is incorrect, but it is true that there is no developed notion of the self or of interrelationships between selves in his major later writing, *Philosophical Investigations*. Indeed, Wittgenstein makes statements such as, "always try to get rid of the idea of the private object"[8] or "I is not the name of a person."[9]

Later Wittgensteinians have explained the notion of the pronoun "I" in terms of indexicals. Pronouns such as "I" are place words that do not refer.[10] Such an analysis contributes to anti-egology, but it does little to make sense out of one's intuitive sense of a substantive self or to explain relationships between selves. Thus while Wittgenstein argues successfully against egocentrism, he also appears to question the existence of a substantive self, the self as interiority, as well.

Given this background of some traditional and contemporary issues that plague moral and social philosophy, Levinas's contributions are prescient. In arguing that "[morality] is not a branch of philosophy, but first philosophy," Levinas's objective is "establishing of this primacy of the ethical, that is, [the primacy] of the relationship of man to man—signification, teaching, and justice—a primacy of an irreducible structure upon which all other structures rest" (TaI 79). This objective, I will argue, finishes or is the starting point for Wittgenstein's analysis.

How does Levinas accomplish this? Levinas does not work his way from a starting point such as the ego, the individual, or the cogito. Nor does he begin, as Wittgenstein does, with community, language, or convention. Nor does he start from a metaethical intuitive foundation such as Rawls's statement that "[justice] is the first virtue of social institutions." Rather, Levinas begins with "face to face," the confrontation with the Other (OB 18-19). This confrontation is both descriptive and normative, and who one is and how justice is defined become realized only in this confrontation. As I understand *Otherwise than Being*, the confrontation with the Other is both irreducible and linguistic. Saying, or more literally translated, "to say" (*dire*), is the mode of face to face of which the Said (*dit*), language, is the outcome. This point is reminiscent of Wittgenstein's assertion that language is constitutive of human experience, but Levinas goes further. Levinas says, "[saying] (*dire*) is communication, to be sure, but as a condition for all communication, as exposure" (OB 48). Exposure to the Other is both constitutive of human experience and its ground, constitutive of language which is integral to that exposure and its ground as well. Levinas writes, "Being is [at least in the first instance] exteriority" (TaI 290). Confrontation is between two exteriorities who, as Others, cannot be thematized, objectified, or totally defined. "Face to face founds language" (TaI 207), and "saying states and thematizes the said, but signifies it to the other, a neighbor, with a signification that has to be distinguished from that borne by words in the said" (OB 46). As one commentator, Simon Critchley, puts it, "The Saying is the sheer radicality of human speaking, of the event of being in relation with an Other; it is the non-thematizable ethical residue of language that escapes comprehension, interrupts philosophy, and is the very enactment of the ethical movement from the Same to the Other."[11] Translating "*dire*" as "to say" captures better what Levinas is trying to convey, because the infinitive expresses in addition to the act of saying that which underlies this act.

Without challenging what has been called the "linguistic turn" in philosophy by beginning from a prelinguistic confrontation, Levinas posits "To Say" and "Said" as the ground of exposure. Moreover, "face to face" is irreducible, because the Other is "inexhaustible," "reced[ing] from thematization" just as *Dire* is not absorbed in the *Dit*, in grammar, rules, and themes of language. *Dire* is that which is not thematized, which is both transcendent and immanent in language. Yet because the confrontation or exposure in question here is linguistic in the way Levinas explains "linguistic"—exposure to the Other being an inexhaustible linguistic face-to-face phenomenon—*Dire-Dit* accounts for the universality, sociality, complexity, and inexhaustibility of language as well.

Unlike Wittgenstein, however, Levinas does not sacrifice what is intuitively important—the notion of the self and the world of selves. One's exposure to the Other captures the notion of the Other as being ambiguous, irreducible, independent, transcendent, and not absorbable into the world of the self or redefinable as an object of or for the self. At the end of *Totality and Infinity* Levinas summarizes this point:

> the face to face is a final and irreducible relation which no concept could cover without the thinker who thinks that concept finding himself forthwith before a new interlocutor; it makes possible the pluralism of society (TaI 291).

In *Otherwise than Being* Levinas implies, if I read him correctly, that this confrontation or exposure to the other is the condition on which subjectivity, the ego, the self becomes exposed, uncovered to itself (OB 48). "Face to face" confronts the ambiguity of the self as freedom and facticity without reverting to traditional dualism or solipsism. Being "exposed to the gaze" (TaI 289) as exteriority reverts to the interiority of the I that becomes articulated as self and as another Other as a result of this confrontation without the negation or objectification of either. The self is never reduced or reducible to the Other (nor the Other to the self), and the self, like the Other, is equally inexhaustible. The self that is exposed as exteriority in face to face develops its interiority from confrontation, so that its interiority is the other side of exteriority and thus not dualistic. Despite the fact that the self is never thematized, it is not, nor can it be, pure ego, since it depends on confrontation for its very exposure as self.

Like Wittgenstein, Levinas has clearly understood and absorbed in his philosophy Heisenberg's argument. Wittgenstein argued that the notion of a rule can never be isolated apart from rule following in language. Similarly, *Dire* and *Dit* are intrinsically interconnected. While neither can be reduced to the other, one cannot isolate "To Say" without Saying and Said, and the Said, in turn depends on "To Say;" neither makes sense or can be articulated without the other.

What Levinas has done is to provide a descriptive analysis of how it is we find ourselves in the world and in a community constructed by the conventions of symbols and language, and in a world of others each of whom is not merely exhaustively descriptive but is in some sense transcendent or irreducible as well as of how we find ourselves as interiority. By starting with "face to face," the *Dire* phenomenon, or "primary sociality" (TaI 304), one avoids the justificatory problems of constructing a community out of an egocentric perspective or, alternatively, an ego out of a conventionalist or social point of view.

Face to face confrontation with the Other is not merely descriptive, however. The normative is embedded in this confrontation, in the sort of experience the face to face embodies, and does not merely reveal the ego as interiority but defines sociality, the nature of human responsibility, and the limits of the normative as well. About social relations Levinas writes,

> Social relations do not simply present us with a superior empirical matter.... They are the original deployment of the relationship that is no longer open to the gaze that would encompass its terms, but is *accomplished* from me to the Other in the face to face (TaI 290).

Levinas is careful not to classify "face to face" as a relationship as it is ordinarily conceived. The exposure to the Other is neither a reciprocal relationship nor a utilitarian one. It is exposure or confrontation of the Other-as-Other. That exposure reflects on oneself as self, but the Other remains that—Other; she does not become absorbed in the self but remains irreducible to her usefulness and transcendent to reciprocal exchanges or duties that are sometimes defined as part or necessary to human moral interactions. Levinas is critical of the notion of reciprocity, because it implies that humans are interchangeable, that one may substitute one person for another, trade off rights for goods, making exploitation or worse justifiable (TaI 298).[12]

Levinas articulates another sort of relationship, that of "substitution." "Substitution" describes contact with the Other which "is conceived as a behavior—that of substituting oneself for another."[13] This form of taking an ethical stance vis-à-vis the Other is to put oneself in another's place (in her shoes, so to speak), taking responsibility for the Other as if one were the Other (OB 113-17). So one is responsible, morally responsible not merely *to* the Other but, more important, *for* the Other. In fact, Levinas seems to argue that one's responsibilities for the Other are prior to responsibilities to oneself.[14] This normative conclusion circumvents another problem of egology, the claim that all my interests are interests *of* the self, since my moral responsibilities are in the first instance *for* the Other. Bernhard Waldenfels argues in this volume that substitution grounds responsibility and that

I exist only because of and in the first instance for the Other. I read Levinas as arguing that this is more of a dialectical confrontation such that face to face grounds both the Other and oneself without reducing or absorbing either to the other.

Justice is part of face to face and sociality, although Levinas's definition and analysis of justice is not altogether clear. In *Totality and Infinity* Levinas writes, "Justice consists in again making possible expression, in which in non-reciprocity the person presents himself as unique. Justice is a right to speak" (TaI 298). In *Otherwise Than Being* Levinas implies that justice arises out of the exposure to the Other in which there is a surplus of duties over rights. That is, one has a commitment to the Other-as-Other that is nonreciprocal, so one always has duties to and for the Other as Other even when one's rights are not reciprocally recognized or honored.

The issue of justice becomes critical and is linked in a more complex manner with responsibility upon the appearance of a third party, a community of others. Justice is necessary because of the multiplicity of relationships but is not meant to degrade or objectify them. "[Justice] remains justice only in a society where there is no distinction between those close and those far off, but in which there also remains the impossibility of passing by the closest" (OB 158). Justice reminds us of our nonreciprocal responsibilities to and for others, but justice also recognizes me as one of those to be counted. Because of justice I am thought of as an Other, I am allowed to speak.

Justice, then, does not arise from an ego, from a decentering ideal speech situation, from a disinterested perspective behind a hypothetical veil, or merely out of community. Rather, it is the normative aspect of exposure to the Other who is neither merely an ego nor a radically situated self. Justice is not the first virtue of social institutions but the ground and normative side of sociality that is neither egocentric nor merely communitarian.

One may wonder whether Levinas's notion of justice provides an adequate route category to certain didactic conclusions that Levinas wants to elaborate regarding, for example, the horror of the Holocaust. I would argue that it does, but only when one takes a metaethical perspective. Levinas seldom steps back from his normative perspective to take a critical point of view on its conclusions and didactic critique. From the ground of morality as first philosophy there is a sense in which one can never step back into a purely metaethical stance. On the other ground of first philosophy, face to face is both descriptive and normative but is not reducible to either. Because face to face as *Dire* is never totally definable or thematized, and because the Other is transcendent to confrontation, the *ideal* of a transcendental, in this context metaethical point of view presents itself as that—an ideal. But the ideal is possible, so one can take a flawed, partial, disengaged meta-view on one's philosophy, one's philosophical method, and one's normative conclusions. Unfortunately, Levinas sometimes blurs the descriptive, normative, and more explicitly didactic instead of appealing to this partial metaview.

By sorting out the descriptive and the normative and pointing out how they inescapably entail each other, Levinas could make stronger claims for his notion of justice. Justice for Levinas is a normative term; it prescribes human responsibility and proscribes egocentrism in its mode of substitution and in its demands *for* the Other. But justice depends on "first philosophy," the prior claim that confrontation with the Other, the *Dire-Dit* phenomenon, grounds who we are as selves and who we are as Others out of which community emerges. The *Dire-Dit* phenomenon, then, is the descriptive/normative ground for justice as responsibility for the Other and justice in community. As ground it escapes explication, definition, reducibility, and finiteness just as objective reality escapes the grasp of science yet is its first condition. Confrontation with the Other is not reducible to the descriptive, since it is a condition expressed normatively through the notion of justice. Justice, in turn, the normative mode of *Dire-Dit*, is not *merely* normative, because it is a way of exemplifying confrontation.

Justice becomes inescapably part of being. To be unjust, to refuse responsibility for the Other is to bring into question one's self, because just as the Other is exposed through confrontation, that self cannot be as interiority, it has meaning only through confrontation with the Other. In actions beyond one's imagination such as the Holocaust, the notion of injustice was played out from an egocentric condition. But it was ultimately self-defeating, since the conquerors could not be or have meaning without the conquered, the Other.

Levinas's philosophy goes some way toward resolving problems of egoism, the issue of the individual versus the community, and radical conventionalism not by ignoring the partial truth and power of these theses or by resolving one in terms of another; rather, Levinas redefines human relationships as irreducibly social and linguistic exposures of face-to-face confrontations with Others who are irreducibly independent, transcendent yet inescapably in communication. Levinas concludes that any theory of morality which tries to reduce that relationship or absorb it into another sort of principle is simply not first philosophy. The history of humankind is, in part, a history of battles between the egologists, crude consequentialists, conventionalists, and communitarians. Levinas has been able to capture our intuitive sense of frustration about these points of view with a substantive position that brings into question these theories by simply overcoming them. Morality as first philosophy establishes a ground that preempts raising these issues.

Notes

1. See Gregory Kavka, *Hobbesian Moral and Political Theory* (Princeton: Princeton University Press, 1986), especially chapter 2, and Bernard Gert, "Hobbes and Psychological Egoism," in *Hobbes's Leviathan: Interpretation and Criticism*, ed. Bernard Baumrin (Belmont, Calif.: Wadsworth, 1969), 107-26.

2. Adriaan Peperzak, *To the Other* (West Lafayette, Ind.: Purdue University Press, 1993), 46.
3. See especially, Michael Sandel, *Liberalism and the Limits of Justice* (Cambridge: Cambridge University Press, 1983) for an analysis of this difficulty.
4. See John Rawls, *A Theory of Justice* (Cambridge: Harvard University Press, 1971). In later writings Rawls tries to answer criticisms of his notion of the self, but not with perfect success. See Rawls, *Political Liberalism* (New York: Columbia University Press, 1993).
5. Jürgen Habermas, *Moral Consciousness and Communicative Action*, trans. Christian Lenhardt and Shierry Weber Nicholsen (Cambridge: MIT Press, 1991), 168.
6. Rawls, *A Theory of Justice*, 3.
7. Ludwig Wittgenstein, *Philosophical Investigations*, trans. G. E. M. Anscombe (New York: Macmillan, 1953). See also G. E. M. Anscombe, "The Question of Linguistic Idealism," in *Essays on Wittgenstein in Honour of G. H. von Wright*, ed. Jaakko Hintikka (Amsterdam: North Holland Publishing Co., 1976), and Patricia H. Werhane, *Skepticism, Rules, and Private Language* (Atlantic Highlands, N.J.: Humanities Press, 1992), especially chapter 7.
8. Wittgenstein, 2: 207.
9. Ibid., § 410. The literature on first-person pronouns in analytic philosophy is as vast and informative as that on *Dasein* in phenomenology.
10. See especially G. E. M. Anscombe, "The First Person," in *Mind and Language*, ed. Samuel Guttenplan (Oxford: Oxford University Press, 1975).
11. Simon Critchley, *The Ethics of Deconstruction* (Oxford: Blackwell, 1992), 7. See also Levinas, OB 18.
12. That this is not just a seventeenth-century problem is illustrated in Robert Nozick's book *Anarchy, State, and Utopia* (New York: Basic Books, 1974), winner of the 1974 National Book Award, in which Nozick argues that a rational person can voluntarily trade herself into slavery, and indeed, that another person can accept that trade and become a slaveholder.
13. Alphonso Lingis, in his introduction to *Otherwise Than Being* (OB xxii).
14. See the papers by Waldenfels and Miller in this volume for a more detailed interpretation of Levinas's notion of the priority of one's responsiblities to the Other or others.

7

The Notion of Persecution in Levinas's *Otherwise Than Being or Beyond Essence*[1]

Elisabeth Weber
Translated from the German by Mark Saatjian.

The expert testimony William G. Niederland, in his capacity as psychiatrist, provided in the so-called reparations trials in post–World War II Germany is documented in the book *Consequences of Persecution: The Survivor-Syndrome Soul Murder*. In the postscript one reads: "Not least among the numerous damages incurred by the Ego-structure through persecution is the harm to the sense of time; therefore the affected persons come either too early or too late to the doctor's visiting hours, they become confused while relating whether they were interned in the concentration camp in 1942 or 1943 and so on. In the reparation hearings such slips usually work to the disadvantage of the plaintiff."[2]

The fact that the survivors can no longer exactly reconstruct in their memories the temporal continuum of the persecution they endured and the fact that later the cohesive bond of their lives often slips away from them, is for some official medical experts, as Niederland shows, reason enough to doubt the believability of their reports of persecution. This in turn provides reason enough to classify the existing suffering as "not persecution related," to identify instead a "predisposition," by the "cruelly inevitable law of a hereditary constitution," as responsible for the suffering, thereby annulling any right to reparation, which, when awarded, is in most cases extremely meager.[3] The violence that inflicted the "break in the cohesive lifeline"[4] (the break which caused harm to the sense of time) is ignored, and the symptoms are traced back to a lack of intelligence, to a predisposition, or to age-related fatigue. The disturbance to the sense of time caused by persecution, cynically enough, has legal consequences, namely, the rejection of legal recognition of the suffering as persecution related. The dogma on which the judgment rests is then that a complaint can only be recognized on the condition of proof of a coherent, linear chronology of experienced injustice; on the presupposition that *chronos* is subject to *logos* and that for the just decision there can only be truth in the realm of chrono-logy. It is chronology, however, whose idiom was made inaccessible to the plaintiff under the most terrible violence. There exists here a *differend* in the sense that Jean-François Lyotard gives this term.[5]

As the "main cause of the various pictures of mental disruption in the formerly persecuted," Niederland's expert testimonies present "the fact that the cohesive lifeline of their past was severed completely, and often in the most terrible way, by persecution. This is how a usually irreparable *cut interrupts the lifeline*."[6] In crass contrast to the break in the lifeline, which has been continually noted, is the likewise continually returning opinion of most official medical experts that "according to experience, psychic suffering is ameliorated and does not become worse in the course of time" and that consequently "a request for reparation is ungrounded."[7] The dogma that "every psychic trauma, including the most severe, fades when the traumatizing influence ceases"[8] assumes without ado that the course of time heals all wounds and that time causes one to forget even what one of the official medical experts unhesitatingly refers to as the "uncomfort" of the concentration camp.[9] Here the conception of the time-constituting continuum is adopted: the "stream of a constant production of modifications of modifications"[10] will carry away even a trauma as deep as this. However, it is exactly this stream of time that was interrupted. The dominant discourse of psychiatry proves itself to be complicit with the discourse of the prevailing juridical opinion: in neither of the two discourses is it possible to articulate, and that means recognize, a break in the continuous temporality.

One of the factors, perhaps the decisive factor, causing the "absolute break in the lifeline" lies, as emerges from the testimonies of the survivors, in the "necessity" of "reconciling oneself with the certainty of being condemned to death."[11] In this sense there was no future for the concentration-camp prisoners, there was "no tomorrow."[12] There was then no continuity stretching into the future, no time line, no stream of time, no possibility of traveling somewhere else in time. On the contrary, time was inexorably closed; as a survivor, one was only late to this verdict. Niederland introduces the testimony of a former prisoner: in Auschwitz, as he appeared for the daily roll call, it seemed to him as if he "were following behind his own corpse."[13] It was the "encounter with death in its most dreadful forms" that inflicted the break in the lifeline.[14] In stark opposition to the "unteachability" of the unconscious, which, as Freud postulated, cannot be convinced of its mortality, there stands the absolute certainty of having been condemned to death, of the impossibility of a tomorrow. Death thus breaks into the present.

Emmanuel Levinas has placed his book *Otherwise Than Being or Beyond Essence* under a twofold dedication to the victims of the National Socialist persecution. The "concepts" that mark this book as no other of Levinas's texts, "persecution," "obsession," "trauma," and even "psychosis," are all defined by a break in coherent linear chronology. Through this interruption of the time of clocks, however, concepts such as "proximity" and "vulnerability" as well no longer belong to a philosophical discourse driven by the question of being or essence. But it is precisely because "concepts" like "persecution," "trauma," and "proximity" (in general, the relation to the other) are defined by a break in the temporal succession that they are ambivalent.

Let us first examine Levinas's description of "proximity."

> Proximity as a suppression of distance suppresses the distance of consciousness of.... The neighbor [*le prochain*] excludes himself from the thought that seeks him, and this exclusion has a positive side to it: my exposure to him, antecedent to his appearing, my delay behind him, my undergoing, undo the core of what is identity in me. Proximity, suppression of the distance that consciousness of ... involves, opens the distance of a dia-chrony without a common present where difference is the past that cannot be caught up with, an unimaginable future, the non-representable status of the neighbor behind which I am late and obsessed by the neighbor. This difference is my non-indifference to the other. Proximity is a disturbance of the memorable time. One can call that apocalyptically the break-up of time. (OB 89)

This an-archy of the other, the impossibility of taking him up into the presence of consciousness, of thinking, of memory as internalization, this impossibility determines, on the one hand, as the passage cited shows, proximity but also, on the other hand, that which Levinas calls "persecution":

> In the form of an ego, anachronously *delayed* behind its present moment, and unable to recuperate this delay—that is, in the form of an ego unable to conceive what is 'touching' it, the ascendancy of the other is exercised upon the same to the point of interrupting it, leaving it speechless. Anarchy is persecution. Obsession is a persecution where the persecution does not make up the content of a consciousness gone mad; it designates the form in which the ego is affected, a form which is a defecting from consciousness. (OB 101)

> The persecuted one cannot defend himself by language, for the persecution is a disqualification of the apology. Persecution is the precise moment in which the subject is reached or touched without the mediation of the logos. (OB 121)[15]

This "precise moment," in which there is no mediation of the *logos*, cannot be reached by a discourse that thematizes it, or if so then only under certain conditions. Levinas mentions at one point the "pain of expression," which he says occurs in a philosophical attempt like the one that characterizes *Otherwise Than Being*. The central chapter, which Levinas himself calls the "germ" of the entire book, concerns "persecution," and this in spite of the constantly emphasized fact that persecution leaves the subject speechless, without *logos*, without successive temporality in the present, even without consciousness.

Levinas writes that it is only the trace, the one left behind by persecution, that language in the "pain of expression" can attempt to say (OB 194 n. 4). This, for its part, leaves traces in the philosophical discourse. The striking syntactical and stylistic figures of *Otherwise Than Being*, like repetition, "raising to a power" (as in the case of "suffering of the suffering," "passivity of the passivity," etc.), hyperbole, and superlative construction follow these traces. They allow a second voice to become audible, one that tears up and drowns out the first; they stand for a wound, a scar, a trauma, for the possibility of such an injury to the philosophical discourse. They mark the places where this speech swerves into a region in which, no longer offering support, the traditional philosophical terminology needs other idioms. These figures can consequently be called "metaphors" in the following sense: they bring into the text traces of a real before which the functions of mediation and representation of consciousness fail. The footnote to one of the first pages of the book describes the almost methodical function of one of these stylistic figures: "it is the superlative, more than the negation of categories, which interrupts systems, as though the logical order and the being it succeeds in espousing retained the superlative which exceeds them. In subjectivity the superlative is the exorbitance of a non-place [*non-lieu*]" (OB 187 n. 5).

The exceptionally frequent use of superlatives in *Otherwise Than Being* carries traces of "non-places" in the text, of the inability of the *logos* to say these "non-places," but also of its inability to say the nontimes or untimes, the temporal breaks. While the superlative is used again and again in connection with the "persecution," and while the superlative thereby opens in the text a trace of the nonplace par excellence to which the subject of the persecution is exposed, it is also used in the description of proximity, touching, and of tenderness. The ambiguity of the concept of persecution lies then in the fact that on the one hand—in a book dedicated to the victims of National Socialism—it cannot not speak of this "historical disaster," it cannot have been chosen without reference to the Shoah, but on the other hand, and *at the same time*, it names the interrupted ego, the one left speechless, a core which always splits itself further in the "exposition" to the other, the in-dividual. Following Levinas, the persecuted as well as this subject are both "already identified from the outside" (OB 107), without the possibility of defense. Is the subject then always already persecuted and therefore only exposed to concrete possibilities of persecution? Why is the encounter with the other described in the same figures of interruption as persecution?

Concepts like "trauma," "psychosis," and so on, carry into the text the trace of a real that left many of those who survived it insane, and left others tormented for the rest of their lives. They had suffered the utmost violence of being so very *nothing* for an other that his violence wasn't even based on a face, which is to say, was not even violence, since, as is stated by Levinas in *Totality and Infinity*, violence can only base itself on a face. And further, they were so very *nothing* that they could not even be killed, first because murder, as it is said in the same text, is directed toward a face, which disappears in mass murder, and second for the following, so to speak, "more principal" reason. In the National Socialist "logics," "the authority of the SS," as Jean-François Lyotard writes in *The Differend*,

> comes out of a we from which the deportee is excepted once and for all: the race, which grants not only the right to command but also the right to live, that is, to place oneself at the various instances of phrase universes. The deportee, according to this authority, cannot be the addressee of an order to die, because one would have to be capable of giving one's life in order to carry out the order. But one cannot give a life that one doesn't have the right to have. Sacrifice is not available to the deportee, nor for that reason accession to an immortal, collective name. One's death is legitimate because one's life is illegitimate. The individual name must be killed (whence the use of serial numbers), and the collective name (Jew) must also be killed in such a way that no we bearing this name might remain which could take the deportee's death into itself and eternalize it. This death must therefore be killed, and that is what is worse than death. For, if death can be exterminated, it is because there is nothing to kill. Not even the name Jew.[16]

The real, whose trace the "metaphors" of *Otherwise Than Being* intimate, is this threat of the killing of death, and it is to this threat that these metaphors attempt to respond.

The "reason" for the close connection in *Otherwise Than Being* between persecution and the encounter with the other is found in the threat of "psychosis." With the concept of psychosis a real crashes into the text that does not become visible in any mirror of the sovereign subject and its sciences: the threat of the killing of death.

The book responds to this threat, especially in the chapter concerning persecution, "Substitution." First it does so in a nearly imperceptible way. It places itself under a motto from Paul Celan's poem "In Praise of Remoteness:" "Ich bin du, wenn ich ich bin." "I am you when I am I." With that, the text places itself beneath a poem in whose sixteen lines the phrase "in the wellspring of your eyes" is called on four times. "In the wellspring of your eyes" is a place in which reversals occur: "Blacker in black I am more naked / Unfaithful, I am true / I am you when I am I"; and "In the wellspring of your eyes / A hanged man strangles the rope." While the poem bears the title "In Praise of Remoteness," it is also a praise of the "wellspring of your eyes." Could it be that this spring is the spring of tears, which as the tears of the other are always inaccessibly strange and distant? The motto with which the chapter "Substitution" begins situates the latter in the "wellspring of your eyes," which if "I am you when I am I," becomes the wellspring of *my* eyes. The substitution attempted here can be read as an attempt to meditate on "persecution" and thus as an attempt to answer that which, as Levinas underlines, cannot be known, even if this attempt is threatened by the breaking of speech. This substitution begins in the wellspring of your/my eyes, begins in the ability to cry, in an opening before words, in the possibility of mourning. This motto, this "*hors-texte*" gives then perhaps a hint as to how the text should be read.

As Levinas emphasizes at the beginning of *Otherwise Than Being*, it was a wound that brought the subject to expose his thoughts. In other words, the wound preceded the ego who writes and bears witness.

As wounded subject I am in the "wellspring of your eyes," in the mourning and in the attempt to remember the immemorial. As writing and testifying ego the ego is, however, already "late" to that which affects, which touches it. The ego's speech preserves at most the trace of being affected, and the trace of being possessed. It *betrays* these traces, however, and this betrayal is unavoidable in bearing witness: "Unfaithful, I am true." The anamnesis of persecution can only occur in words, the interruption of language cannot remain absolute.

If for the subject in *Otherwise Than Being* the wounding par excellence is the silence of the other, if it is the silence of the dead and the impossibility for the survivors to say what happened to them, if this silence and this impossibility have traumatically touched the subject, then the encounter with the Other repeats this trauma, for the subject is left "without words" by this encounter. This connection between persecution and other is significant: the trauma which is repeated, or, more exactly, the trauma which in the encounter with the other recalls an earlier trauma, is trauma *because* it is reminiscent of an immemorial trauma. But then it breaks, it *opens up* the impossibility of remembering this speechlessness. *Otherwise than Being* "stands" in this opening. In the trauma of this opening *there are words*. That distinguishes it from the trauma of persecution, and only *because* there are words is it reminiscent of the absolute lack of words. This trauma is trauma because it opens anamnesis. This trauma is trauma because it recalls the attempt undertaken in persecution to kill death, but it does so by making mourning, and hence death, again possible: the trauma of the encounter with the other is trauma of absolute responsibility, which is traumatic only because the one encountered can die.

The trauma of absolute responsibility comes in contact with the absolute trauma of persecution to the extent that the former situates itself before the authority which enacts law and language and which persecution intends to destroy. To speak to the other implies the recognition of this law and of death. The encounter with the other is called "traumatic" because it is the sole path of an anamnesis of the trauma of persecution, of the killing of death. This encounter touches the trauma, but exactly in this contact opens trauma, since, in encountering the other, the subject encounters, as Levinas says, his or her extreme vulnerability, and that means his or her mortality.

The connection between persecution and other allows then the *possibility* of mourning. The impossible mourning, which corresponds to death killed, is opened onto a possible mourning. Only in this opening are anamnesis and bearing witness possible. The giving of testimony in *Otherwise Than Being* will be designated implicitly as "betrayal," however, even if as necessary betrayal. If the text is able to bear witness, it condemns bearing witness at the same time. This impasse and this hesitation mark the book *Otherwise Than Being*, and if Levinas writes in another place, "forgetting is the law, the happiness and the condition of life. But here life is wrong (DF 149)," then this sentence underlies as a palimpsest many passages in this book.

The wrong of life is the wrong of surviving. The mourning that could become possible is a betrayal, a betrayal committed in survival, as other testimonies constantly attest. Niederland reports that the "survivor syndrome" manifests itself, among other things, in the "deep guilt of having survived," a guilt which reveals the "macabre irony" that "not the perpetrators and executioners of Nazi crimes but rather their victims seem to suffer the guilt of having survived."[17]

"Anamnesis," the anamnesis of the impossible death, that is, the death of the other as well as of one's own death, is what is demanded in *Otherwise Than Being* in order to make the death of the other as well as one's own death possible. Sentences like the following therefore have a very real background: "The soul is the other in me. The psyche, the-one-for-the-other, can be a possession and a psychosis: the soul is already a seed of madness" (OB 191 n. 3). The soul, as an impossibly solipsistic soul, as a soul always already with others and with the "other other," with death,[18] needs the other, the ability to die and also the other human being's ability to die. In persecution this "we" is meant to be destroyed, this we, the most ephemeral and the deepest, I am you when I am I.

Notes

1. The reflections of the following paper find more thorough elaboration in Elisabeth Weber, *Verfolgung und Trauma: Zu Emmanuel Lévinas' "Autrement qu'être ou au-delà de l'essence"* (Vienna: Passagen Verlag, 1990).
2. William G. Niederland, *Consequences of Persecution: The Survivor-Syndrome Soul Murder (Folgen der Verfolgung: Das Überlebenden-Syndrom Seelenmord)*, (Frankfurt am Main: Suhrkamp, 1980), 231.
3. See ibid., 8, 12-13, 128, 192, 220, and passim. See also William G. Niederland, "Psychiatric Disorders among Persecution Victims," *Journal of Nervous and Mental Disease* (Baltimore) 139 (1964), 458.
4. E. de Wind, "Begegnung mit dem Tod," *Psyche* (June 1968): 437. See also W. R. von Baeyer, H. Häfner, and K. P. Kisker, *Psychiatrie der Verfolgten* (Berlin: Soringer, 1964), 221.

5. Jean-François Lyotard, *The Differend*, trans. Georges Van Den Abbeele (Minneapolis: University of Minnesota Press, 1988).
6. "...ein zumeist unheilbarer *Knick in der Lebenslinie*" (Niederland, *Folgen der Verfolgung*, 229).
7. Medical experts quoted in Niederland, "Psychische Spätschäden nach politischer Verfolgung," *Psyche* (1965): 888, and "Psychiatric Disorders," 458. See also Kurt R. Eissler, "Die Ermordung von wievielen seiner Kinder muß ein Mensch symptomfrei ertragen können, um eine normale Konstitution zu haben?" *Psyche* (1963): 241.
8. Medical experts quoted in Niederland, "Psychische Spätschäden," 891.
9. "In a case described by Eissler the medical expert spoke of the 'uncomforts' [*Unannehmlichkeiten*] of the concentration camp," (ibid., 892). In 1966 William Niederland expressed the fear that psychiatry in German-speaking countries, through the influence of the Nazi ideology, seemed in some cases to have remained "at the level of the scientific knowledge of the 1920s." See Niederland, "Ein Blick in die Tiefen der 'unbewältigten' Vergangenheit und Gegenwart: Anläßlich der Besprechung von W. Ritter von Baeyer, H. Häfner und K. P. Kisker, Psychiatrie der Verfolgten," *Psyche* (June 1966): 466.
10. See Edmund Husserl, *Zur Phänomenologie des inneren Zeitbewußtseins*, ed. R. Boehm (The Hague: M. Nijhoff, 1966), 100.
11. E. de Wind, "Begegnung mit dem Tod," 437.
12. Ibid.; see also William G. Niederland, "Diskussionsbeitrag zu E. de Wind: Begegnung mit dem Tod," *Psyche* (June 1968): 445.
13. Niederland, "Diskussionsbeitrag," 444.
14. Niederland, *Folgen der Verfolgung*, 232.
15. The English translation reads erroneously "with" instead of "without" (*sans*).
16. Lyotard, *The Differend*, 101.
17. Niederland, *Folgen der Verfolgung*, 232.
18. Weber, *Verfolgung und Trauma*, 196. See also Rainer Marten, "Heideggers Heimat—eine philosophische Herausforderung," in *Nachdenken über Heidegger: Eine Bestandsaufnahme*, ed. U. Guzzoni (Hildesheim: Gerstenberg, 1980).

8

"Only the Persecuted…": Language of the Oppressor, Language of the Oppressed

Robert Bernasconi

The basic framework that Levinas employs to describe the encounter with the Other in the face to face is well known. "Ethics and the Face," the second chapter of the Third Section of *Totality and Infinity*, gives the now classic explication of how I discover my responsibility in the face of the Other who appeals to me in his or her destitution and hunger (TeI 175; TaI 200). In a world of hunger, I am an oppressor. Sometimes Levinas portrays the full force of that responsibility, as when he cites the saying of Rabbi Yochanan that "to leave men without food is a fault that no circumstance attenuates; the distinction between the voluntary and the involuntary does not apply here" (TeI 175; TaI 201). I discover myself to be "murderous" (TeI 56; TaI 84). By contrast, the Other reveals himself or herself as "the primordial phenomenon of gentleness" (TeI 124; TaI 150).

The familiarity of this account makes it easy to forget that elsewhere Levinas takes up the seemingly very different case of my responsibility for the one who persecutes me: "the persecuted one is liable to answer for the persecutor" (AE 141; OB 111). This is to be found not in an isolated text but in "Substitution," an essay from 1968 that in 1974, in a revised version, became the central chapter of Levinas's second magnum opus, *Otherwise Than Being*. Furthermore, Levinas again draws on rabbinic literature, citing Rachi's commentary as saying that one is responsible "to the point of being delivered over to stoning and insults" from those for whom one answers in one's responsibility (AE 110n; OB 192 n. 24). If, to the best of my knowledge, nobody has succeeded in reconciling the two different analyses or languages to be found across Levinas's two major works, it should also be said that most commentators seem untroubled by this issue.[1]

If one were to speculate on the general lack of concern for this issue among Levinas's readers, one might attribute it to their familiarity with the ambiguity of the face from *Totality and Infinity*. In *Totality and Infinity*, the Other, who commands me not to kill, also threatens me with violence. If the face is always ambiguous in this way, then am I not correspondingly both murderous and subject to violence? Early in *Otherwise Than Being* Levinas again took up the ambiguity of the face of the neighbor as both the one "*before whom* (or *to whom*, without any paternalism)" I answer and the one "*for whom*" I answer: "For such is the enigma or ex-ception of a face, judge and accused" (AE 14; OB 12). One finds a variation of this developed precisely in respect of persecution for the chapter "Substitution" in *Otherwise than Being*: "The face of the neighbor in its persecuting hatred can by this very malice obsess as something pitiful. This equivocation or enigma *only the persecuted one*, who does not evade it, but is without any references, any recourse or help (that is its uniqueness or its identity as unique!), is able to endure" (AE 141; OB 111; emphasis added). By an extension of this line of thought, perhaps I am both persecuted and oppressor to the extent that the face which confronts me is both judge and accused.

However, even were one to reconcile the apparent inconsistency between the dominant analysis of *Totality and Infinity* and that of the "Substitution" chapter by appeal to the ambiguity of the face, it would still be necessary to establish the status of this ambiguity. Levinas does not provide very much guidance here. Is one to say that it is a fundamental datum about the face that it is two-faced in this way? Or is Levinas taking two contrary tendencies that can be observed in human beings and referring them back to the face as their transcendental condition? Does the answer lie perhaps in the claim that the persecuted one alone can endure the enigma of the face (AE 141; OB 111)? Furthermore, once one had answered that question, it would still leave intact the fact that in *Totality and Infinity* the alterity of the Other arises for a separated I, whereas the analysis of substitution has recourse to Rimbaud's "Je est un autre." This formulation, like Celan's "Ich bin du, wenn ich ich bin," is an affront to the logic and grammar of the Western philosophical tradition. The question of the reconciliation of the language of the oppressor and the language of the persecuted might seem at first to be no more than that of reconciling two models, but what appears to be at issue now are two logics. The account of the face in *Totality and Infinity* seems to have as its framework the philosophy of identity: it is with reference to the same, the I, that the Other is encountered. By contrast, the notion of substitution is introduced precisely to contest the logic of identity. To be for the other is to be without identity (AE 73; OB 57).

Of course, the situation is far more complex than that for at least two reasons. First, Levinas already challenges the identity of the I in *Totality and Infinity*, albeit in the very different context of the discussion of fecundity (TeI 250; TaI 272). Second, even while seemingly relying on the logic of identity in the central portions of *Totality and Infinity*, Levinas does not hesitate to announce his departure from what he calls "formal logic" (TeI 77; TaI 104). The crucial point is, however, that a comparison of the two books shows that they do not represent two elaborations of a single scheme.

In *Otherwise Than Being* Levinas does more than translate an already completed thought into a new idiom. Whereas in *Totality and Infinity* Levinas stresses the distance and height of the stranger, in *Otherwise Than Being* the focus falls on the proximity of the neighbor. Whereas according to the earlier analysis I found myself put in question in the face of the stranger, in the later analysis I am "like a stranger" (AE 117; OB 92). My home is no longer the site of inwardness and hospitality (TeI 126; TaI 152); it has become the site of contestation. Furthermore, the introduction of persecution alters the status accorded to apology. In a passage from the 1968 essay "Substitution," in lines that were expanded but not radically altered for *Otherwise Than Being*, Levinas writes: "Accused beyond any fault, to be persecuted is to be unable to defend oneself in language. The disqualification of the apology is the very characteristic of persecution" (S 504). Compared with the later works, the treatment of apology in *Totality and Infinity* appears somewhat ambiguous: the I both asserts itself and inclines before the transcendent (TeI 10; TaI 40). By contrast, in *Otherwise Than Being*, the apology is the means by which consciousness regains its self-control (AE 130; OB 102). Persecution interrupts every apology, every *logos* (AE 156; OB 197 n. 26).

Levinas's own testimony in the augmented version of "Signature" is that in *Otherwise Than Being* he succeeds in freeing himself from the ontological language of *Totality and Infinity*. "The ontological language which *Totality and Infinity* still uses in order to exclude the purely psychological significance of the proposed analyses is henceforth avoided. And the analyses themselves refer not to the *experience* in which a subject always thematizes what he equals, but to the *transcendence* in which he answers for that which his intentions have not encompassed" (DL 379; DF 295). What can Levinas mean when he describes *Otherwise Than Being* as free both of ontological language and the language of thematized experience? The answer to that question is perhaps best approached by understanding how both these languages already operate in *Totality and Infinity*. I have argued elsewhere that in *Totality and Infinity* the language of transcendental conditions and the language of empiricism are juxtaposed without being reconciled in an attempt to point beyond both of them.[2] One merit of this reading is that it helps explain how Levinas could in his later works still retain so much of the language of *Totality and Infinity* while at the same time recognizing the need to *avoid* it. It should not be overlooked that the language of *Totality and Infinity* remains the dominant language he employed for the exposition of his thought, even after he had completed *Otherwise Than Being*.[3] A brief examination of how Levinas avoids the language of thematized experience specifically is in order.

The logic of substitution transforms the apparent suggestion of the earlier analyses that the Other came on the scene to address an I that had already attained the level of a subject. In some passages in *Otherwise Than Being* Levinas contests the dominant account offered by *Totality and Infinity* simply by reversing the order in which the protagonists might be said to have arrived. "Absolving himself from all essence, all genus, all resemblance, the neighbor, *the first one on the scene*, concerns me for the first time (even if he is an old acquaintance, an old friend, an old lover, long caught up in the fabric of my social relations) in a contingency that excludes the a priori" (AE 109; OB 86).

Levinas does not seem to be troubled by the fact that he is still here giving a representation of a scene. He even evokes the "fabric of my social relations," although they are at once transcended. This enables Levinas to reintroduce into the new context his earlier analysis of the face (AE 112; OB 88). Elsewhere in *Otherwise Than Being*, however, Levinas goes further. In keeping with his stated aim to move away from the "narrative, epic way of speaking" that was still dominant in *Totality and Infinity* (AE 16; OB 13), he redescribes the "being put in question by the alterity of the other" of *Totality and Infinity* so that it takes place "before the appearing of the other" in sensibility (AE 95; OB 75). One of the primary effects of the term "substitution" is to combat the ingrained presumption that the story that must be told is that of how an already formed subject turns toward the neighbor. As a result, the language of alterity falls under suspicion. Levinas by no means abandons this language altogether, but in *Otherwise Than Being* he questions it on the grounds that it is susceptible to ontological categories (AE 19; OB 15-16). What is at stake is both a terminology and a logic.

Within this context, how radical is the change of emphasis brought about by the introduction of the heavily charged term "persecution"? In "Language and Proximity" Levinas repeats with specific reference to *Totality and Infinity*, that "in the face cognition and the manifestation of being or truth are engulfed in an ethical relationship" (DEHH 229; CP 120). He then adds, in what to my knowledge is the first use of the term "obsession" in his philosophical writings, "Consciousness reverts to obsession." Because "language, contact, is the obsession of an I 'beset' by the others" (DEHH 233; CP 123), there is some suggestion that this responsibility "for the pain and fault of others" is a persecution. Indeed, Levinas writes: "Obsessed precisely with responsibilities that do not go back to decisions taken by a freely contemplating subject, and thus accused with what it never did, persecuted and thrown back upon itself, backed up to itself, ipseity 'takes on itself,' in the absolute inability of slipping away from proximity, from the face, from the dereliction of the face where infinity is also absence" (DEHH 233; CP 123). It might seem that Levinas is saying no more than that to be obsessed by the Other is to be persecuted by the other. "Obsession is a persecution where the persecution does not make up the content of a consciousness gone mad; it designates the form in which the ego is affected, a form which is a defecting from consciousness" (AE 128; OB 101). There would be no reference to what ordinarily passes for persecution. Obsession would be "unassumable like a persecution" (AE 110; OB 87). The continuity with *Totality and Infinity* would not be threatened.

Does persecution serve as a formal notion? Does *Otherwise Than Being* set out universal structures that can be applied to anyone independent of their condition? When Levinas says that the Other is a stranger who has no other place, that the

Other is "uprooted, without a country, not an inhabitant, exposed to the cold and the heat of the seasons" (AE 116; OB 91), he is saying, among other things, not only that the Other makes a claim on me irrespective of his or her nationality but also that the Other has the claim on me that the nationless, the refugees, and the homeless have. "Misery and poverty are not properties of the other [*Autre*], but the modes of his or her appearing to me, way of concerning me, and mode of proximity" (HS 32; OS 18). Does not this make the poor one, the homeless, the Other par excellence? "To be reduced to having recourse to me is the homelessness or strangerness of the neighbor" (AE 116; OB 91). What if I too am poor and homeless? Am I still then responsible for the Other? Levinas gives no indication that my responsibility is in any way limited either by my objective condition or by that of the Other, who may be better off than I am. But even if to exist is to be called into question, would one want to say also that to exist is to be persecuted? If persecution is to be understood as a universal structure, it would be hard not to conclude that Levinas had simply introduced an ontological language of his own, much as Heidegger did in *Being and Time*, where a term like "solicitude" was said to bear an ontological sense, divorced from any ontic reference. However, to understand Levinas in that way would be to ignore his attack on Heidegger's division of the existential from the concrete *existentiell* (TeI 250; TaI 272). It is true that when Levinas writes of my responsibility "for the persecution, with which, before any intention, he persecutes me" (AE 212; OB 166), this seems to set the notion of persecution, as Levinas employs it, apart from what ordinarily passes for persecution. But would Levinas, looking for a purely formal notion, select the term "persecution," when it is what defines his life—"the presentiment and the memory of the Nazi horror" (DL 374; DF 291)—and the fate of so many members of his family?

The phrase "only the persecuted" (AE 141; OB 111) quoted earlier differentiates the persecuted from the persecutor, but it is at least on the face of it possible that it could still be made to conform to the formal interpretation of persecution, where to be persecuted means no more than to bear responsibility and so refers to everyone. But the same phrase also occurs in another context, where it does not admit of such a reading. In "Judaism and Revolution," a Talmudic reading that dates from 1969, Levinas writes: "To bear responsibility for everything and everyone is to be responsible despite oneself. To be responsible despite oneself is to be persecuted. *Only the persecuted* must answer for everyone, even for his persecutor" (SS 46; NTR 114-15; emphasis added).

These three sentences have the appearance of a non sequitur, but on closer examination they convey the logic of substitution and thus clarify the transition from *Totality and Infinity* to *Otherwise Than Being*. The passage occurs as part of a discussion of the destiny of Judaism, thereby excluding a straightforward formal interpretation. Levinas identifies Judaism with "responsibility for the entire universe, and consequently, a universally persecuted Judaism" (SS 46; NTR 114). The destiny of Judaism is the missing premise supplied by the context which establishes the consequence in that chain of thought, although even with the premise supplied it remains to be shown that Levinas's logic does not revert to that of identity. The three sentences on responsibility and persecution can be understood as an attempt to translate this Hebraic wisdom into the *logos* of the Greek language. But it is a translation which is imperfect in the very specific sense that the thought is rendered incoherent in the absence of any specific reference to the destiny of Judaism. Levinas's understanding of the destiny of Judaism underwrites the sequence of thought giving rise to the conclusion "only the persecuted must answer for everyone." The reference to Judaism does not render Levinas's thought exclusive; the paragraph from which the sentences just quoted are drawn ends with the statement "non-Jews can also feel this Jewish particularism" (SS 47; NTR 115). It would be entirely inappropriate to attempt to identify the persecuted and so reimpose the very logic of identity that the logic of substitution as it arises from persecution challenges. Similarly, solidarity with the persecuted does not render one persecuted oneself.[4] Persecution is an election and to declare that each and every one of us is persecuted is tantamount to denying persecution.

Levinas does not attempt to explain clearly in "Judaism and Revolution" what it means to say that the tension between Judaism and universalism confers on Judaism "a meaning beyond universalism," but he does explore it further elsewhere, for example, in "From the Rise of Nihilism to the Carnal Jew," which, like the first version of "Substitution," was first published in 1968.[5] In it Levinas offers a description of persecution as "an invisible universality" (DL 290; DF 225) while not ignoring the persecution that exists at the level of fact and which in the form of Nazi persecution was evoked on the opening page (DL 285; DF 221). These are not easy to reconcile. Levinas marks the difference between "the Israel that is interpreted spiritually, where there is an obvious equation between Israel and the Universal" and "an Israel of Fact, a particular reality that has traversed history as a victim, bearing a tradition and certainties that did not want to win acclaim from the end of History" (DL 288; DF 223). But is it possible to give a universal meaning to persecution? Persecution is not directed at the universal: the Inhuman does not have humanity as its target. One is persecuted as a Jew, an Arab, a heretic, or for one's color.

The problem arises acutely in the context of the dedication to *Otherwise Than Being*, "To the memory of those who were closest among the six million assassinated by the National Socialists, and of the millions on millions of all confessions and all nations, victims of the same hatred of the other man, the same anti-semitism." The dedication to the millions on millions of all confessions who are victims of "the same anti-semitism" is problematic not least because it seems to attempt to subsume all persecution and all hatred under one form of hatred. Not everyone who is a victim would welcome being told that they were victims specifically of anti-Semitism. It is especially problematic at the beginning of a philosophical text, and one that challenges the logic of identity. Is this "sad privilege" to which the Jews are elected (DL 361; DF 281) evoked at the point where the reading begins out of sentiment? Or does it not address the book to those who can supply for themselves the missing premise of Jewish destiny without which the book would remain incoherent? And is it not ultimately this Jewish destiny of persecution that according to

Levinas, enables the enigma of the face to be endured? Only the persecuted can endure this enigma, just as it is only the persecuted who must answer for everyone. In other words, only with reference to persecution does the logic of *Otherwise Than Being* emerge, a logic that avoids the philosophy of identity as traditionally conceived and so allows the notion of substitution to be expressed.

One can see what Levinas is attempting to do when he looks to Judaism to negotiate the relation between the particular and the universal. Judaism is a particularity that promotes universalism (DL 28; DF 13), conditions it (DL 39; DF 22). This is not to say that Levinas's attempt to negotiate the tension between Jewish election and Jewish universalism is clear. His insistence that this "universalist particularism" is not Hegel's concrete universal is stated rather than explained, but Levinas does establish its relation to a people who for centuries confronted "the danger of persecution" (DL 128; DF 96). The privilege Levinas assigns to Judaism might indeed be difficult for some other peoples to accept, but reading the dedication in the context of the confessional writings, one encounters a thought that finds its basis in the persecution of the Jewish people and yet explicitly extends its application to other persecuted peoples. The second dedication to *Otherwise Than Being* guards against losing touch with the particularity of a strictly Jewish destiny. Written in Hebrew, it is inaccessible to many of Levinas's readers. It records the names of Levinas's father, mother, brothers, father-in-law, and mother-in-law, in whose memory the book is offered. Perhaps one can use this more personal dedication, written in memory of these victims of Nazi persecution, to suggest that the concept of persecution to which Levinas appeals is not a generalization but is always rooted in a certain specificity.

The fate suffered by the persecuted—the Jewish people and all those who are victims of the same anti-Semitism—underwrites Levinas's philosophy in a rigorous sense. That is to say, Levinas does not just draw on persecution in developing his thought. It is more even than an ontic fundament. Responsibility for everyone, as opposed to some more circumscribed or delimited conception of responsibility, arises only among the persecuted. Persecution, as Levinas conceives it, is not therefore a formal structure or an elaborate metaphor employed to describe the way in which the Other puts me in question.

And yet, in both "Language and Proximity" and "Substitution," Levinas warns against understanding his ethical language as arising from a special moral experience independent of the descriptions elaborated in those essays (DEHH 234; CP 124 and AE 155; OB 120). This warning must be considered carefully. As Levinas explains elsewhere in *Otherwise Than Being*, the ethical language he employs is not added to the phenomenological descriptions but is said to be the only language "equal to the paradox which phenomenological description enters when, starting with the disclosure, the appearing of a neighbor, it reads it in its trace, which orders the face according to a diachrony which cannot be synchronized in representation" (AE 120n; OB 193 n. 35). In other words, Levinas finds ethical language "adequate" to the description of the approach in its contrast with knowing and of the face in its contrast with the phenomenon (AE 155; OB 120). Furthermore, Levinas explains that the experience from which his use of ethical language arises is what Alphonse de Waehlens called a "nonphilosophical experience." The context in which de Waehlens uses the phrase is Marx's contestation of Hegelianism.[6] It parallels Levinas's evocation of the nonphilosophical at the end of "God and Philosophy" when he appeals to the cry of revolt of those who mean to change the world and describes it as a challenge to Hegel's statement that the real is rational and the rational alone real (DVI 126; CP 172).[7] My claim is that in "Substitution" nonphilosophical experience again challenges philosophy but that this time the experience is that of persecution.[8] An experience is nonphilosophical for Levinas, on my interpretation, if it is not one of those experiences on which philosophy as constituted by the tradition has been based, such as *theoria* or *poiesis*. Heidegger's procedure of destructuring has exposed the relation between these experiences and the philosophical tradition. An experience might have been discussed philosophically, or might be textually and historically saturated, as is the case with "persecution," but it would still be nonphilosophical insofar as it had not given rise to a philosophy.

The analysis I have presented here is no doubt controversial, and not just as a reading of Levinas. On this occasion I shall limit myself to the question of the implications of my analysis for the conception of philosophy itself. There is a great deal of resistance among philosophers generally to the idea that any individual philosophy might be rooted in a specific kind of experience. It is held to be an affront to philosophy's claims to universality. The objections are no doubt multiplied further when the suggestion is made that the experience from which Levinas's philosophy draws is in some sense a Jewish experience and that this is a Jewish contestation of the logic of identity, just as Marxism provided an "ethical" contestation of Hegelianism. Does not this inevitably have the effect of in some way limiting Levinas's philosophy? One can even imagine the accusation being leveled that this amounts to a ghettoization of Levinas's thought, an attempt to keep it apart from a mainstream which is allegedly universal.

I would argue in response that my account of the relation between philosophy and the nonphilosophical experiences from which it arises might be understood as a new way of understanding the possibility of pluralism in philosophy. In an essay on Jean Wahl, Levinas celebrates the pluralism of philosophy: "the pluralism of philosophy does not signify a regrettable fragmentation of a totality, but that multiplicity of modes of transcendence that are persons" (HS 113; OS 77). In support, Levinas quotes Wahl as saying that "the metaphysician is someone who experiences other experiences, and who expresses in him- or herself these other experiences and thereby attains a second level of consciousness."[9] Levinas construes this as a statement about the history of philosophy, but it applies even more readily to the pluralism of philosophies arising from different cultures. However, to my eyes quite scandalously, Levinas excludes the possibilities of most cultures from contributing to philosophy. He refuses the possibility of developing his conception of the pluralism of philosophy on the basis of the model of pluralism developed in *Totality and Infinity*. Levinas is not always Levinasian. He does not acknowledge the existence of philosophies outside the Greek and Hebraic traditions; still less does he admit the possibility that they might put in question the dominant tradition, as a "Levinasian" hermeneutics—were such a thing admitted—would surely proclaim.[10]

Levinas's achievement is that he has developed a philosophy that arises from the non-philosophical experience of being persecuted. It presents itself as a philosophy for the millions on millions of all confessions and all nations that are victims. One should not be surprised if Levinas does not attempt to identify them. Nor for that matter does he attempt to identify the millions on millions of all confessions and all nations that are their oppressors. To do so would be to revert to the philosophy of identity that Levinas seeks to avoid, however insistently it threatens to return. One can never claim oneself immune from this threat, which also surrounds the effort to acknowledge what is Jewish in Levinas. It must be risked because the debt Levinas's thought owes to a Judaism that reflects Jewish destiny can serve other peoples as a model of how philosophy arises from nonphilosophical experiences. This is of particular importance to those peoples whose voices have been suppressed by the dominant language and logic of the tradition, especially to peoples who have also suffered persecution but whose philosophical presentation of it might be different from that found in Levinas.

Notes

1. It could be said that Blanchot recognizes the problem of the two languages, but by characterizing the relation with the stranger or dispossessed as a relation of myself to the Other and the relation with the persecutor as a relation of the Other to me, he comes to understand the problem as being how the latter relation is still a relation to the Other. It is apparent that I see the problem rather differently. Maurice Blanchot, *L'écriture du désastre* (Paris: Gallimard, 1980), 36-38; *The Writing of the Disaster*, trans. Ann Smock (Lincoln, University of Nebraska Press, 1986), 19-20. Michel Haar recognizes parallel questions to those raised in this essay in his "L'obsession de l'autre," in *Emmanuel Levinas*, ed. Catherine Chalier and Miguel Abensour (Paris: L'Herne, 1991), 444-52. In particular, the present essay could be understood as a response to the problem that "persecution" is "pre-originary" but inevitably haunted by diverse historic faces (see Haar, "L'obsession," 447).
2. Robert Bernasconi, "Rereading *Totality and Infinity*," in *The Question of the Other*, ed. A. Dallery and C. Scott (New York: SUNY Press, 1989), 23-40.
3. I am not claiming that in using the language of *Totality and Infinity* in later works, Levinas always interwove the empirical and transcendental languages. The claim is only that the philosophical integrity of such expositions is para-

sitic on their systematic juxtaposition in *Totality and Infinity*.
4. In "Substitution" Levinas suggests a very different derivation of solidarity: it is "as though persecution by the Other were the basis of solidarity with the Other" (S 491; AE 130; OB 103).
5. Emmanuel Levinas, "De la montée du nihilisme au Juif charnel," in *D'Auschwitz à Israël. Vingt ans après la Libération*, ed. I. Schneersohn (Paris: Centre de Documentation Juive Contemporaine, 1968), 244-49; reprinted in DL.
6. Alphonse de Waehlens, *La philosophie et les expériences naturelles* (The Hague: Martinus Nijhoff, 1961), 13.
7. See also Richard Kearney, *Dialogues with Contemporary Continental Thinkers* (Manchester: Manchester University Press, 1994), 69; DVI 19; LR 238.
8. The nonphilosophical should not be confused with the prephilosophical. In Levinas, the pre-philosophical as "the immediacy prior to philosophy," as naive consciousness, is put into question by the nonphilosophical, the passivity of obsession (AE 116; OB 91).
9. Jean Wahl, *L'expérience métaphysique* (Paris: Flammarion, 1965), 221. Levinas misquotes Wahl slightly. Instead of saying that the metaphysician expresses (*exprime*) these other experiences, Wahl actually said that the metaphysician tries (*expérimente*) them. Levinas presents it as a statement about the history of philosophy, whereas it is clear from the context that Wahl had in mind artistic, scientific or religious experiences.
10. See R. Bernasconi, "Who Is My Neighbor? Who Is the Other? Questioning 'the Generosity of Western Thought,' Ethics," in *Ethics and Responsibility in the Phenomenological Tradition*, Ninth Annual Symposium of the Simon Silverman Phenomenology Center (Pittsburgh: Duquesne University Press, 1992), 1-31.

9

The Riddle of the Pre-original

Fabio Ciaramelli

Why is Levinas's very notion of the "pre-original" or "pre-originary" an enigmatic one? What does "pre-original" mean? And what does *énigme* mean?

Through the analysis of these questions, I would like to highlight Levinas's claim of the anteriority of the ethical ("ethics as first philosophy," according to his formula) in connection with the originarity of ontology, and consequently of the political.

One could find in Levinas's work numerous quotations concerning the originary character of ontology. Even if ontology is not fundamental (EN 13-24), it is originary and primordial. For instance, in *Otherwise Than Being*, Levinas says that the manifestation of Being, the appearing, is "indeed the primary event" (AE 31; OB 24). Consequently, the ontological Said "in which everything shows itself is the origin... of philosophy" (AE 118; OB 192). And according to Husserl's phenomenology—as an accomplishment of the Western philosophical tradition—"in evidence the spirit is the origin of what it receives" (DEHH 24).

But the plexus of such notions—origin, Being, phenomenon—is always followed by another plot, or *intrigue,* that of terms as pre-original, meaning or signification, enigma (DEHH 203-17; CP 61-74). For instance, if the Said is the place of manifestation and therefore the origin of philosophy, signification is nevertheless articulated in the "pre-originary" (AE 108; OB 192). Thus "the very primacy of the primary" is only "in the presence of the present" (AE 31; OB 24), but the pre-originary is not a present, it "occurs as a divergency [*écart*] and a past," a radical past, the past of the other that "must never have been present" (DEHH 210-11; CP 68).

In this sense, the pre-originary is in no way a beginning, an *arché*; it does not have the status of a principle, but comes from the dimension of the "an-archic," which must be distinguished from that of the "eternal" (AE 30; OB 187-88).

In *Totality and Infinity* Levinas had already said that Infinity "does not first exist, and *then* reveal itself" (TeI xv; TaI 26): in the same way, we must not understand the pre-originary in *Otherwise Than Being* as something which "is" before origin, which is more originary than origin, for instance, a more ancient origin. On the contrary, the pre-originary produces itself as the deconstruction of origin, as its destructuration and interruption. Therefore it precedes the origin only after the event, *après coup*, according to the scheme of what *Totality and Infinity* called the "posteriority of the anterior" (TeI 25; TaI 54). If the anterior only occurs a posteriori, it presupposes—and at the same time escapes or gets out of—origin.

The pre-originary is the dimension of meaning that is irreducible to the dimension of manifestation and in this sense, to the orders of both ontology and politics. The very enigma of the pre-originary is its nonphenomenality interrupting the phenomenal order of appearing, which is in its turn originary. *Otherwise Than Being* stresses very clearly and very strongly that the "origin of appearing [*l'origine de l'apparoir*]," which is "the very origin of an origin [*l'origine même de l'origine*]," is "the apparition of a third party [*l'apparition du tiers*]" (AE 204; OB 160). This apparition is the permanent entry into the intimacy of the face to face, which is not an empirical event but the ontological principle of human society, the constitution of the political. The immediacy of the ethical responsibility for the other—an "immediacy antecedent to questions" (AE 200; OB 157)— is the pre-original meaning that precedes origin without being in its turn origin.

From responsibility to problem: that is the way which Levinas indicates in this section of *Otherwise Than Being*. Here responsibility is not "justice," because the latter implies that originary "comparison of incomparables [*comparaison des incomparables*]" (AE 201; OB 158 and passim) which is absent in the pre-originary dimension of proximity. The slight difference between, on the one hand, the anteriority or precedence of the ethical and, on the other, the originarity of the ontological and of the political generates an insurmountable "anachronism," an overlapping between two irreducible time orders which collide without coinciding, which stay together in their nonsynchronizable diachrony.

These themes are well known, and it is not necessary to recall them at greater length.[1] Here I would merely like to defend the following thesis: namely, that the riddle of the pre-originary—irreducible to the phenomenon of origin—is the mise en scène, the staging—and not the conceptual representation—of a necessary condition of the political (and of its ontological constitution), which is also its limit. The very notion of mise en scène is certainly a phenomenological one, but it applies itself to what occurs on the borderline of phenomenology, according to an original gesture that has become familiar to Levinas's readers.[2] It allows him to describe the *déformalisation*—the signifying concreteness—of what interrupts phenomenology. This interruption of the articulated order of phenomena and beings can only be understood and signified by a step backward that attends to an implication which is on the horizon of manifestation but which makes sense without showing itself.

So the enigma of the pre-original is not a phenomenon, does not occur in a present, is not the activity of a consciousness but insinuates itself within phenomena, as their very condition and their limit.

If the pre-originary is the immediacy of the ethical responsibility before freedom, in what sense does this enigmatic immediacy "stage" the condition and the limit of the political that is in its turn originary?

I would like to show that the enigma of the pre-originary is the deconstruction of the ontological identity of origin, of an inner duality that is always an ontological articulation, a duality within the immanence of origin. In this sense the pre-originary means the opening of origin to a radical alterity that is irreducible to the circle of origin. The radical alterity disturbing the immanence of origin is the very complication of human plurality, its paradox , a paradox that breaks the originary identity of totality.

But what is origin? It means that from which something springs into existence. The search for origin is always transcendental and ontological: it looks for universal conditions of the possibility of Being. But the first thing springing from origin is the origin itself. The *Ur-sprung*, the primordial jump or leap, is one's emerging from oneself. To be origin, therefore, means to begin in a present, that is, to avoid the causal chain of mediations, interrupting it at its origin, in order to start immediately from oneself without deriving from anything else. But, at this very moment, such an immediacy of origin implies a sort of paradoxical duality, an inner articulation. Levinas evokes it in *De l'existence à l'existant*, in his analysis of the instant that, in its ontological sense, is not instantaneous (DE 129-32; EE 75-77).[3] Origin can arise or spring from itself only if it originarily implies a reference to itself as to its own alterity, from which it emerges. Thanks to this inner articulation, thanks to this originary complication of the simple or to this circularity of the initial, origin originarily comes to itself without starting from anywhere. Thus origin, as origin of itself, precedes itself, presupposes itself, as it cannot presuppose anything else that would be only its external starting point. The self-originating origin implies the alterity of itself with regard to itself, an immanent alterity coming to Being in the same movement of the primordial leap.[4]

But this ontological inner duality of origin is not adequate to the genuine complication of human plurality, which implies a radical alterity, irreducible to the alterity immanent to the origin that occurs only as a condition of its totalization.

Totality and Infinity had already stressed the irreducibility of human plurality to totality, in which the same and the other remain correlative. The paradox of human plurality lies precisely in the impossibility of deducing it from an external origin yet at the same time in the inadequacy of the ontological and immanent duality of origin to do justice to the difference between social pluralism and totality.

This difference can only be safeguarded by a deconstruction of the ontological identity or immanence of origin. And it is precisely the enigma of the pre-original—its irreducibility to a more originary starting point or origin—that stages the condition of the political and its limit. In other words, thanks to this notion of the pre-originary, the political—which does not find its starting point outside of itself, which is in its own dimension originary—can mean a kind of human relationship which is not absorbed by totality, that is, by an anonymous despotism of universality over individuals.

"There exists a tyranny of the universal and of the impersonal," writes Levinas in *Totality and Infinity*, and, he adds, "an order that is inhuman though distinct from the brutish" (TeI 219; TaI 242). This universal and totalizing order is not given, is not natural, and constitutes itself through the totalization of individuals, through their reduction to empirical moments or elements of a generality. But human society is human precisely because it is "a multiple existing—a pluralism"—distinct from "numerical multiplicity," that "remains defenseless against totalization" (TeI 195; TaI 220). So we have to think of the political in its difference from such a totalization.

Now, the specific operation of the political in human society is understood by Levinas as the institution of equality among separated and different individuals. It is the institution of an equality that is precisely the result of a "struggle for recognition": indeed, "politics tends toward reciprocal recognition, that is, toward equality; it ensures happiness. And political law concludes and sanctions the struggle for recognition" (TeI 35; TaI 64). But "politics left to itself bears a tyranny with itself; it deforms the I and the other who have given rise to it, for it judges them according to universal rules, and thus as *in absentia*" (TeI 276; TaI 300). This danger is linked to "politics left to itself," without reference to the pre-originary meaning implied within its horizon.

But the political, in its difference from tyranny, has to imply the institution of a universal order which is not a totality, which is not a totalization of individuals, which reflects and respects human plurality, that is, pluralism.

Politics—as distinct from totality, distinct from tyranny—is the institution of a society of equals. In *Totality and Infinity* the political operation (the same operation that will be called in *Otherwise Than Being* a "comparison of incomparables") already has its starting point in the relationship of the face to face with a third party, and we know that this relationship is originary. Levinas writes, "In the measure that the face of the Other relates us with a third party, the metaphysical relation of the I with the Other moves into the form of We, aspires to a State, institutions, laws, which are the source of universality" (TeI 276; TaI 300).

But the difference between the political universality whose "latent birth" (AE 200; OB 157 and passim) is the ethical proximity originarily troubled by the entry of a third party and the general anonymity of a tyrannical totality is precisely laid bare by a reference to a nonpolitical condition and limit of the political. This is the very role of the pre-originary, which stages the ethical meaning of this condition. We read in *Totality and Infinity*: "The distance which separates happiness from desire separates politics from religion. ... Religion is Desire and not struggles for recognition. It is the surplus possible in a society of equals, that of glorious humility, responsibility, and sacrifice, which are the condition for equality itself" (TeI 35; TaI 64). I would like to stress strongly this last point: "religion"—in the very sense of "the bond that is established between the same and the other without constituting a totality" (TeI 10; TaI 40)—is a condition for political equality itself. Without this relation among separated terms able to absolve themselves from relation, there would be no equality in human plurality but just the formal totalization of an anonymous generality. This conjuncture in which proximity does not abolish distance is irreducible to totality and always subtends any formal totality (TeI 53; TaI 80-81).

But this conjuncture always presupposed by totality is not in its turn an origin. It precedes origin, it prevents politics from becoming the false communion of totality, and at the same time it does not allow politics to find outside of itself any general criterion for deducing its rules. This last point becomes very clear in *Otherwise Than Being*. The permanent appearance of a third party within the intimacy of the face to face gives birth to the political problem as the problem of justice, as the search for equality. The comparison of incomparables, the becoming equals of individuals who are radically other, is the originary operation of the institution of society. Individuals who are radically other, who are not actually equal to one another, are "equalized" and *become* equals through a comparison which we have to distinguish from a totalization but which we cannot derive from any more originary origin.

Of course, the tyranny of totalization is an ever-present danger, and the very task of a radical reflection on the political has precisely to avoid any reduction of the political to totality. The originary comparison of incomparables is a political operation because it establishes a symbolic order or dimension generated by society but not reducible to the given reality of society. We meet here what Claude Lefort has called the "enigma of society," an enigma related to the "idea of a social order that is of necessity instituted politically [*l'idée d'une nécessaire institution politique du social*],"[5] which is to say, to the fact that it is impossible "to precipitate what belongs to the symbolic order into the real."[6]

This overlapping of the self-origination of the political and its enigmatic relation to the pre-originary is not a theoretical construction but—still quoting Claude Lefort—"the experience of a difference which is not at a disposal of human beings…; the experience of a difference which relates human beings to their humanity, and which means that their humanity cannot be self-contained, that it cannot set its own limits, and that it cannot absorb its origins and ends into those limits." Finally this experience implies the acknowledgment that "human society can only open onto itself by being held in an opening it did not create."[7]

The very notion of the pre-originary makes reference to this passivity at the core of the originary self-constitution of human society. It makes reference to the impossible reification of the political, to the unassumable exteriority of society with regard to itself. Beyond and before (*en deçà de*) any constituted social totality, the asymmetric relation to the other as the "religious" or "ethical" condition and limit of the political signifies the impossibility of absorbing in a phenomenological network of relations the invisible source of meaning which escapes manifestation, which has its roots in the absolute past of the other.

Indeed, the other escapes always, gets out of reality, absolves himself or herself from relation. The desire of the other is irreducible to any need that we can satisfy, precisely because the other does not give himself or herself in reality. In this sense, religion—which is the place of such a "Desire of the Other that is our very sociality" (DEHH 193)—would be the symbolic figuration of the exteriority of society with respect to itself.

I would read the enigmatic resort to God, very often or almost always between quotation marks, in the last chapter of *Otherwise than Being* in connection with this search for a symbolic staging of the pre-original condition of the political.

The resort to God alludes to the enigma of the pre-originary implied by the originary constitution of a political space, which is the space of social equality and universal laws. In an earlier article, "The Ego and the Totality," where Levinas says that " 'We' is not the plural of 'I,' " he evokes God as "the fixed point exterior to society, from which the law comes" (EN 49, 34; CP 43, 32).

This radical transcendence with regard to society prevents the latter from degenerating into an impersonal totality and offers a figure of the symbolic exteriority of society with regard to itself insofar as this exteriority is precisely irreducible to the inner and immanent duality of the origin. The resort to God in *Otherwise Than Being* occurs as a deconstruction of the originarily ontological character of the political, in order to avoid the neglect of difference in favor of unity or fusional community. "It is only thanks to God that, as a subject incomparable with the other, I am approached as another by the others, that is for myself.... The passing of God of whom I can speak only by reference to this aid or to this grace, is precisely the reverting of the comparable subject into a member of society" (AE 201-2; OB 158).

For Levinas the institution of the "original locus of justice"—that is, the political realm which enables the social exchange among separated and incomparable subjects—is only possible "with the help of God" (AE 204; OB 160). In order to understand this enigmatic resort to God, I propose to read it in connection with the overlapping—*l'empiètement*—of two features of the political: its instituted dimension and its symbolic character. "The help of God" is a way of saying the pre-originary meaning implied and "staged" by this originary operation of doubling, which occurs when society becomes exterior to itself, in order to posit the universal and common plan of justice. The symbolic and instituted exteriority of the social with regard to itself is at the core of the event of the political, by which the face to face, starting from the originary apparition of a third party, "moves into the form of We" (AE 204; OB 160), which has to be distinguished from a plural of I, for otherwise human pluralism would be reduced to an impersonal totality. In this sense, the universality of law comes to itself without having started from outside, but in its self-origination it continues to allude to its "*latent* birth" in a pre-originary doubling of the social, where its instituted character means the irreducibility of the symbolic order to reality. Therefore social and political equality can institute the phenomenal order of appearing without destroying "the attention to the Other as unicity and face (which the visibleness of the political leaves invisible)" (TeI 276-77; TaI 300). The tyranny of the political thought of in terms of totality is precisely the reduction of the instituted and symbolic order of the political to a neutral anonymity eradicated from its "latent birth" in the pre-originary meaning of the ethical, where proximity and distance go together, where nobody is at the starting point of institution, but where among separated beings the apparition of a third party requires the creation of a common plan, external to the terms of relation without being in its turn a term, without being a projection of one of them, without being objectifiable and reified.

Therefore the resort to God may suggest this necessary implication of a symbolic dimension as the condition and the limit of the political institution of equality. But this condition, because of its pre-originary character, cannot be precipitated into the real, cannot become an ontological *arché*, cannot be reduced to a mythical origin before society or beyond it from which society would be derived as a consequence. The pre-originary is not the origin of origin: "it is a hither side not presupposed like a principle is presupposed by the consequence of which it is synchronous. This an-archic hither side is borne witness to, enigmatically, to be sure, in responsibility for others" (AE 203; OB 160).

The pre-originary is not the ontological essence of the political, but it makes sense only in its "*reprise*" within the social order, where the ethical responsibility for others "deformalizes" the reference to it. And this reference becomes an enigmatic allusion to a symbolic dimension from which no institution is deducible but of which each institution must be a creative "*reprise*." The political institution of equality must aim at this pre-originary dimension of the ethical, which is the only warranty of its difference from totality.

Notes

1. For a more detailed analysis of this point, see Fabio Ciaramelli, "*L'anacronismo*," in E. Levinas and A. Peperzak, *Etica come filosofia prima*, ed. F. Ciaramelli (Milan: Guerini, 1989), 155-80; "Levinas's Ethical Discourse between Individuation and Universality," RL 83-108; "Remarques sur religion et politique chez Levinas," in *Religion, société, démocratie* (Bruxelles: Ousia, forthcoming).
2. See, for example, the preface to DVI.
3. See also Fabio Ciaramelli, "Il tempo dell'inizio. Responsabilità e giudizio in H. Arendt ed E. Levinas," *Paradigmi* 9 (1991): 477-504.
4. For a more general development, see Fabio Ciaramelli, "The Circle of the Origin," in *Political Theory*, ed. S. Watson and L. Lagsdorf (Albany: SUNY Press, forthcoming).
5. Claude Lefort, *Ecrits sur le politique* (Paris: Seuil, 1986), 10; *Democracy and*

Political Theory, trans. D. Macey (Minneapolis: University of Minnesota Press, 1988), 3.
6. Claude Lefort, *L'invention démocratique* (Paris: Fayard, 1981), 150.
7. Lefort, *Ecrits sur le politique*, 262; *Democracy and Political Theory*, 222.

10
On Resorting to an Ethical Language

Paul Davies

At issue is a question arising from whatever it is Levinas means by "ethical language," a question that seems to challenge a long-standing reading of Levinas. That Levinas's work has increasingly warranted being read in this way is, for me, one of the things that has made it so distinctive, giving it the aura of a difficult but appealing reflexivity. Now there is this question and I am not sure how it is to be answered. It might be that such uncertainty is the result of a deliberate move on Levinas's part, and this is the direction we will be moving in here. But we begin with the reading itself, in full flow...

An ear and an eye for what most attracts Maurice Blanchot to the work of Emmanuel Levinas will always return one to the passively insidious effects of the *il y a*, not simply to what Levinas's work says of those effects but, more important, to what the introduction of the *il y a* does to that work. For as Levinas, in the wake of this introduction, continues to philosophize, his work must run the perpetual risk of paralysis and must, too, perpetually problematize the reading of the various steps it would invite us to take: from ontology to ethics, from meaning to sense, from phenomenon to face, from knowledge to approach. In each instance it is a matter of a step from linearity to the nonlinearizable, and inasmuch as we are asked to move from the place where the negative is at work (differentiation in the service of a totality, differentiation as circumscription) to somewhere and something else, inasmuch as we are asked to move from negativity to not negativity, it would seem as if the step is best written as the step *from "from...to" to*, the step from any sort of productive stepping to what must remain unnamed. This impossible formula, at the very moment it prevents our arrival at a new term or terminus, enables us to address the paradoxical weakening of negativity that, for Blanchot, lies at the heart of Levinas's work. It marks the difficulty of the ubiquitous "not negativity," the implicit illegibility of which can only be protected when read through the filter of Blanchot's logic of the *pas au-delà*. It underlines the irreducible significance of the *il y a* always crucially linked to the occurrence of this weakening, and it also allows us to see why Blanchot seems to prefer *Otherwise Than Being* to *Totality and Infinity*.

Without rehearsing Blanchot's reading of Levinas, let us note that whereas *Totality and Infinity* seems first to situate the *il y a* by allotting it a negative function (the inevitable failure of ontology, the relentlessly destructive character of the "philosophy of the neuter") and then to stage a step away from it (i.e., breaking with "the philosophy of the neuter"), *Otherwise Than Being* seems more willing to sustain an ambiguity and to acknowledge the consequences of such a sustaining. Levinas writes, "The rumbling of the *il y a* is the non-sense in which essence turns and in which thus turns the justice issued out of signification" (OB 163). And he continues, "There is ambiguity of sense and non-sense in being, sense turning into non-sense" (OB 163). Ventriloquized by Blanchot, this "turning" is heard and written throughout *Otherwise Than Being*. It determines its tropes, prefigures its figures. Think of the extraordinary syntax, the series of names (substitution, obsession, responsibility, trauma, psychosis, hostage, one-for-the-other, etc.), each replaced and interrupted by the others before it can harden into a theme, a definition, or a term. It is surely not going too far to suggest that this never quite coming to (a) term, this never quite terminating, is indebted to the unstageable turning of essence and in essence here named and held to be indissociable from the *il y a*.

Against this sort of reading there are those who, applauding Levinas for recalling philosophy to an originary ethical concern, grow impatient with the time spent addressing the question of the status and the very possibility of the language in which that call is uttered. They feel that a reminder of what Levinas said about the prefatory word in *Totality and Infinity*, about the "prephilosophical" in the "itinerary" to *Otherwise Than Being*, and an account of the distinction between the saying and the said must always suffice to settle the matter. They distrust, too, the reluctance to surmount or to contain the issue of the *il y a* and its particular alterity or version of non-sense. This tension and disagreement has some bearing on the following discussion.

Levinas sometimes refers to what he calls an "ethical language," a language adequate to a predicament in which philosophy must inevitably find itself. Every nuance is crucial here: that the language suffice to describe a particular situation in a particular fashion; that the situation be characterized as irreducibly enigmatic, that is, as a situation of and for which philosophy can give no account; and that philosophy's encounter with this unaccountable, enigmatic situation also be unavoidable. Philosophy has recourse to a "language" in which this paradoxical encounter is re-presented, read, or described as the encounter with the face. Thus, in "Language and Proximity," we read: "Ethical language alone succeeds in being equal to the paradox in which phenomenology is abruptly thrown: starting with the neighbor, it reads this paradox in the midst of an absence which orders it as a face" (CP 124). And in *Otherwise Than Being*: "The tropes of ethical language are found to be adequate for certain structures of the description: for the sense of the approach in its contrast with knowing, the face in its contrast with a phenomenon" (OB 120).

To speak of "ethical language" rather than "ethics" already suggests that anything we might wish to identify as a Levinasian "ethics" can never have done with the issue of language. Levinas makes things even harder, insisting that ethical language "does not proceed from a special moral experience, independent of the description developed until then. It comes from the very meaning of approach, which contrasts with knowledge, of the face which contrasts with phenomena" (CP 124). And what it does proceed from, namely the ethical situation of responsibility, "is not comprehensible on the basis of ethics" (OB 120). An examination of the sort of resource this "ethical language" is seems to bear out the idea that in introducing this phrase Levinas is willfully complicating his own procedure. It is clear that no simple step is being proposed from knowledge to approach, from phenomenon to face, and that whatever ethical language does by way of contrasting these terms cannot support any sort of linear narrative.

One of the most striking things about this ethical language is the strange way in which it combines a negative and a positive function. On the one hand, as a language judged capable of enabling a philosophy thrown into paradox to continue, it would seem to provide a way out of the paradox. On the other hand, its object and addressee is nothing but this paradox. On the one hand, it is said to order or to reconstitute the paradox by permitting it to be read as "face," that is, by enabling us to think the predicament as inherently ethical. On the other hand, in having always to read "face" on the hither side of a determinable content or datum, "ethics" itself is to be thought henceforth as inherently this predicament. Ethical language, as a language committed to responding to what renders appearance (the appearing of a phenomenon) enigmatic, always returns us to the scene just prior to its introduction, and it is this impossible scene which it, and Levinas, would have us read.

The manner in which "ethical language" would both address and produce a predicament for its reader is mirrored in "God and Philosophy" with the introduction of the very idea of a specifically Levinasian *exposition*.

> The exposition of the ethical signification of transcendence and of the Infinite beyond being can be worked out beginning with the proximity of the neighbor and my responsibility for the other.
> Until then a passive subjectivity might seem something constructed and abstract.... The passivity "more passive than all passivity" consisted in undergoing ... a trauma that could not be assumed; it consisted in being struck by the "*in*" of infinity which devastates presence and awakens subjectivity to the proximity of the other ...
> [This trauma], inflicted by the Infinite on presence, this affecting of presence by the Infinite... takes shape as a subjection to the neighbor. It is

thought thinking more than it thinks, desire, the reference to the neighbor, the responsibility for another. (CP 166)

What sort of beginning or point of departure is invoked in the opening, single-sentence paragraph here? What does it mean to start out from "the proximity of the neighbor," "my responsibility for the other," terms and phrases that surely already require some sort of Levinasian exposition? Note the ambiguity operative from the very first. The sentence implies that Levinas's exposition (of "the ethical signification of transcendence and the Infinite beyond being") must begin with an exposition of the proximity of the neighbor and my responsibility for the other, but it actually says that any exposition at all must begin with the proximity of the neighbor itself, must begin with my responsibility for the other itself. The exposition of the ethical signification of transcendence must also be an exposition of the proximity of the neighbor and my responsibility for the other insofar as everything Levinas will say of the former involves a perpetual appeal to and account of the latter. And yet this cannot suffice to make the signification "ethical." If it could, the ethical signification of transcendence would be no more than one way of presenting things. The point is that this whole procedure, Levinas's philosophical exposition as such, must start with the proximity itself, the responsibility itself. It must begin here. But where? And with what? With a description of a particular situation? With some sort of proof that this exposition, this text, this sentence is somehow responsibility in action, an autopresentation of "proximity" and "responsibility"? The next paragraph seems in part to resolve the issue. But it does so by implicitly turning in on itself, by drawing attention to Levinas's own vocabulary and the strange way in which it *works*. If "the proximity of the neighbor" and "my responsibility for the other" refer both to what is an essential and sustaining moment of the exposition and to what must remain outside the exposition as its provocation or spur, then to use such terms is not only to problematize the very idea of a philosophical exposition and its beginning but also to problematize the way in which such terms are to be read. The step Levinas takes is from abstraction to alteration. A passive subjectivity will seem an abstraction unless we realize that it is an already altered subjectivity; the phrase "passive subjectivity" will seem the most familiar of philosophical abstractions unless we realize that Levinas's enterprise requires an alteration in and of the very language of philosophical exposition. Transcendence and infinity wrought from ontology and thought in terms of a beyond being, that is, thought in their ethical signification, must thereby become what thought cannot think. They are thought in and as their affectivity. The exposition must arise from a thinking beset by what exceeds it and by what, in exceeding it, obsesses and traumatizes it. Thus the beginning, to which the exposition would bring us and which would finally allow us to see what lies behind the apparently abstract terms of the exposition must also cause the exposition to falter, for the terms of this beginning, "the proximity of the neighbor," "the responsibility for the other," and the terms that would here mark its nonabstractness, "trauma," "affectivity," and so on, must be read as though they were written on the hither side of exposition. The product of the exposition here naming its true beginning would perpetually postpone all access to it. To encounter Levinas's vocabulary and to begin to learn how to read it is to be constantly returned to this puzzling exile. The exposition only gets going by never quite getting going.

In offering neither solace nor solution, in providing no means of moving beyond the scene of an enigma, Levinas's vocabulary and his "ethical language" can only serve endlessly to extend and to exacerbate the enigmatic quality of that scene: the irrecusable faltering of philosophy. Yet it is at this juncture that Levinas sometimes seems to confound the dictates of his own discourse. We have already noted his comment on the "origins" of ethical language as it appears in "Language and Proximity": "The ethical language to which we have recourse does not proceed from a special moral experience, independent of the description developed until then. It comes from the very meaning of approach, which contrasts with knowledge, of the face which contrasts with phenomena" (CP 124). The first sentence reappears almost word for word in *Otherwise Than Being*. But here Levinas continues: "The ethical situation of responsibility is not comprehensible on the basis of ethics. It does indeed arise from what Alphonse de Waelhens called nonphilosophical experiences, which are ethically independent" (OB 120). In "God and Philosophy," too, having shown the reader the full paradoxical effect of the beginnings of exposition, Levinas goes on to remark that what is expressed in the seemingly abstract passive subjectivity is "familiar to us in the empirical event of obligation to another" (CP 166).

What are we to make of these sudden irruptions of the straightforward? It cannot be enough to argue that the "empirical event of obligation," for example, must be read in terms of what we already know about Levinasian "obligation," what we already know about how this word is to be read. If the text does seem to support such a move, immediately returning us to the confines of Levinas's vocabulary and so to the predicaments described and celebrated above, the problem is that in hurriedly renegotiating the reference to the empirical, we are simply not reading it. We are replacing the phrase "the empirical event of obligation to another" with the single term "obligation" and drawing no consequences for our understanding of the latter, not least that the replacement would have to work the other way as well. We would have to hear "the empirical event of obligation to another" in every "obligation" Levinas writes.

But is the matter really this complicated? Do not Levinas's seemingly ingenuous appeals to something like the real simply follow from the argument that any unprejudiced description of my being responsible for another must recognize the impossibility of determining the limits of this responsibility? It is the imposition of a moral theory that enables philosophy to demarcate the realm of particular responsibilities in particular situations. Responsibility and obligation already denote and call for the thought of asymmetry. When I am responsible for another I am also responsible for his responsibility. The responsibility is already excessive. It is philosophy which attempts theoretically to mitigate this excess, and it is (this) philosophy which is undone by the empirical event of obligation to another. That event requires Levinas's vocabulary: obsession, substitution, hostage, the Other, and so on. The hyperbole seeks to answer and to relate the urgency and the intensity of these "nonphilosophical experiences"; "the tropes of ethical language are found to be adequate for certain structures of the description." This is a legitimate and helpful way of introducing Levinas's concerns, a nice starting point. But there is a danger of forgetting that although Levinas speaks of nonphilosophical experiences and the empirical event of obligation as starting points, he does not himself begin with them. We read the references to them as starting points long after we have started to read Levinas and, more pertinently, immediately after we have followed the being thrown into paradox of exposition and description. If we were to start with a description of a simple example of obligation and were then to show how extraordinary the description is forced to become in order to do justice to that example, we would still have only demonstrated a feature of a particular type of experience. We would have shown something interesting perhaps about certain phenomena but would have said nothing about phenomenology itself, and would certainly not have shown that those phenomena somehow ceased to be conceivable as phenomena. For Levinas, it is not enough to say that when I think about what it is to be under an obligation to someone I find myself caught up in the throes of an enigmatic and pre-originary responsibility. That enigmatic binding does not simply apply to a particular type of thinking but impinges on the essence of thought itself. In order to understand this larger claim the references to "nonphilosophical experiences" and "the empirical event of obligation" must be read in context and that context must both make them shocking and make it impossible to free them from the paradoxes we have already outlined.

One way of playing down the element of surprise here is to recall the closing pages of Derrida's "Violence and Metaphysics" and the suggestion that Levinas's project must involve, whether wittingly or not, a renewal of empiricism. Empiricism would be the proper philosophical name for all the falterings, betrayals, and inconsistencies that befall Levinas's "ethics" and to which Levinas and his "ethics" are explicitly resigned, and its renewal can never entirely avoid the argument that it remains dependent on the very thing it would renounce: the concept, philosophy. Thus when Derrida, ostensibly describing the more familiar pre-Levinasian empiricism, contrasts the profundity of that empiricism's intention with "the naïveté of certain of its historical expressions" (WaD 151), nothing in Levinas's subsequent use of the term can prevent the description from being extended to him. It is with regard to language that the shared naïveté is most apparent. Empiricism "is the *dream* of a purely *heterological* thought at its source.... We say the *dream* because it must vanish *at daybreak*, as soon as language awakens" (WaD 151). Whatever Levinas says about language, no matter how complex or how self-deprecating, and however much what he says about language contributes to his bringing philosophy, in the very undoing of philosophy, to the thought of the face, that thought (that encounter) can only reproduce in philosophy, and so in Levinas's own text, an always recognizably philosophical naïveté. Accordingly, the fundamental hesitation to which philosophy would be returned remains accessible to a continuing philosophical analysis. It can never be quite fundamental enough.

It is tempting to suppose that we could simply incorporate Derrida's remarks into a discussion of Levinas's writings after *Totality and Infinity*. But is that fair? After all, is not language everywhere awake in *Otherwise Than Being*, "Language and Proximity," "Meaning and Sense," and "God and Philosophy"? Nonetheless Derrida's argument claims to hold, however sophisticated or deliberate the treatment of language, wherever and whenever the linguistic predicament, the linguisticality of the predicament, is set aside. And is it not set aside when "nonphilosophical experience" and "the empirical event of obligation" are used to translate Levinas's difficult sentences? Is there not a lessening of attention here? One can envisage how a Derridean skepticism might be sustained throughout a reading of *Otherwise Than Being* even at those places where Levinas seems closest to Derrida. For example, when Levinas speaks of the unconditioned yes prior to consent, the yes echoed and traced in every actual situated yes, he insists that this pre-originary affirmation indicates a pre-originary exposure to critique. In keeping with so much of the more recent work on language, here linguisticality goes all the way down. Might Derrida not insist, though, that this double affirmation also expose to critique everything Levinas wants to protect under the "sincerity" of this exposure, the sincerity of saying? Even if Levinas has developed a far subtler account of the failure of language to the extent that we can now say that it is language itself which brings this failure, its own failure, to thought and to utterance, the assumption that something still falls outside the drama or the intrigue of language, a pre-origin (a peaceful an-archy) guaranteeing the sincerity of saying, means that a particular version of the failure of language is being privileged over any other. If language in failing nevertheless provides access to its own excessiveness, if it continues where and when continuing would be impossible, what determines that this excess and this continuing bear the trace of an unambiguous and pristine sincerity? Whatever the answer here Derrida would suggest that it must resuscitate empiricism and thus "naively" suspend or frame all the preceding remarks about language.

Note that on this reading our central question (how to read and to think together the meaning of "approach" and "face" on the one hand and "non-philosophical experiences" on the other, "the proximity of the neighbor and my responsibility for the other" on the one hand and "the empirical event of obligation" on the other) is not really an issue. Levinas's work simply requires and relies on this inconsistency, the essentially ambiguous over and against the essentially unambiguous. The inconsistency or indeterminacy is a constitutive moment in the production of Levinas's text. The legibility of "approach" and "face" depends on the illegibility, the impossible naïveté, of "non-philosophical experiences." The complexity and the paradoxical illegibility of the former, the requirement that these terms are never taken on board as philosophemes, depends on the legibility of the latter. But even if it is the case that an astute reader of Levinas should realize that the gestures toward empiricism are completely in keeping with the ethical project itself, such a structural and diagnostic account has nothing to say about how, where, and when the actual references occur.[1]

If ethical language enables us (philosophy, phenomenology) to read a paradox, then, as a result of that reading, surely either one moves away from the paradox or one does not. So far, and maybe with good reason, we have been disinclined to accept the possibility of a step away or beyond. But let us reconsider this matter of the turning of phenomenon into enigma, phenomenology's falling into paradox, the moment of Levinas's recourse to an ethical language. However paradoxical the account of this moment, and we have tried to show just how convoluted Levinas's text is here, it would seem as if one would have to be able to differentiate between the philosophy that is perpetually bound to encounter this paradoxicality and the thought of its so doing. One can go further, to differentiate between a philosophy rendered ever more restless by the failure of its projects and by the always ambiguous nature of this failure and a reading or remarking of this restlessness. For the latter, the former's inability to arrive at a thesis concerning language is not simply due to the nature of language, which would after all be just one more thesis, but is rather an unease, an ethical unease, to which the nature of language attests. Hence we have Levinas's idea of saying as an orienting, and presumably we also have a distinction between philosophy as an always oriented said and the thought of the said as oriented, where although this would itself necessarily be said, it would mark differently and *as* different the predicament to which the said is always already destined. On the one hand, then, we have ambiguity and on the other hand, we have the orienting of ambiguity, the thought that ambiguity is oriented and that this orientation determines both the essence of ambiguity and the ambiguity—the becoming ambiguous—of essence. Even though it is formulations of the latter sort which must sound strangest and which must be the hardest to read, it is they that seem to benefit from the perennial possibility of a translation into familiarity: the empirical event of obligation to another, nonphilosophical experiences. Querying anything at all here is tantamount to realigning oneself with that skepticism which in refusing to accept its logical refutation may well serve as evidence of the irreducibility of philosophy to logic, and of language to the said but which cannot do so in a way that benefits itself. No traditional skeptical undertaking is aided by Levinas's reading of skepticism, just as no Cartesianism can garner support from Levinas's retrieval of the idea of infinity in the third meditation. The difficulty of Levinas's discourse might be said to arise from the way he must continually refigure a paradox endlessly ruinous of philosophy. Those who seek to return Levinas's text and his "ethical language" to that ruination might best be seen as exemplifying the very thing that that language would read, a relentless and increasingly sophisticated critique, intensely aware of the fundamental undecidability of logic and ontology but always as yet incapable of construing itself as "obliged," as "responsible." This argument suggests an ingenious means of excluding oneself or one's own text from an otherwise necessarily all-encompassing reflexivity. It thereby seems to provide a check to the reading with which we began and with which we sought to emphasize the self-referentiality of Levinas's discourse. It can even be put more succinctly: instead of showing that there is no stepping away from the scene of a ruinous paradoxicality, and instead of leaving the reader endlessly caught up in that scene, Levinas's recourse to an "ethical language" involves the realization that these predicaments are strictly logical. Paradox is after all a figure and a problem in and for logic. The confounding of logic, even a phenomeno-logic, by paradox must never be thought as the confounding of ethics. To the question of how the "must" in the preceding sentence is to be understood (Is it ethical, logical, undecidable? And if undecidable, is it not thereby *logically* undecidable, or is this "undecidable" itself undecidable? And so on and so on, in an infinite and paralyzing regress), to all of this the Levinasian response is to signal to another language, an ethical language, as a means of freeing oneself from regress, from ceaseless repetition, from all arguments of this form.

Yet if the name "ethical language" already embodies this clear-cut protection from logic, if it already attests to the step away from the paradox, then there is no real need for the references that have been puzzling us: nonphilosophical experiences, the empirical event of obligation. But perhaps that is the point of this interpretation. In themselves such references are neither necessary nor particularly puzzling; they merely draw out what is already implicit in the phrase "ethical language" and in everything Levinas says about the language of his own expositions. This, however, brings us to the major stumbling block. If, from the first, Levinas's "ethics" can be written as an "ethical empiricism," written with direct reference to the real, the nonphilosophical, the empirical, then how are we to begin to justify the extraordinary difficulty of his language? What are we to say about the intricate self-undoings that clearly do characterize at least a part of Levinas's work? If the translation of the hardest constructions into the most straightforward of empiricisms is always somehow on the cards then why postpone it? And why bother with those constructions in the first place? Is there not something seriously troubling— logically and ethically—about this inability to justify or to account for the difficulty all readers of Levinas's texts are bound to encounter?

Even if we were to accept this state of affairs and entertain the idea that certain arguments and questions are to be cut off or suspended *for ethical reasons*, Levinas's ethical language would seem to rely unequivocally on a moralizing tone. It would be brought to bear on a situation (philosophy's being thrown into paradox) as though it did arise from a moral experience, a knowledge of how one ought to behave.

If the difficulty of Levinas's own discourse, the deliberate convolutions of his own vocabulary, must always work against a straightforward attempt to present that discourse as a new philosophical "ethics," it cannot, in the end, simply be a matter of illustrating and describing that difficulty. There must be something wrong with this way of remaining with the paradox. One worry about our opening remarks concerning *Otherwise Than Being* and our readings of "ethical language" and "exposition" that would have to give pause even to those broadly in agreement with them is the danger of reintroducing the most conventional conception of a form being appropriate to its content. To describe *Otherwise Than Being* as, say, an always interrupted and interrupting text designating the perpetual interrupting and having-been-interrupted of a subject, to argue that here the textuality of the text itself somehow conveyed the subjectivity of the subject, is to celebrate a coinciding of form and content that must sit uneasily with the very idea of originary response and responsibility, with the insistence on the noncoinciding of the saying and the said, with everything in fact that *Otherwise Than Being* seeks to teach us about language. To see the "success" of this text in which so much is said about asymmetry and heterogeneity as deriving from the way in which its form mirrors its content is to remain dependent on the safest of homogeneities, an aesthetic symmetry.

How then are we to conclude? It seems as though we fail as readers of Levinas whether we attend to the letter of his text and so recognize the extent of our predicament as readers or whether we endeavor to free ourselves from that predicament by making a once-only appeal to the spirit of the text, to what it is we know Levinas is trying to say. Note, though, that the references to nonphilosophical experiences and the empirical event of obligation to another only come as a shock to readers taking the first of these two options. Let us insist on this point. The references *must* come as a shock. They must come as a shock to those readers attentive both to the formal intricacies of Levinas's text and to the way in which those intricacies seem to be called for by what the text says about language and by its philosophical claims about the nature of the philosophical said. And here the "must" is logical and ethical. Nonphilosophical experiences, the empirical event of obligation: one of the most startling things about these terms is their unoriginality. In one instance the unoriginality is specifically indicated, Levinas refers to Alphonse de Waelhens without developing the matter and without letting the reference harden into an interpretation or engagement. In another instance Levinas employs what Derrida in "Violence and Metaphysics" had called the most familiar philosophical pretention to nonphilosophy, empiricism. Levinas is not drawing these words and phrases back into the language of the paradox, back into "ethical language." He is not concerned with radicalizing "experience" as Blanchot does with "limit-experience." Nor is he engaged in retrieving "*empeiria*" from a traditional or Aristotelian interpretation. In simply letting these words stand, Levinas confronts the attentive reader with a dilemma. It is an unsettling but exemplary moment: one in which this complex text is not allowed to close in on itself; one in which it is obliged to lose something of its authority, to be unsure of how it is to see or to present itself. It is a sort of secession.

Notes

1. It is worth remembering that when Derrida comes to write on *Otherwise Than Being*, he does not simply expand or apply the points made in "Violence and Metaphysics." What fascinates him are the self-reflexivity, the obsessive fidelity to an ethicolinguistic predicament, and all the necessary minutiae of Levinas's discourse, in other words, the places where the appeals to the empirical and the nonphilosophical will always ring strangely and surprisingly.

Part Three: Psychism

11
Nonintentional Affectivity, Affective Intentionality, and the Ethical in Levinas's Philosophy

Andrew Tallon

Introduction: There Are Two Affectivities in Levinas

How do affectivity and intentionality relate to one another and to ethics in Levinas's philosophy? The first and most important point to be made is that there is both affective intentionality and an affectivity that is nonintentional.[1] Thus we first need to clarify just how affective intentionality *connects* with nonintentional consciousness in giving rise to responsibility to and for the other and how we might find, *in other words* than Levinas's own, namely, those of Jungian psychology, an explanation and confirmation of his thesis.

From his dissertation onward, Levinas took as established by Husserl and confirmed by Heidegger not only the intentionality of the representational consciousness of cognition but also the intentionality of the nonrepresentational consciousness of affectivity, including feelings and even moods. In its own way, Max Scheler's phenomenology had also affirmed the intentionality of feelings as both apprehensions of and responses to value. Within French phenomenology the intentionality of higher affections is not controversial. Sartre and Merleau-Ponty, for example, use the language of affective intentionality without ever deeming it necessary to argue its existence or nature. When I visited Levinas in 1975, he said that between the wars the most exciting topic of discussion in the soirées at Gabriel Marcel's house on the boulevard Port-Royal was in fact this idea that affectivity shared in the intentionality of cognitive consciousness. We therefore take the intentionality of affectivity as something we need not argue here but only understand and apply.[2]

To speak of intentionality is to speak of meaning. To intend is to mean. To intend affectively is to mean through feeling. To say the face means responsibility is shorthand for an affective intending or meaning that in the face-to-face relation one feels responsible for the other. It is not something first understood in concepts or reached as a conclusion in judgments, nor is it freely chosen or decided on after deliberation. Rather, one is affected by meaning, one is commanded by proximity, held hostage by an experience, not after representation but before it, in presence, presentation, vulnerability, embodiment, in affectivity as its own kind of intentionality, its own access to meaning. But the questions of this paper are How? and Why? How does affective intentionality work? Why does the face communicate and command responsibility?

The answers lie in the fact that there are two affectivities in Levinas. He speaks not only of the face of the other affecting me in the present but also of another kind of "being affected," one that reaches back into a preconscious and preintentional past, before knowledge, volition, or freedom. This preintentional or nonintentional consciousness, furthermore, is not a lower kind of consciousness, like that mentioned by Scheler and Dietrich von Hildebrand when they speak of mere physiological or organic appetites or of mere teleological orientations, vectors, or trends, such as fatigue, thirst, and so on; while those affections are conscious, their explanation is causal, and entirely from below; they are not affections that occur *because of* relations to objects in conscious intentions.

The claim that there is a *non*intentional affectivity has in Levinas's employment of it the structure of a practical postulate offered to explain the feeling of responsibility occasioned by the face of the other. Why and how does the face have this power, or rather this authority?[3] The way Levinas uses the language of hyperbole (words like obsession, persecution, hostage) to describe this nonintentional affectivity, especially under the name of the presence of the idea of the infinite (the biblical "image of God" translated into the Cartesian idea of the infinite) in consciousness, opens the way for us to call responsibility a projection onto the other of one's own interior archetype, to use the language of psychology—the "in other words" to which I return in the second part of this paper—understanding such archetypal projection itself as one kind or part of a general mediation of a diachronic nonintentional affectivity by a synchronic affective intentionality like the face.[4] The face operates as a symbol, and as a symbol it unites a feeling with an image.[5] The feeling of responsibility is attached to an archetypal image, rooted in the diachronic past of creation. It is this creation that places in oneself, like Descartes's idea of the infinite, an image of God, an image one finds in oneself and in the other. Let the foregoing suffice as an introductory summary of this paper and its thesis. Now, how might we understand these two affectivities and the relation between them?

How Affective Intentionality Connects with Nonintentional Consciousness

Thesis: Together affective intentionality and nonintentional affectivity explain Levinas's philosophy of the face as ethical responsibility in that the synchronic affective intentionality of the face-to-face relation draws its authority from a diachronic nonintentional affectivity.

We can try to explain the authority of the face in terms of the two affectivities in either or both of two ways: it makes appeal to our created solidarity as one species and/or to the image of God in oneself and in the other.[6] One can postulate this, and stop there; but we can also try to understand the postulate by pointing to the trace of everyman and everywoman in us all. I am reminded of a *Star Trek* episode in which the crew of the *Enterprise* is indicted for the sins of humanity before a court of sentient species representing all the galaxies. The crew is led from initial rejection of responsibility for its species to a grudging acceptance—while denying any personal knowing or voluntary culpability—under the protest that humanity as a species had progressed beyond its early barbarism. They denied individual guilt while admitting solidarity with the species "human."

What escapes cognitional and volitional intentionality is, however, accessible through affective intentionality, and the classical name for this, as Ricoeur points out in *Fallible Man*, is "*affective connaturality.*" There has to be some link between the before-the-prehistoric nonintentional origin of our affectability, on the one hand, and each present event of one's consciousness of being affected in the face-to-face relation, on the other. If we had no such consciousness, no intentionality to which Levinas could appeal, then his work and his message would remain inaccessible to consciousness and thus outside assent by his readers. We who hear him must find resonance within ourselves of what he proclaims to us, such as the image of God (the idea of the infinite) found within us—and also met in the other—so long as we remember that the image of God is not God nor the idea of the infinite (the) infinite. Now, affective connaturality explains the way affective intentionality actually works and operates as a connaturality based on a common affectivity, linking the intentional back to the nonintentional. So how do these two affectivities interact?

Let us analyze affective intentionality. Affective intentionality has two moments; according to Ricoeur, feeling is "an affection plus an intention," the first is a "being affected" (affection) and the second is the affective response (intention). The first presupposes an affectability, an ability to be affected; the second presupposes a responsibility, an ability to respond. It is to being as important, as good, but especially as value that feeling responds.

But value imposes a demand, obligation, or call for an *adequate* response, unlike a good that is merely appealing or subjectively satisfying and to whom or which one's response is entirely optional. A value puts a claim on us; value commands. The face is in the class of value, demanding an adequate response once one is affected. This is the dual structure of affective intentionality, that is, affectability plus responsibility. But *why* is one so affectable by the face?

It is because affectability itself—the ground of responsibility—is based on something prior to itself, namely, a nonintentional connaturality, affinity, kinship, solidarity with the other: something in me resonates with the other and I am spontaneously affected and so commanded to respond—obsessed, Levinas says, and therefore free. (There is also, of course, an affectability that is intentional, when through our own actions we acquire habits, a second nature. Levinas is addressing the origin of our first nature, in a nonintentional affectivity that is a pure passivity, the absolute receptivity or our very existence, prior to all action.) Recall the story Joseph Campbell tells of the Hawaiian policeman: a deep solidarity with a fellow human, who was in the act of committing suicide by leaping off a cliff, precipitated the policeman into risking his own life to save another's, and even drew, with a strange magnetism, a second policeman into the chain reaction. Clearly this is a substitution, a spontaneous action before voluntary deliberation, beyond willingness. Why did the policeman feel so responsible? How did his affective response override reason and will? Campbell quotes Schopenhauer to the effect that at a moment like that, a deep metaphysical (his word) resonance between one's consciousness and the deeper unconscious self that Jung calls the objective psyche occurs within one's subjectivity; this identity with the other is rooted more deeply than rational, discursive thought or deliberative, voluntary will. One could invoke the Platonic "like known by like," but it is more than a knowing; it takes affective connaturality to explain how the solidarity, already there beneath and before cognition and volition, breaks through into consciousness as feeling.

Let's further analyze the structure of feeling as affective intentionality. A response is not an operation in the sense of cognitional and volitional operations. We must distinguish between operations—such as looking, seeing, thinking, forming concepts, judging, deciding—and responses. Feeling, as affective intentionality,[7] has something specific to it as affection, namely, the dual structure of feeling whereby the feeling or emotion is always a feeling of some moving agent, namely, the other, but also a feeling or emotion for oneself, where the emotion consists in being moved, being frightened, made to rejoice or to be sad, and so on; there is a double intentionality of the "of" and of the "for," a participating in affectivity from two sides, since the event in oneself depends on being affected by the other. The essence of affective intentionality is that the term of the intention is not a concept or an act of will but a being-affected, in the first passive moment, and an affective response, in the second, spontaneously active moment.[8]

My response, then, while produced by me, depends on the other to whom it is a response and who has affected me in such a way as to engender this response. But the point of dual affectivity, nonintentional and intentional, is that the face is a symbol that acts not only with its own present power but also as and with the deeper force of an archetype whereby there occurs a deep communicating between the diachronic past and the synchronic present.[9] As face it speaks for itself, but as symbol and archetype it says much more than itself through its affective link to all humanity, "affective" because I am passive to this being-affected with a passivity that doesn't even presuppose my existence as a subject, for it is the passive reception of that very existence in my being created in the human species. Thus the face, while not "only" or "merely" a symbol, operates as if it were one, that is, with the overdetermined force of one, that is, by being more than itself, by being itself plus the trace.

Thus I am affectable because out of my own immemorial past, I project onto or transfer to the other something (the image of God, like the idea of the infinite) from that deep objective psyche that the other and I share as human. The transfer works and has the authoritative power it does because it is grounded in our common created solidarity, coming to consciousness as a link between a nonintentional affectivity and an affective intentionality, making the experience possible as qualitatively what it is. It is not an empty projection because the image found in the face is first found nonintentionally in myself. Thus, rather than take the power of the face as a "mere" projection in any pejorative sense, we should understand projection itself as a subset of the face as the most fundamental occurrence of an affective intentionality of which projection and transference are instances—in the way psychology speaks of projection as the first attempt of the Self to bring its unconscious (objective) past to present (subjective) consciousness—and these instances are themselves explainable on the basis of the dual structure of affective intentionality. Thus Levinas's projection of responsibility to and for the other is rooted in the archetype postulated to begin in a diachronic nonintentional affectivity. This aboriginal affectivity is projected onto the other from a past too remote to be accessed directly by cognition and volition.[10]

Further, if we take Ricoeur's definition of symbol as "meaning other than what is said," then Levinas's face can be taken as a symbol in that sense also, that is, as a saying other and more than its said, as commanding, "Thou shalt not kill," which by interpretation sends us back to the nonintentional affectivity of the trace that is the true diachronic saying embodied in every synchronic said. Symbols, like the face, represent the fullness of language in that a symbol, much more than a word, contains an overdetermination of meaning. As Ricoeur says in his *Freud and Philosophy*, speaking of full language, "The movement that draws me toward the second meaning assimilates me to what is said, makes me participate in what is announced to me. The similitude in which the force of symbols resides and from which they draw their revealing power is not an objective likeness; it is an existential assimilation, according to the movement of analogy, of my being to being."[11]

This means that the reason why the face communicates more meaning than itself is that there is an affective connaturality not between my knowing and the other but between my being and the other. It is what Ricoeur calls an "existential assimilation," or what Sartre calls an affective intentionality when he says that "Heidegger's being-with is not knowledge,"[12] and what I would call an affective connaturality.

We can therefore see in Levinas a reversal of the Freudian reduction, which is of a present to a past by way of a hermeneutic of suspicion that empties meaning from immediate consciousness in favor of an archaeology of the subject who is a pure self-obsessed narcissist. In Levinas we find a hermeneutic of recovery, and the self-obsessed narcissist becomes an other-obsessed altruist. The meaning of the present still returns to an immemorial past, but its sign is reversed. Freud's irreligious egoism, which saw in religion "the universal obsessional neurosis of mankind,"[13] is replaced in Levinas by an obsession with the other whose authority comes from connecting with the infinite, the vertical infinite of God, the creator, and the horizontal infinite of a humanity of the other, the created image of God, where creation is the event of a nonintentional affectivity (i.e., where one's creation is something one undergoes without intending to—an unintended being-affected). The for-itself of Freud's amoral egoism becomes the for-the-other of Levinas's moral altruism. The two affectivities are linked by the face as real symbol, almost as sacrament, effecting what it signifies.

So there is also a telos in Levinas, a reference of the face to the future that complements its archaeological roots in the prehistoric past. Its name is substitution as the future to-be-done, the action that complements the passion of having-been-affected by having been created in the immemorial past. Thus the face as symbol is a Janus face, both a looking back and a looking forward, a trace and a project, a nonintentional affectivity and an affective intending of the other. The face has this double intentionality, repeating our childhood, anticipating our adulthood, a present extending back into our past and forward into our future, an archaeology and a teleology.[14] Affective intentionality is the present face-to-face moment that links an archaeology, created in a nonintentional affectivity, to a teleology, creative responsibility for the other. Archaeology and teleology connect through a passivity of the past and an activity for a future still to come, the advent of the other.

Similarly, the dual function of face as symbol shows in that the face conceals and reveals, hides and shows the infinite. The face makes present an immemorial past, but for the sake of a present that becomes its future. Thus the face is not a *re*presentation but a *present*ation, a presenting and presencing of what can never become old, namely, the other who addresses to me the ever new imperative "Be responsible." Each meeting face to face with the other is an epiphany both of myself and the other; the question is never asked once and for all but always anew: Do you accept this responsibility or not?

Finally, we must make even more explicit why this event is experienced as ethical. The psyche—to speak now with Jung, not Freud—as sum of conscious and unconscious life, includes the ego and the Self. Affective intentionality, as one of consciousness's three intentionalities, is an activity of ego, taking the ego as the center of consciousness. *Non*intentional affectivity, however, is a passivity of the Self, taking the Self as the center of the whole psyche, of which consciousness is a small part. Ego and Self are complementary and connected because both are of the psyche. If we accept that the psyche communicates within itself, namely, between ego and Self, through symbols, and accept the face as a real symbol, and further accept that the unconscious psyche as unconscious has no intentionalities (for intentions are experiences of consciousness), then we have at least a formal structure for explaining not only the connection of ego consciousness and its intentionalities with the deeper Self but also the possible content or quality of the connection as ethical. What would have to be articulated is some conflict between conscious ego and unconscious Self that admitted now of an ethical interpretation.

Levinas offers many descriptions of conflict brought on by the advent of the face. One such is the analysis of metaphysical desire. Desire, as Levinas has so forcefully explained, moves the Self, as center of the psyche, toward the other, and when the Self meets the other in the face-to-face relation, the unconscious and nonintentional affectivity of the Self is revealed as meant for the other. This meeting is an event which by transcending the ego calls forth from the Self a response that exceeds and dethrones the ego—precisely by driving it out of the paradise of enjoyment as the center of consciousness back to an anarchic "past" so remote as to arise from a nonintentional, nonconscious affectivity—and places it into question in such a way that one experiences it as answer-ability, respons-ibility. If the event did not touch oneself twice or in two ways or two places—or times, synchrony and diachrony—then the face *as* responsibility, as called to respond, obliged to respond, would not make sense. It would have no ethical value or moral force. We would have no explanation adequate to its authority and power as commandment. There would be no experience of imperative or of being accused or of having one's naive transcendental ego discover its murderous potential. There has to be this dual consciousness of ego and Self, of affective intentionality against the ground of a nonintentional affectivity. The Self of nonintentional affectivity, awakened from dogmatic slumber by the ego of affective intentionality, face to face with the other, puts the ego in its place—or rather out of its place. The reason that the face can cause or occasion this awakening is because the Self is created for this, lives just for this, becomes human in these birth pains. It is the ego claiming its place in the sun, says Levinas quoting Pascal, that is hateful.

In this way the movement from the ego to the Self can also be seen as a fundamental movement toward the mature appropriation of one's own affectivity, from exterior to interior; Levinas's novelty is to see this movement as occuring for the sake of the exterior,[15] not for one's own idealistic *Beisichsein* but for the other. Not one's own death, as Levinas says, contra Heidegger, but the death of the other, should be the human obsession. For Levinas, the face evokes the trace, because the finite is an epiphany of the infinite, as the face met in affective intentionality connects with a nonintentional affectivity, and as exteriority connects with an infinite interior, to another Self-consciousness that transcends ego-consciousness. Thus the movement initiated by the face of the other does not end with my interiority but through a deeper exteriority (the infinite within me but before my freedom) returns to the other as responsibility for the other, in the completion of affective intentionality as affective response, the second moment of affective intentionality after the being-affected by the face. So the movement that begins when the ego is affected by the other finds itself complete only when it is the Self that responds to the other rather than the ego, where the affective intentionality toward the other connects with a nonintentional affectivity in the Self that issues in responsibility for the other. It takes both affectivities, one intentional and one nonintentional, and both moments of affective intentionality, to account for the event of the face experienced as responsibility. It is a movement away from naive consciousness to responsible consciousness, from an unquestioned ego-centeredness to a question that commands a response and to an awareness of the primacy of the other, from affectability to being-affected and from responsibility to affective response.

Thus, to conclude this main point, there would be no experience of responsibility, no sense of responsibility, were it not for the dual structure of affectivity, the dual structure of the Janus face as symbol tracing its power and authority to an affectivity before time, in the solidarity of our creation as one species, for the sake of the other. This archaeological-teleological dialectic is experienced as a present ability to answer for a future because of a past that can only be present in this face as real symbol overdetermined with meaning. To employ another language, affectivity, unlike cognitional and volitional intentionalities, is the heart, that is, a capacity to respond that depends on being affected by the other. As Ricoeur says, a feeling is a mélange of affection and intention; something in the present symbol communicates with a past for a future. Past, present, and future unite in the face; one is affected and made able to respond, affected because the face as symbol communicates with an immemorial past affectivity, and intending because the transcendence of ego toward Self is felt as a command to respond to the other. As created, we are one species; the Self (not the ego) is an other. Transcendence of the ego is the advent and epiphany of both Self and other. The ego of cognitional and volitional intentionality must be overcome by the Self-Other structure of affective intentionality, and out of this dialectic comes the ethical.

Levinas's Dual Affectivity in Other Words

Levinas's analysis of responsibility as based on a preconscious nonintentional affectivity admits of comparison with the concept of the complex and its central element, the archetype, in Jungian analytical psychology.[16]

The concept of the archetype offers a model for understanding how the face operates to evoke the structure of responsibility. If responsibility is a nonintentional affectivity until the face awakens it, then there must be a common something shared by both, a bond between them that is the basis of their ability to communicate. Affectivity is that element, as affective connaturality, their felt common nature, which is both nonintentional in the aboriginal diachronic event of creation of oneself as a member of the human species, and intentional in the synchronic event of the face. The face is the symbol that bears—in the sense of meta-phor, that is, bearing more than it can bear (of itself), carrying a force beyond itself—the feeling of responsibility. It does so without reduction to representation, to cognitional or volitional intentionality; that is, it operates by affective intentionality. But in a second, reflective moment it is analyzable in cognitional and volitional terms, of course, and we eventually have to analyze the symbol in order to offer an argument in support of this thesis. What is a symbol? A symbol is a nonrational, intuitive, affective means of psychic functioning, where "psychic" comprises unconscious and conscious.[17]

As Jung explains, "the drive or complex always reveals itself initially, in the primitive stages, as though it came from the other person, because whatever is unconscious, whatever we are identical with, is projected."[18] Rimbaud's saying "The Self is an other" has new meaning in light of this concept. Levinas wants to take us back to a nonintentional primitive state of being affected by otherness at the very core of oneself. This nonintentional affectivity, one's very creation in the image of God, then surfaces up from (or "down from," thinking of the idea of the infinite) the objective unconscious psyche to become subjectivity in an affectivity that is intentional, namely, the face of the other, onto whom the fundamental complex of responsibility is projected. Note that this responsibility is not found first in the other but in the Self, after Descartes's idea of the infinite, but—and this is the point of my recourse to Jung—it is also felt as coming from the other as face. Further, "since a projection is always visualization of a complex, it makes itself felt by a strong affect charge. In plain English, whenever a projection is involved, it 'gets' us, it 'gets under our skin.' Our reaction is affect-determined and we are therefore unable to react adequately to a person or situation; we can neither accept nor modify nor leave that person or situation. This is one of the few basic laws of the psyche which is, without exception, one-hundred-percent foolproof."[19]

Levinas's language of violence, wound, obsession, hostage, the trauma of persecution, substitution, and so on, is illustrated and confirmed in other words by Jungian psychology.

Further, there are connections between the psychological model and Levinas's face as real symbol. Of human faces we could say, "They are symbolic inasmuch as the objective psyche does not conceptualize; it does not speak English or French or German or Chinese; it speaks images, which are aboriginal forms of perception and expression."[20] Levinas's attempts from the first to find a language adequate to the face as symbol of an anarchic nonintentional affectivity resemble the objective psyche's attempt to become a subject; the concept—the said—is never equal to the saying. The ego is never equal to the Self and the tension between them is experienced as the ethical ought.

Levinas is quite clear that responsibility (i.e., as an ability to respond) anticipates the advent of the other, like a *Vorgriff* that projects a horizon of possibility which becomes conscious when a real other appears against it. Affective intentionality operates when the face of the other shakes us from dogmatic slumber and the dreamer awakens, because an anarchic nonintentional affectivity connects us to this real other through an archetype, the other as image of God, commanding responsibility. "Projection is therefore the first stage of awareness, the actualization of a psychic content or of a complex as if it adhered or pertained to an external object. We might describe a projection as a vision or inner image which is evoked by outward elements that correspond to the energy field of a complex and is as yet experienceable only in terms of these outward elements."[21]

The nonintentional affectivity of our creation as one species, each in the image of God, is actualized by the affective intentionality of the face, and thus a solidarity with the other is felt as responsibility. Please note that this model is not presented as a simple-minded psychologistic reduction; it is not an attempt to explain away responsibility as "nothing but" this or that. Quite the contrary, Levinas is showing us the radical truth of an ultimately untranscendable structure writ in the bone and sinew of human existence. He has perhaps shown us precisely why a Freudian reduction to symptomatic mechanism compares so poorly with a Jungian model of symbolic dynamism. Why is this so? Because Levinas spends his efforts in teaching us to differentiate the nonintentional affectivity of creation from the affective intentionality of the face in the cause not of reducing the latter to the former, thus divesting it of its actuality, but of teaching us to recognize the very meaning of the anarchic dream of nonintentional affectivity in the actual other whose face awakens us to a responsibility for this real other. "A capacity for moving towards differentiating and transforming the drive will not arise until the state of identity has been dissolved. This requires a confrontation of the drive as a Thou, as something that is not I, as something separate from ourselves. Until then the drive remains unconscious, primitive, and destructive. Only after the identity has been dissolved by learning to experience the drive as an autonomous entity that is separate from the ego, despite its tendency to engulf the ego, do we get a chance to choose a right time and place and to develop the positive potential of the drive."[22]

In Levinas's works we find a dual movement, one a permanent reaching back to an immemorial past, the other an almost excessive vulnerability and extreme sensitivity to a morally unavoidable present. Only the conscious connection of present affective intentionality with the aboriginal nonintentional affectivity of human, created solidarity can make sense of the tremendous power of this weak and needy other facing me. Only the archetypal solidarity of a race in which all others are myself can bend the interpersonal space into an ethical transformation so as to make the other embody all the others.

Conclusion

To say that Levinas has written a philosophy means that he has worked to bring to consciousness the structures and operations of human life, to take them from their subjective operational functionality, and to objectify them. It is true that the trace left in nonintentional affectivity does not need to become conscious in order to be operative in one's encounter with the other in the face-to-face relation. The other will affect me ethically, Levinas would say, without my knowing how or why. But Levinas has written a philosophy of that prephilosophical life, and to write such a philosophy is to try explain the how and why, and that requires recourse to a philosophy of affectivity which finds in the totally passive event of creation the origins of one's being affectable in just this way by connatural others, others also marked by the trace. A psychology that has something to say about obsession and projection can throw light on the way one might become conscious of how the diachronic trace works, can help one become conscious of why and how one is so affectable by the other. Possession is a first stage that leads to projection as a middle stage toward objective consciousness: possession → projection → consciousness.

So how does one become possessed? That is the question of nonintentional affectivity and it is as important a question as how the other (the face) arouses me to responsibility, which is the question of affective intentionality. For a philosophy has to ask these earlier questions of how responsivity becomes responsibility. And further, how does the ability to respond become the obligation to respond? And even further, how does this obligation to respond become an obligation to respond well, to do good? If there is obligation coming from somewhere (who knows where?), why does this obligation become ethical? The one answer Levinas gives to all these questions comes down to a practical postulate to the effect that in the diachronic origin that is my creation, the creator infected me with an affectivity and affectability that I did not intend, making me affectable by an other who is connatural to it, namely, by the also-created others met in the face-to-face relation. Levinas does not claim a direct face-to-face relation with God and yet is wary of any relation that would get in the way of such a relation, including the neighbor. So there is an inevitable but fruitful tension between the face and its meaning, which is more than itself. The trace is ambiguous: is it *il y a* or *il*? Again it seems that Levinas's answer comes to a practical postulate: the diachronic event of creation is a nonintentional affectivity that marks me as someone who will henceforth be affectable by others similarly marked. Like a palimpsest, each of us bears the trace of the Scribe who first wrote; but the very existence of the palimpsest is also, itself, the nonintentional affectability.

Notes

1. There is a phenomenological and a nonphenomenological meaning to the key term "intentional." Within phenomenology, intentional means "of consciousness" or "existing as an object of consciousness," without prejudice as to one kind of consciousness over any other. Thus one can speak of feelings and moods as affective intentionalities, as ways of being conscious, just as one can speak of ideas, concepts, judgments as cognitional intentionalities and of decisions as volitional intentionalities, as other ways of being conscious. But the usual, nonphenomenological meaning of intentional is "on purpose" or "willed" or "desired." One of the sources of confusion about Levinas's position on nonintentional consciousness stems from the author's awareness of the usual meaning of intentional and his desire to make sure his readers do not think that the experience of the face is intentional in that usual, nonphenomenological sense. We do not desire or intend the other to affect us ethically, and he uses his most forceful language (hostage, obsession, persecution, allergy, epiphany, advent, substitution, etc.) to describe the event. So he has to call the face a nonintentional consciousness. The confusion comes from the fact that he also insists that the face is an instance of affective intentionality in that the face affects oneself not within the representational intentionality of (preexisting) concepts or willed acts of freedom; the face's authority is preconceptual and

prevolitional. So long as we recall the dual meaning of intentional we can speak of a nonintentional, affectivity and an affective intentionality.

Levinas holds that affectivity is the basis of responsibility; that is, one's ability to be affected in vulnerable embodiment grounds one's ability to respond. Being created is the event of our most aboriginal affectivity: one exists only as recipient of being given existence, as a result of being affected by God; this is a radical affectivity, a passivity that presupposes no activity, not even a previously existing being to be affected. The first affectivity is nonintentional: one's very existence is due to a nonintentional (in both meanings: unconscious as preconscious, and unintended) affectivity, one that presupposes no subject or agent. The second affectivity is intentional (not in the sense of willed but in the sense of conscious): as embodied one is already in motion toward others, moving in space and time in a world already peopled with others. Diachronic nonintentional affectivity becomes synchronic affective intentionality when the trace of the infinite left in us by creation meets the other person in time and becomes the face to face of my neighbor.

2. See Edith Wyschogrod, *Emmanuel Levinas: The Problem of Ethical Metaphysics* (The Hague: Martinus Nijhoff, 1974) for more on affective intentionality. Levinas's occasional denials of intentionality all refer to a rejection of representational, cognitional intentionality; see, for example, OB 47: "the 'inversion' of intentionality," and OB 49: "prior to any intentionality"; see also OB 189 n. 24, 192 n. 20, and 193 n. 35. This was also true in TaI (e.g., 27).

3. Levinas speaks much of the face in the interview in PL.

4. There is precedent for addressing Levinas in the "other words" of psychology. See, for example, Monique Schneider, "La proximité chez Levinas et le Nebenmensch freudien," EL 431-43; and Michel Haar, "L'obssession de l'autre. L'éthique comme traumatisme," EL 444-53. See also Noreen O'Connor, "Who Suffers?" RL 229-33.

5. "A symbol is an image or a real or imaginary object [e.g., a face] that evokes a feeling or is evoked by a feeling." Bernard J. F. Lonergan, *Method in Theology* (New York: Herder and Herder, 1972), 64.

6. When Levinas says "same" and "other" he has to mean "same nature" but not "same person," otherwise there can be no communication or commerce between human beings. Human solidarity is not denied by affirming the otherness of the other. That the other and I are not the same leaves intact that she is my sister, he my brother. Nonintentional affectivity affirms our original solidarity, a humanism of the other and an otherness within humanity. This humanism makes possible a hospitality to the stranger at the same time that it can declare the *totaliter aliter* an absurd notion. It is not that otherness is contained within and by sameness—rightly called totalitarian—but that it is on another plane, having the intelligibility of judgments of existence rather than that of essence, concepts, definitions, that is, having the meaning of the saying

not of the said, of actuality not possibility, of person not nature, of who not what.

7. In an affective intentionality we have four elements. By accounting for them we account for the nature of affective intentionality as the experience of feeling of the *other*. We have (1) the object intended (the other; the *quod intenditur*); (2) the subject intending (oneself, the *qui intendit*); (3) the act of intending (the *intendere*), an act known both as the act of the subject and of (4) the being intended, that is, one's being affected by the other (the *intendi*). As a subject of cognitional intentionality, I know myself knowing something or someone; as a subject of volitional intentionality, I know myself willing something or someone; as a subject of affective intentionality, I know myself feeling something or someone.

   I can also *reflect* on these intentions and *represent* them; I do this by attending not to the *other* but to *myself*, that is, not to the data of sense (e.g., listening to someone, being in a face-to-face relation with someone) but to the data of consciousness. It is to this second, reflective stage that Levinas is anxious to deny primacy; but that denial leaves direct affective intentionality undenied. There would be no *other* without it, nor would there be a conscious subject, only a substance. Substance becomes subject *when it acts*, not when it becomes an object of someone's knowledge. I am therefore in a nonrepresentationally intentional relation with the other affectively *and* know myself to be affected by the other purely and simply in the feeling itself, and only later do I turn that nonrepresentational intentionality into a representation when I think about it, understand it, form a concept of it, reflect on it, judge it. When I do this latter set of operations, I am not attending directly to the *other* in my presence, near me, whom I see, address in saying, and so on, but am now attending to *myself*, that is, to my consciousness of my seeing, addressing as said, and so on.

   In other words, I do not *have* to turn myself into an object (although I can) in order to know myself as a subject: I need only *be in act, be intending, be conscious*, including being conscious of an other. I can do that affectively, cognitively, volitionally. In my intending, *because I am in act*, I know *myself* once. In *reflecting* on my intending, I know myself *twice*, but now I have lost the *other*, because now indeed I myself am the object of my intending. It is this *second* moment Levinas wants to dethrone from the primacy it holds in *representational* intentionality.

8. It is incorrect to say that Levinas's ethics depends on a nonintentional affectivity exclusively or that he denies an affectivity that is intentional. His rejection of intentionality is a rejection of *representational* intentionality, the reflective, second-order intentions mentioned above, along with a somewhat irrelevant allusion to a nonphenomenological meaning of intention having to do with *purpose, willing,* and *volition*; this latter rejection of the term "intention" is apparently aimed at those of his readers who do not understand the proper

phenomenological sense of intentionality as consciousness of an object rather than as a term used to describe the "doing something intentionally," meaning voluntarily; obviously he wants to deny that our being affected by the other is under our direct voluntary control. A proper understanding of affective intentionality preserves both elements of this phenomenon, both the affection, whereby the agency of the other is affirmed, and the intention, whereby one's consciousness of the face is also given.

In an act of affective intentionality, the subject is known not as an object but as a subject, for the act already has an object, namely, the other. Levinas is obviously doing away with a superfluous representational intentionality; he doesn't need a cognitional intentionality to have a subject and is wary of anyone inserting one. Why? Because that puts freedom first, before responsibility.

9. The human face, as no other, functions as the symbol par excellence, evoking the feeling of responsibility, where "feeling" changes its meaning as the quality of consciousness changes, especially in persons of more maturity and affective development. Now, "symbols obey the laws not of logic but of image and feeling. ... The symbol, then, has the power of recognizing and expressing what logical discourse abhors: the existence of internal tensions, incompatibilities, conflicts, struggles, destructions. ... Finally, it does it in a way that complements and fills out logic and dialectic, for it meets a need that these refinements cannot meet. This need is for internal communication. Organic and psychic vitality have to reveal themselves to intentional consciousness and, inversely, intentional consciousness has to secure the collaboration of organism and psyche. Again, our apprehensions of values occur in intentional responses, in feelings; here too it is necessary for feelings to reveal their objects and, inversely, for objects to awaken feelings. It is through symbols that mind and body, mind and heart, heart and body communicate" (Lonergan, *Method*, 66-67).

10. The thesis of the projected archetype is illustrated in the pages on paternity in *Totality and Infinity*. My son and daughter are my vulnerability incarnate in a space and time other than my own yet somehow still my own. We get an insight into affective intentionality seeing it writ large in the other. I suffer for the other who is me and not me, as my own embodiment is a kind of vulnerability of me outside me, at least outside the me who is capable of thinking this distinction. In living paternity, just as in living embodied, I live an intention to be affected by an otherness I have partly generated.

11. Paul Ricoeur, *Freud and Philosophy*, trans. Denis Savage (New Haven: Yale University Press, 1970), 31.

12. Jean-Paul Sartre, *Being and Nothingness*, trans. Hazel Barnes (New York: Washington Square Press, 1953), 331.

13. Ricoeur, *Freud and Philosophy*, 147.

14. "Relationship with the future, the presence of the future in the present, seems all the same accomplished in the face-to-face with the Other. The situation of the face-to-face would be the very accomplishment of time; the encroachment of the present on the future is not the feat of the subject alone, but the intersubjective relationship" (TO 79).
15. *Totality and Infinity* is subtitled *An Essay on Exteriority*: the exteriorization of the infinite is the face of the other; the divine is found nowhere better than in the human other.
16. "The term *complex* denotes the basic structural element of the objective psyche, and the central element of the complex is the *archetype*." Edward C. Whitmont, *The Symbolic Quest. Basic Concepts of Analytical Psychology* (Princeton: Princeton University Press, 1969), 57. ("Objective psyche" was Jung's term for the unconscious in his later writings.) Projection can be seen as an attempt of the unconscious or objective mind to become conscious, to enter subjectivity.
17. Ibid., 15.
18. Ibid., 60.
19. Ibid., 60.
20. Ibid., 37.
21. Ibid., 37.
22. Ibid., 59-60.

12
The Irresponsible Subject

William J. Richardson

Like many others, I have had the privilege of meeting Emmanuel Levinas personally. I propose to describe that meeting, to reflect on its implications, and to conclude by raising some questions that it leaves for all who admire his work and wish to draw on its capital. Unfortunately, it is impossible to describe this encounter without writing about myself. For that I apologize and ask the reader's indulgence.

To avoid misunderstanding and make the argument easier to follow, since it must move along rather quickly, let me sketch it in advance. The incident I shall recount raises an obvious difficulty that admits of two interpretations. One, a psychoanalytic one that I favor myself, offers a benign, very indulgent reading; the other, a Levinasian one, seems to offer, prima facie at least, no benign reading, if it has room to consider the difficulty at all. My concluding question will be, What, if anything, can be done about this ambiguity?

Thirty years ago, almost to the day, Martinus Nijhoff published a book I had written entitled *Heidegger: Through Phenomenology to Thought*. The book had grown out of research for a doctoral dissertation for the Higher Institute of Philosophy at the University of Louvain (Belgium), as a consequence of which I had been invited to become a candidate for the title of *maître agrégé*—a promotion roughly comparable to the *doctorat d'état* in France or the *Habilitation* in Germany. The candidacy required, among other things, a solemn public defense of the book before a jury of internationally known scholars. The candidate had the right to make recommendations as to who these scholars might be and, with proper approval, to extend the invitation to them in the name of the Institute. Because the book dealt with Heidegger's phenomenology, it seemed appropriate to invite a renowned phenomenologist to be a discussant, and who better than Emmanuel Levinas? He had in effect introduced Husserl into the French-speaking world, had written one of the best books on the early Heidegger ever to appear, and was a much respected friend of the Husserl Archives at Louvain. The authorities of the Institute thought it a great idea for him to come, but would he come? The book on him said that he was probably very busy (*Totalité et infini* had appeared the previous year), and passionately anti-Heideggerian. But the authorities agreed that he would be an excellent choice and encouraged me to invite him—after all, it was their guts and my blood.

Levinas received me very courteously. His manner was grave and reserved, but one got an immediate sense of the intensity of his intellectual and spiritual life. He seemed puzzled that I should ask him but accepted the reasons mentioned. He said that he would be willing at least to read the book, if I left it with him, and give me an answer in a few weeks. When I returned, he received me again most graciously. He agreed to be a member of the jury but warned me that he was no friend of Heidegger and would speak his mind. I assured him that that was why we were inviting him and thanked him sincerely for accepting.

The ceremony of the defense is quite solemn and may be best described perhaps as a one-man commencement ceremony: the entire faculty of the Institute gathers in its academic robes and enters the ornately decorated seventeenth-century hall in formal academic procession. The candidate takes his place at a podium surrounded on three sides by the faculty in tiered wooden benches, with the four critics in front on either side. When it came time for Levinas to speak, he was, again, very gracious. I had been prepared to take a hard shot, but, as a matter of fact, the harshest thing he said about the book was that it was very "scholastic" and "pedagogical." As I recall, he then asked a fairly general question as to why a believing Christian would spend so much time with someone like Heidegger in the first place.

After the defense, there was the usual reception for faculty and dignitaries at the president's official residence. I felt relieved, of course, but a little numb, to say the least, and was soon caught up in the ritual of greeting people, thanking them for coming, and so on. Suddenly I felt a very vigorous poke on my shoulder from someone who came up from behind. I turned, and who was it but Professor Levinas! I was delighted to see him, and stretched out my hand to him in order to tell him again how grateful I was personally for his coming and being so generous in his remarks. But I didn't get the chance. He ignored my outstretched hand and, looking me straight in the eye, said, "I was just talking about your book." "That's nice." "I was talking with some old friends, regaling them with stories—had them all laughing. I thought you might like to know what they were laughing at." "Sure." "Do you remember that place in your book where you say '1943 was a very prolific year'?" "Yes I do," and I did. I had a quick flashback, remembered trying to find some fresh way to open up yet another chapter by referring to other things Heidegger was doing at the same time that he was composing the text I was about to comment on. How could I refer to all that in one comprehensive word? Should I call it a "busy," "productive," "eventful," "fruitful" year? How about "prolific"? That should do it—let's go with "prolific" for now and get on with it. Levinas continued, "In 1943, my parents were in one concentration camp and I was in another. It was a *very* prolific year, indeed." And he turned on his heel and walked away. He was gone. I could not follow him into the crowd—I was surrounded by others. All I could do was continue the routine: "How do you do?" "Glad to see you again." "Thank you for coming."

My question is, Who did that ("that" being the entire gesture beginning with the poke on the back down to the turning away)? There seemed to be two dimensions in the one person. For this angry man was a different person from the courteous savant who had addressed me quite respectfully one hour earlier in public. If he had wanted to launch a salvo like that, why didn't he do it during the defense? That's what it was for. He would have had an audience in a prestigious academic setting, and many of those present would have been happy to see a real confrontation of that sort, just for the excitement of it. But now that moment had come and gone. My own spontaneous reaction was purely instinctual. Wasn't it a blindside hit (hit-and-run) after the game was over? Like a schoolboy, I felt it wasn't "fair."

But we are not schoolboys, we all know that life is not as simple as that. The only legitimate reason for recalling the incident now after thirty years time lies in seeing it as a symptom, for it suggests a problem, I think, that any ethical thought which wants to be radical ought to take into account. For there is a discrepancy, it seems to me, between Levinas's thought, with its focus on the infinite responsibility of one for the other—any other—and his action in this instance, which I experienced, in the blindness of a purely visceral response, as an unnecessary act of violence (as he uses that term). So I recount the matter in order to be able to ask the question, Where do we find room to account for this discrepancy in Levinas's practical thought?

Other ethical thinkers, after all, offer us a place to discuss behavior of this kind. Aristotle, you recall, when speaking of the "mean" in Book II of the *Nicomachean Ethics* cites, among other things, anger as an example of what can be felt "too much or too little," adding that to feel it "with reference to the right objects, towards the right people, with the right motive, and in the right way—this is what is intermediate and best" (1106b), all these factors being judged by a rational principle, of course, and involving some kind of deliberate choice.[1] If one were to assess this action in strictly Aristotelian terms, the issue might well turn around its deliberate/indeliberate character. For my part, I would argue that it was almost certainly an indeliberate act, set off by Levinas's "forgetting himself," as we say, when the word "prolific" threw him into a skid. I don't think that explanation would work in a court of law, of course, for it does not explain why one simple word chosen haphazardly by a then unknown other in a different context and different time, apparently had such explosive force there and then. Aristotle does not talk about unconscious motivation, and I think we have to go that far to explain this form of embodied speech. My question then becomes, Does Levinas offer us a place to talk about unconscious influences in his protoethics?

I don't know anything about Levinas's personal life other than what is obvious to anyone. What his early relations with his mother and father were like, I have no idea—all pertinent psychoanalytic questions remain unanswered. Born in Lithuania, then moving to the Ukraine, he experienced the Russian Revolution at the age of eleven before moving to France, where he finished his higher education. I am aware of no anecdotes, such as we have in the case of Freud, that tell of any concrete experience of anti-Semitism. But we do know the story of the Holocaust. Recent images prompted by the dedication of the Holocaust Museum in Washington together with televised records of "ethnic cleansing" in Bosnia make vivid even to us what that event must have meant to someone intimately involved in it, as Emmanuel Levinas was. In a brief autobiographical note he remarks laconically how his life has been "dominated by the presentiment and the memory of the Nazi horror" (Si 177). Though his esteem for the philosophical power of the author of *Being and Time* never wavered, the debacle of 1933 was shattering. A propos of Heidegger's use of the term *es gibt*, he observes sardonically, "No generosity which the German term 'es gibt' is said to express showed itself between 1933 and 1945" (Si 181). Prolific!

In this light it is easy to imagine how it may have rankled him to read a seven-hundred-page book on the evolution of Heidegger's notion of thought that did not confront directly the issue of the philosopher's political involvement. One can see how the residual anger of many years might descend on the head of a young man who had just sustained a public defense at the Catholic University of Louvain, one sponsored by the national hierarchy of the same church that gave us the Inquisition. And this man was not only a cleric but a Jesuit too—Jesuits are just as bad as Dominicans—and an American to boot. "Prolific," indeed! And there he is being congratulated for it all, without the least awareness of the scandal his words contain. Maybe he ought to be told.

All of this is sheer fantasy, of course, but it is one scenario that might make sense out of why the word "prolific" was so explosive. For the unconscious I am referring to functions like that, through the power of words. Psychoanalysis as a method is essentially the "talking cure." In psychoanalytic terms, the unconscious I am speaking of is "structured like a language." This terminology was introduced, of course, by Jacques Lacan in his effort to reread Freud, and I know you are familiar with his basic ideas. Recall his fundamental categories of the psyche: symbolic, imaginary, and real. The symbolic (the term comes from Lévi-Strauss) is the order of law(s) that governs the structure of language, and this is what Lacan, strictly speaking, identifies with the unconscious. The symbolic order functions in inseparable conjunction with another component, the order of imaged representation named the "imaginary," both orders together forming the structure of what we normally refer to as "reality." Reality in this ordinary sense is distinct from the third component of the psyche, one knotted together with the other two, called simply the "real"—that dimension of experience which defies representation of any kind, whether by the images of the imaginary or by the articulation of the symbolic. It is the place where trauma resides, where the unspeakable/unimaginable/unthinkable defies any attempt to domesticate it—e.g., what Levinas calls the "Nazi horror." The real is also where the undiscovered secrets of nature lie hidden, maybe even the place to which God withdraws.

In this conception, what Freud calls the "other scene" of conscious life Lacan calls the Other. It is not simply the unconscious of the subject but the unconscious *as* subject, insinuating itself into the "I" of the "I"-speaking, conscious subject, sabotaging its best intentions. The unconscious thus understood is more than the set of laws governing the symbolic order. These laws are inscribed in history and transferred through language in the heritage of our race and in every influence of family, culture, and personal biography that forms and informs who we are.

I would suggest that the unconscious which flared up in Levinas's symbolic action that afternoon was sedimented with his entire heritage. The affect of anger it expressed was an effect in the imaginary when the old, still unintegrated trauma jutted into his "reality" again by reason of the explosive ambiguity of the word "prolific." Levinas's expression, then, would have proceeded from the Other of the unconscious, articulated in Levinas's name through his gesture and speech. This, I say, is my hypothesis. If it seems tenuous, I will concede that the incident in question here does not provide the best example imaginable of the functioning of the unconscious. In fact, this particular example is in no way essential to the question I am trying to raise, but it does have value as an ad hominem argument that adds cogency to my proposition. Let it stand, then, at least as symptomatic of the problem posed for ethical thought by the unconscious as such. In any case, it is this other Other that I have ventured to call, at least provocatively, "the irresponsible subject."

The question becomes, then, How do we account for the functioning of this other Other in the protoethics of Emmanuel Levinas? As far as I can see, he rarely addresses the matter explicitly. The issue seems not to have interested him, perhaps because of the early influence of Bergson as mediated by Charles Blondel. At the age of nineteen while studying in Strasbourg, as Levinas told Richard Kearney, Blondel "developed a specifically Bergsonian psychology quite hostile to Freud—a hostility which made a deep and lasting impression on [Levinas]."[2] We get a good sense of his opposition to it from the following:

> [If psychoanalysis is to be believed,] we can no longer speak. Not because we no longer have an interlocutor but because we no longer take his words seriously, and because his inwardness is purely epiphenomenal. ... Psychoanalysis casts a basic suspicion on the most unimpeachable testimony of self-consciousness. That the clear and distinct consciousness of what was formerly called a psychological fact is now taken to be only the symbolism for a reality that is totally inaccessible to itself, and that it expresses a social reality or a historical influence totally distinct from its own intention, is what voids the very return of the *cogito*. So the distinction between phenomenon and noumenon can even be introduced into the domain of self-consciousness. The *cogito* then loses its value as a foundation. (CP 34)

For all the radicality of his reading of Husserl, Levinas remains, it seems, a Cartesian in his bones. I shall return to his criticism in a moment, but first let us recall the essentials of Levinas's own conception of language to see if the notion of an unconscious as "structured like a language" might find a surreptitious place there.

In *Totality and Infinity* language is understood as a "recourse to a system of signs" (TaI 206). Its primordial essence is to be sought "not in the corporal operation that discloses it ... but in the presentation of meaning" (TaI 206). But "meaning is the face of the Other, and all recourse to words takes place already within the primordial face to face of language" (TaI 206). Meaning, however, emerges from signifying acts, so for signification, too, the "primordial event is the face to face— not the effect of signs but what makes them possible" (TaI 206). What Levinas calls here "expression" is the manifestation of the presence of the Other's face as signifying source, that is, immediately—without the help of some mediating sign (TaI 181-82). And "speech [I am taking *la parole* to mean the word as spoken] is a manifestation beyond compare: it ... unlocks ... every sign ... by making the signifier *attend* [*assister*, 'be present at'] [the] manifestation of the signified" (TaI 182).

The issue of language is orchestrated more fully in *Otherwise Than Being*; the axis around which the book turns is the difference between what is Said and the Saying of it. That there is some correlation between the two is obvious. What Levinas means by the Said is also relatively easy to grasp. According to his method of intentional analysis, every thematizing identification of a phenomenon implies an anticipatory word that suggests a kerygmatic function in consciousness, by reason of which consciousness can proclaim a phenomenon to be what it is *as* this or that. This proclamation is essentially a Said, the apophantic disclosure of the phenomenon in its being—its *logos*.[3] More broadly conceived, the Said includes the entire spectrum of beings thus disclosed, Heidegger's "beings in their totality" (*das Seiende im Ganzen*). This is the region of the Third. The intelligibility of this totality would be its "systematic structure," and all subjectivity would be thought of in terms of its power to represent this intelligibility (OB 132). This is the domain of thought and science, of truth and untruth (like distortion, deception, and lies). It is here, no doubt, that belong the findings of linguistics, cultural anthropology, and psychoanalysis, for it is only here that one can begin to speak of knowledge as explicit or implicit, as conscious or unconscious. In fact, however, the unconscious I am speaking of is not a Said but a Saying. What, then, is Saying?

Surely, the power of Saying is not exhausted by its apophantic function (OB 6), and the infinitive form of the French (*dire*), which we translate as a noun, that is, a gerund (saying), rather than as an infinitive (to say), suggests that its action, as such, is undetermined by either object or subject. Levinas approaches it as if making a formal reduction: "The movement back toward Saying is the phenomenological reduction in which the indescribable is described" (OB 53). Why indescribable? Because to describe the Saying would be to thematize and identify it, hence to reduce it to a Said. The task is to pass beneath (*en deçà de*) or beyond (*au delà de*) the Said to that dimension of experience which transcends the realm of the Said toward the Other in its infinite unspeakability, for among human beings Saying is, before all else, a saying of someone to someone, that is, to the transcendent, unthematizable Other. But where does the reduction lead us? Or rather, to fall back into ontological language, who does the saying? Some kind of self (*soi*), it seems, an irreducible point of reference/response that is prior to the origin (*pré-originaire*) of the subject as conscious of itself, prior to any freedom or nonfreedom it may eventually exercise, though not prior to desire.

But how is this ultimate point of reference a Saying? Saying, Levinas tells us, is essentially handing over meaning to another (*bailler signifiance*)—and this, not simply in the sense of delivering over signs (as if the signs already existed waiting to be delivered) but in the sense of making this delivery possible, as the "condition of all communication [in the regime of the Said]." It is primordial exposure (*exposition*) in its purest form (OB 48). "In Saying, the subject approaches the neighbor by ex-pressing itself, in the literal sense of the term, by being expelled from any locus.... [It] does not give signs, it [itself] becomes a sign" (OB 48-49). Sign of what? It is a "sign given to the Other and already sign of this giving of signs, pure signification" (OB 143). It is "to exhaust oneself in exposing oneself" (OB 143). This expropriation of the pre-originary self is a total passivity—"not the passivity of a 'language which speaks' without a subject (*die Sprache spricht*)" (OB 54), to be sure, but a passivity nonetheless. Passivity, vulnerability, substitution, and all the rest—this is the ultimate Saying, the very heart of what Levinas calls responsibility.

How does this pre-originary self express itself? As someone, experienced as an Ego (*Moi*) but on a level prior to (i.e., beneath and beyond) any awareness of itself as self and expressed only by articulating the total exposure of the self-signifying sign to the Other in saying, "me voici," that is "vois-moi ici," "see me here," "here I am." Here, "the pronoun 'I' [*Moi*] is in the accusative [case], declined before every [other] declension, possessed [as it is] by the other" (OB 142). It is in this prevoluntary submission in complete passivity to the Other that the uniqueness of the self consists. "In the signification [of my signifyingness as direction (*sens*) toward the Other] I am disengaged as unique" (OB 139).

That is as much as time permits. I conclude with a few questions that remain. With regard to Levinas's fundamental objection to psychoanalytic theory, that it "casts a basic suspicion on the most unimpeachable testimony of self-consciousness," one must admit he is right. Freud was the first to tell us that his insight was comparable to that of Copernicus and Darwin in deflating man's sense of his own anthropocentric importance, and revealing to him that he is no longer master in his own house.[4] But we need a better reason to reject it than that it forces us to face unpleasant truths. That psychoanalysis must find another way to talk about ethical responsibility than the one Levinas proposes is clear; but it does not thus behoove us to reject the data on which the theory is based. The question is, How else can we explain these data? In particular, what better way can we find to explain the discrepancy between the two dimensions we have seen of the one Emmanuel Levinas than the psychoanalytic one I am suggesting, which accepts the hypothesis of an irresponsible subject?

Problems arise concerning both the relation of Said to Saying and of Saying to Said. One problem I should mention in passing but cannot explore is the little boy's cry "it's not fair." Obviously, this eruption points to the order of justice, of others, of the third party—in a word, to the social/historical dimension of psychoanalysis. Time constraints make it impossible to explore this issue further, but something should be said about the problem of truth that is at stake here. Levinas tells us that exposure to the Other is not an experience of the Other's truth, since truth implies nontruth and such polarities belong to the order of ontology. But whence comes the negativity of this polarity? For example, under the rubric of "nontruth" I assume he intends to include whatever is meant by the "lie." But if we take this "lie" in the broadest sense as some kind of discrepancy between what is meant/intended and what is said, then the concept of the lie extends a broad net: it includes any form of misstatement, distortion, deception, confabulation, misrepresentation, exaggeration, and so on—any form of misspeaking that goes into the nitty-gritty of everyday life and is the stock and trade of psychoanalysis. Now if the lie, given this grab-bag meaning, is no more than "the price being must pay for its finitude" (Si 71), and totally ingredient to the Said, must the negativity in question here not be inscribed somehow in the Saying of it? But how is such inscription possible if primordial Saying finds its signifyingness simply in passive exposure to the Other, where meaning is to be found only in the face to face?

And now, one last word about the Saying of the Said. Whence comes the Saying when the word (*parole*) eventually does get spoken? The question is, Can Levinas tolerate the possibility of another Other infiltrating the "I" who says, "Here I am," sabotaging its intentions? For we are dealing with an "I" here that in fact is *not* in the accusative case as in the French "me voici" but clearly in the nominative. And even if by an acrobatic flip one were to translate "me voici" as "here is me," it would still be that speaking "I" the linguists speak of (*je de l'énonciation*) as distinct from the spoken "I" (*je de l'énoncé*) who both says it and is *represented* in the said.

In any case, my suspicion is that it was this subject of the unconscious that erupted in Levinas one afternoon thirty years ago and revealed a second dimension in him that I, at least, had not witnessed before. Whether or not the surmise holds is for others to judge. At any rate, the "I" of the unconscious, functioning in the manner of a language and following laws beyond our control, an "I" inscribed in the linguistic heritage into which we are born and through which we breathe, is a phenomenon of our twentieth-century experience that is here to stay. If it is difficult to find a place for it in Levinas's thought at the present time, might it be one of those "nonphilosophical experiences" Robert Bernasconi speaks of that could eventually find philosophical articulation coherent with a potential pluralism in Levinas's thought? I hope so, and I am grateful to him for calling our attention to this possibility.

Notes

1. Aristotle, *Nicomachean Ethics*, in *The Basic Works of Aristotle*, ed. Richard McKeon (New York: Random House, 1941).
2. Richard Kearney, *Dialogues with Contemporary Continental Thinkers. The Phenomenological Heritage* (Manchester: Manchester University Press, 1984), 49.
3. Adriaan Peperzak, "From Intentionality to Responsibility: On Levinas's Philosophy of Language," in *The Question of the Other*, Selected Studies in Phenomenology and Existential Philosophy, vol. 15, ed. A. Dallery and C. Scott (Albany: SUNY Press, 1987), 6-7.
4. Sigmund Freud, *Standard Edition of the Complete Works of Sigmund Freud*, ed. and trans. J. Strachey (London: Hogarth Press, 1969), 16: 284-85.

Part Four: Art

13

The Art in Ethics: Aesthetics, Objectivity, and Alterity in the Philosophy of Emmanuel Levinas

Edith Wyschogrod

Two objections arise repeatedly in connection with Emmanuel Levinas's philosophy of language. First, it is argued in the spirit of Jürgen Habermas and K. O. Apel, for whom ethics is grounded in discursive reason, that for Levinas, ethics is an unmediated relation to the Other and, as such, transcends linguistic and conceptual structure.[1] Ethics is not a matter of moral argument but of the solicitation by the Other who by virtue of sheer otherness resists violence. Levinas's access routes to the Other are nonlinguistic: they include the human face, an idea of the infinite that exceeds any description of it, sensation as a noncognitive relation of sensing and sensed. His position is not merely a restatement about the poverty of language with regard to transcendence, one made familiar through negative theology, because for negative theology even if one cannot say what God is, propositional language is not excluded but restricted to statements of negation. In sum, the first argument against Levinas is that if ethics is beyond language, then ethics remains silent and rationally derived moral norms are meaningless. Language has become a liability, a fall, and ethics an inchoate relation to the Other.

A second standard reproach directed at Levinas is that he disparages the aesthetic by relegating art and poetry to a status inferior to that of philosophy and, a fortiori, to ethics. For example, in his early *Existence and Existents* (conceived between 1940 and 1945), art is interpreted as divesting things of their forms so that things cannot be made present as they are in cognition. Although it may seem paradoxical to sever art from form, Levinas explains that form always arises in a context. In cognition and relations of utility we experience objects in a network of relations, whereas art lifts entities out of the world to create a field not of forms but of pure sensations (EE 52-57).

In "Reality and Its Shadow" (1948), Levinas argues that art substitutes images for being. The image is not a transparent sign pointing toward objects through which objects become intelligible; instead, images are the doubles of objects, resemble them, in the sense that shadows resemble things. This duality of thing and image is born in resemblance. A kind of duplicity or evasion is created in that the image neither yields the object nor replicates it in an ontological sense. As a nonobject, the image lies outside the world, is not in time. Because images cannot move along naturally in the stream of becoming, they immobilize time, freezing it. This atemporality, unlike the eternity of concepts, distorts the flow of becoming. The image is trapped and cannot free itself for the world of action (CP 5-12).

Artists are under the sway of images, possessed by them. Insofar as the literary artist is also a purveyor of images, the same criticism applies mutatis mutandis to fiction and poetry. This interpretation presupposes Heidegger's view that the true poet is not a creator but a passageway for being and André Breton and the surrealists' belief that literature is an automatic or spontaneous production, dream rather than work. In sum, Levinas is charged with a Platonic aesthetic: art is infraethical and infracognitive. If art is "legitimate," it is so only as the handmaiden of ethics and requires augmentation by criticism. On this view, Levinas could be seen as endorsing straightforwardly didactic tales or Socialist Realism as the highest types of art; such is far from being the case, however, as Levinas shows in his sympathetic and nuanced analyses of complex contemporary writers and painters.

I shall argue that the objections I have rehearsed can be countered by a new reading of Levinas's view of the "art" of literature. The two frequently voiced objections I have sketched—first, that ethics is an unmediated relation to the Other and, as such, beyond discursive language, and second, that the language of art is infracognitive and dangerously nonethical—are actually linked. When these objections are taken together, the problems that arise in connection with Levinas's view of religious language can be resolved, at least partially, because important clues for the interpretation of ethicoreligious expression can be found in the uses of literary language. This claim can be established by turning to Levinas's treatment of recent French writers, specifically of Proust, master of images and the inundation of subjectivity by pure sensibility; of Leiris, advocate of total freedom; and of Blanchot, artist of the nocturnal, of the nothing that speaks.

I argue further that it is helpful to think of Levinas's rendering of the aesthetic by relating it to the stratigraphy of Kierkegaard's account of life stages. Kierkegaard criticizes the immediacy of the aesthetic from a higher standpoint while at the same time reintroducing immediacy at the still higher level of the religious. For Levinas, aesthetic experience—both as creation and appreciation of the aesthetic object—is a kind of shamanistic seizure of consciousness by being prior to being's assumption of form. But if being as disclosed in art is formless and ethics (for Levinas bound up with and often indistinguishable from the religious) is also beyond form, then common strategies for grasping this immediacy may be developed. Art and ethics in Levinas's sense can be thought of as fields in which disclosures of formlessness occur: in art, the amorphous power of being; in ethics, the Other who calls me to responsibility. Each—possession in the case of art and revelation in the case of ethics—grips the individual, in the one instance dissolving, in the other singularizing individuality by positing the Other in her uniqueness. In the aesthetic of Proust, Leiris, and Blanchot, Levinas finds linguistic strategies of indirection with which to bring out that which, strictly speaking, does not belong to phenomenality but to experiences of formlessness.

Not only is a Kierkegaardlike articulation of the aesthetic and the ethical a structural inference, but Levinas explicitly refers to Kierkegaard's account of faith to shed light on the status of religious language generally. In his brief comments on Kierkegaard in *Noms propres*, Levinas (unsurprisingly), like Buber, faults Kierkegaard, first for describing Abraham as transcending the ethical and thereby falling into violence and second for interpreting the ethical as expressing the universal and thus bypassing the subjectivity of the individual existent. This second point is of greater interest to Levinas in that his own discourse—the entire topos of responsibility and alterity—is based on a contrary premise, that ethics as consciousness of responsibility for the other individuates, "posits you as a singular individual" (NP 113). This difficulty is far from fatal to a comparison of the relation of the aesthetic to higher planes of meaning in both thinkers. Kierkegaard's ethical stage is roughly comparable to what Levinas calls justice, the juridical plane that allows for the settling of actual disputes in social existence, whereas ethics for Levinas is more properly equated with religion or faith in Kierkegaard. It is in this light that Levinas's comments about Kierkegaard should be understood.

Levinas and Kierkegaard

Kierkegaard's unique contribution to philosophy, Levinas asserts, is his account of belief (*croyance*). I shall fasten on this point because features of this analysis are repeated in Levinas's description of the literary languages forged by Proust, Leiris, and Blanchot. If there is a *language* of belief, it can then be argued that there is something like a concept of religious language in Levinas and that the specific character of this language can be explicated. We are then justified in turning to the works of literary figures who have developed strategies of indirect communication to convey what is, to use Levinas's formulation, otherwise than being and beyond essence. In a crucial passage on belief Levinas writes:

> Belief is not [for Kierkegaard] imperfect knowledge of a truth which would be perfect and triumphant in itself; for him belief is not a small truth, a truth without certainty a debasement of knowledge. There is in Kierkegaard an opposition not between faith and knowledge where the uncertain would be opposed to the certain, but between triumphant truth and persecuted truth. Persecuted truth is not simply a truth approached badly [but] the modality of truth. … Transcendent truth

manifests itself as if it would not dare say its name and thus, always on the point of leaving; it does not come to take its place amidst the phenomena with which it would be confused as if it did not come from beyond. ... *[One] can ask oneself whether the incognito would not be the very mode of revelation, if truth which was spoken would not also have to appear as that about which one said nothing.* (NP 114; my translation, emphasis added).

This passage describes the fault lines of transcendence as they are inscribed in language. Transcendence is the subject of belief rather than of knowledge. But Levinas does not appeal to one of two generally accepted positions: either that belief is more certain than knowledge because based on revelation or, by contrast, that belief is a weaker form of knowledge because it is not founded on evidence. Taking issue with both of the received views, Levinas segregates religious from propositional truth, arguing instead that belief has nothing whatever to do with certainty. Religious truth is a function of its mode of self-manifestation, true only if it is not puffed up in presenting itself, "persecuted" rather than "triumphant." Thus religious truths are not warranted beliefs, those resting on evidence showing them to be well founded. Instead the truth of belief lies in its refusal to put itself forward, "to say [its] name." Religious truth appears incognito, shows itself as "that about which one would say nothing."

On Levinas's reading, Kierkegaard's "glimpse of truth" overturns Heidegger's view of truth as unconcealment and points the way toward a new persecuted language that hides and shelters transcendence. This language is the very language developed through the literary artistry of Proust, Leiris, and Blanchot.

Proust: The Diffractions of Self

Levinas reads Proust as a "master of the differential calculus of souls, psychologist of the infinitesimal" (NP 149). But unlike many standard interpreters who hold that in Proust the relation of the soul to itself is that of primary emotion to emotion reflected upon, he contends that Proustian reflection is itself infected with emotion. Levinas writes: "Proustian reflection governed by a split between the self and its state, by a species of refraction, actually puts its stamp on inner life. Everything happens as if another myself were constantly doubling the self, in an unequalizable friendship, but also in a chilly strangeness that life strives to overcome. The mystery in Proust is the mystery of the other" (NP 152; my translation).

Because consciousness works through scission or doubling in Proust, it would seem that images could be interpreted as the relation of reality to shadow mentioned earlier in which the shadow replicates objects but lacks independent ontological status. Despite Levinas's stress on the process of doubling, such an account would be misleading. In Proust the doubled self is a stranger to itself because its two components asymmetrical, cannot be made equal. This inequality is not the result of different intentions of consciousness (to use Husserlian language), the difference between reflection and affect, between reflection and a stratum reflected upon. Instead the emotion of the stratum reflected upon infiltrates reflection: in Freudian terms, reflection belongs to the level of the cathexes. What accounts for this asymmetry—and this is the novelty of Levinas's interpretation—is the Other who can never be reached, the Other that penetrates the heart of the self. Thus Levinas suggests, "Places, things move him by way of the other, ... Albertine, ... his grandmother, ... his past self. To know what Albertine is doing, ... seeing, ... [or] who sees [her] has no interest in itself as a species of knowledge but is infinitely exciting because of the fundamental strangeness in Albertine, this strangeness that mockingly resists knowledge" (NP 153; my translation).

For Levinas, Proust is the writer who shows the inescapability of the Other within solitude, an intrusion of the Other distinguishable from the understanding of the Other in collective solidarity. Like Buber, Levinas argues that the Other who is part of a collectivity cannot be experienced in her alterity. Thus Levinas: "the pathos of socialism breaks against the eternal Bastille where everyone ... finds himself when the party is over, the torches extinguished, and the crowd gone off" (NP 154; my translation). "Genuine" alterity is an absence that rends the psyche, worms its way into the self, and prevents the ego from losing track of the Other who, in her absence, fissures the self in its interiority.

Proust's artistry, often seen as the power to depict sensation, would seem to lend weight to Levinas's theory of the image as subverting form and giving rise to an inundation by sensibility, and *À la recherche du temps perdu* a premier example of that theory. Instead Proust is not the depicter of infraontological shadows but—to coin what now seems less and less an oxymoron—an artist of alterity.

If Proustian fiction evokes alterity, is it possible to think of Proust as a didactic writer, an artist of fabular discourse? But there can be no artistry of fables, because they articulate moral principles and these do not lend themselves to successful artistic rendering. Instead Proust's fiction is a kind of protoethics, a revelation within language of the persecution of self by another. To be sure, in Proust's writing the persecution of alterity is bound up with actual persecution: Albertine as absence and mystery shades off into the Albertine who actually tortures Marcel. However, the point is that Albertine as Other eludes plenary presence, cannot become a datum of consciousness. Proust is the "phenomenologist" of what cannot be recovered, of the Other's concealment, not because of the Other's artifices of camouflage—although there is artifice aplenty in Albertine, Odette, Monsieur Charlus, and the rest—but because to be other is to remain hidden *en principe*.

Biffures: Levinas and Leiris

Levinas interprets the first volume of Leiris's autobiography, *Biffures*, as depicting alterity by unmasking the pretensions of cognition and thereby suggesting a strategy of indirection for religious language, although Levinas does not specifically articulate this link. For Leiris, thought has two intrinsic characteristics that deflect it from achieving clarity and certainty, ideals that are in any case deceptive.

The first, bifurcation (*bifurs*), is the deflection of a line of thought from what appears to be its natural path so that it heads in a new and unexpected direction (NP 146). The second, erasure (*biffures*), is the alteration or rubbing out of the univocal meaning of an idea at the point of its inception. Leiris, Levinas suggests, rejects free association as the primary law of thought and instead attributes the linkage of ideas to erasure. Ideas connected in this way do not dislodge previous ideas: "Thought at the moment of erasure still influences through its erased meaning; its different meanings still participate with one another" (NP 146).

Leiris's notion of erasure creates a space in which ideas nest inside one another rather than a streaming of thought articulated as temporal passage. It is, of course, paradoxical that autobiographical writing should be spatialized, in that it is a depiction of a life as experienced through time. Levinas compares Leiris's spatial conception of ideas to painter Charles Lapicque's "space of simultaneity," a space that "does not delineate volume" and in which lines do not form the framework for objects but suggest multiple hookups.

It is because thought is conceived as a mode of spatialization that Levinas thinks Leiris's art falls short as a discourse of otherness. Only sound as encapsulated in the heard word of another attests the presence of the Other (NP 148). Leiris, he concedes, has brought to light the process that underlies thought's inception, bifurcation, and erasure, but Leiris's insights still presuppose "the primacy of thought in relation to language expressed by the classic notion of what is well conceived" (NP 149).

It is surprising that Levinas's analysis does not take account of the many passages in which Leiris stresses violence and wounding, although these are *echt* Levinasian themes. For example, in *Manhood* Leiris says of the bullfight (*la corrida*), "It is not the spectacle that is essential but the sacrifice,"[2] and again, "Looking back to my earliest childhood, I find memories of *wounded women*."[3] The matter at issue is not this omission but Levinas's retreat from his original insights, his refusal to press the connection between Leiris's account of bifurcation and erasure and the problematic of alterity, in part at least because of Levinas's own inner struggle against image making.

Despite Levinas's downplaying of erasure in Leiris, it is possible to relate the use of erasure to the pregnant concept of the trace, a key Levinasian theme. Not a sign, because signs are transparent with respect to their objects, the trace is the marker of the immemorial past of a transcendence that has passed by. Traces are clues, tracks, or trails that cannot be integrated into the order of the world wherever transcendence inscribes and erases itself, preeminently in the human face. The effort to coerce transcendence into appearing assures its loss; it can only be glimpsed in and through another as Other.

Levinas's use of the trace has been linked to Heidegger's account in *Holzwege* of old forest trails which the experienced woodsman knows how to read but which mean nothing to others. Yet missing in Heidegger's description and found in Leiris's view of *biffures* is the idea of the accretion of meaning, the nesting of one idea in another. This cumulative character is intrinsic to Levinas's trace in that transcendence, expunged from the order of the world, "nests" in faces, sensation, the time between heartbeats, and other Levinasian "tropes" for transcendence. Like the idea of the infinite, there is more in them than can be contained by cognition. (One could argue that Derrida's account of the trace as well as his tactic of placing terms under erasure [*sous rature*] could also be linked to Leiris's *Biffures*.)

But the very spatialization of Leiris's art that makes possible its connection with the trace renders it mute. It is an art of silence. In this context Levinas contrasts and extols criticism, the word, at the expense of the image and thus backs away from the art of Leiris: "The use of the word wrenches experience out of its aesthetic self-sufficiency.... It is in this sense ... that criticism, which is the word of a living being speaking to a living being, brings the image in which art revels back to the fully real being. The language of criticism takes us out of our dreams in which artistic language plays an integral part" (NP 148). For Levinas, criticism is secondarily commentary on the formal aesthetic properties of a work, and primarily the placing of literary discourse within a moral framework.

In sum, although Levinas acknowledges Leiris's breakthrough in seizing the moment of thought as bifurcation and erasure, his suspicion of image making prevents his connecting the former with the trace. Despite Levinas's ambivalence toward Leiris's literary strategies, these find their way into his antiphenomenology of the trace.

Blanchot on Levinas: Tracing the Differences

The influence of Blanchot on Levinas is more complex than that of either Proust or Leiris, in part because it is reciprocal. It may be useful to focus first on Blanchot's *Writing of the Disaster*, a late work (1980) that takes into account not only the large Levinasian corpus available by that time but also Levinas's 1975 work about Blanchot.[4] In *Writing of the Disaster* Levinas may be exhibited through the focus of Blanchot's poetics of negation.

In this work, Blanchot tries to think negation both as actual apocalypse seen through the cataclysmic events of the twentieth century and as the destruction of traditional metaphysical interpretations of being, time, and history or, more primordially, as their aboriginal *Ur*-absence. Defining disaster, Blanchot writes, "I call disaster that which does not have the ultimate for a limit: it bears the ultimate away in the disaster" (WoD 28). Because the disaster is a sweeping away of all limit, there is neither self nor event to describe so that "the disaster does not put me into question but annuls the question, makes it disappear—as if along with the question I too disappeared in the disaster which never appears" (WoD 28). Lying outside the chain of facts and events, the disaster cannot be said to happen in any straightforward sense. Instead it is always behind itself, "always takes place after having taken place," so that it lies outside experience (WoD 28). It should be noted that Blanchot's earlier fiction articulates this post hoc constitution of events which never existed. The question of how to speak about the disaster should not be confused with the speech about an object that is thought to be indescribable because contradictory attributes are ascribed to it. The disaster is an event, yet as pure negation it falls outside the realm of ontology. As an absence that is extraontological it is linked to Levinas's problematic: can there be speech about another who is never present?

Blanchot comments on the problem of ineffability—his own as well as that of Levinas—in his remarks on Levinas. Turning to the question of the relation of the Other and the giving of gifts, he argues that despite their unbreachable differences, the works of Levinas, Georges Bataille, and Heidegger are related in and through the idea of alterity. For Levinas, he claims, alterity means, "the transcendence of another person, the infinite relation of the one person to another [that] obligates beyond any obligation" (WoD 109). This relation opens up the idea of the gift, which for Levinas means "detachment, a disinterestedness which is *suffered*, patient responsibility [for the other] that endures all the way to 'substitution,' 'one for the other'" (WoD 109). By contrast, Blanchot contends, for Bataille the gift is an indication of excessive expenditure and plays a transgressive social role. More important, for Heidegger, the gift is implied by the expression "es gibt," a crucial locution in his account of *Ereignis* (appropriation). The "es gibt" points not to a subject who gives but to the object bestowed: the gift of language (WoD 110).

Heidegger's interpretation of the gift as the bestowing of language reflects a dangerous sanctification of language and, according to Blanchot, one directly opposed by Levinas for whom language is justified by the speaker who provides the warranty for it. In contrast to the cultic idea of language as *in itself* holy, Levinas, Blanchot says, thinks of language as itself always already skeptical, as a self-questioning that opens the possibility of its own unmaking.

Against the backdrop of language as undoing itself, Blanchot describes writing as a "giving withholding," giving because language tries to bring otherness into speech, and withholding because speech tries to justify itself. If "giving withholding" is the work of writing, what is to be written and how is it to be written? If "the object" of writing is the disaster, Blanchot suggests in a terse formulation, the task of the writer is to show "*in*discretion with respect to the *in*effable" (WoD 114). The key words of this phrase are governed by the prefix "in," the same prefix that introduces the word infinity, an "in" shot through with Levinasian resonances: infinity is not only the negation of the finite but also the excess or beyond of the finite. This appears to be its meaning in Blanchot's declaration: "the ineffable, the unspeakable, would be circumscribed by Speaking raised to infinity" (WoD 114). Such an elevation of speaking signifies that what is spoken is not some content that eludes language but unsayability itself, "what escapes all that can be said" (WoD 114).

But why is this saying characterized as indiscreet? Blanchot glosses "indiscretion" by appealing to Levinasian "Saying": the unspoken covenant between speaker and hearer promising that his or her language will be marked by alterity. Unsayability, Blanchot suggests, "escapes," becomes indiscreet, only "under the auspices of Saying" (WoD 114). But the escape of unsayability, that is, the bursting into language of what cannot be said, is also restrained by Saying, by the Other that resists linguistic captivity. Thus, for Blanchot, speech paradoxically breaks forth, is unreserved, and is held back, reserved, by the authority of Saying. From these remarks about writing as a relation to Levinasian Saying, it is possible to assert that for the later Blanchot, writing is an ethics in Levinas's sense.

In Blanchot's comments on unsayability what comes to the fore is not principally Levinas's contrast between Saying, the warranty for speech, and the said, what actually falls into language, but the *movement* from ineffability to speech. In his fictional works (if for him the distinction between fiction and criticism can be maintained), Blanchot fixes on the *escape route* of unsayability, on how it seeps into language without losing its unsayability in a world where distinctions such as inside and outside are eroded. Blanchot's own art explicates this loss of foothold as characters glide from one level to another—death and life, sickness and health—in a world in which levels mingle and are intercalated.

Levinas on Blanchot: Before Language

What makes Blanchot perhaps the writer par excellence for Levinas is that in Blanchot's works meaning is before rather than after language, a "situation" that forces language to a breaking point. The assertion that meaning is anterior to language implies that meaning does not belong to the same topos as language, not because meaning inheres in a world that is prior to language and then represented by it but because meaning is (somehow) inimical to language. Thus in his 1966 essay on Blanchot, "The Servant and her Master," Levinas writes: "Does the meaningful depend on a certain order of propositions, constructed according to a certain grammar so as to constitute a logical argument? Or does meaning cause language to explode and then signify amidst these fragments (grammar remaining intact in Blanchot's case!)—but already in spirit and in truth in advance of any subsequent interpretation?" (LR 153).

If meaning is prior to language, there is no coming to grips with meaning, no arguments that can be brought to bear for or against it. Thus Blanchot reverses a dictum of literary modernism that language dissolves prior meanings by showing that meaning precedes language, paralyzes language even before it speaks. The a-linguisticality of meaning precludes its communication by way of language. "Arrange for me to be able to speak with you," a Blanchot character says in *Waiting Forgetting*, as Levinas notices (LR 152). This citation supports my earlier contention that Blanchot is obsessed with the impassability, the blocking of meaning that is as close by as the Other yet always out of reach.

To depict this blocking of meaning Blanchot is compelled to rely on the bleakness of a speech locked into itself from which the Other is absent and in which, as Levinas says, "nothing extra-ordinary [exterior to itself] occurs." Because language cannot go outside itself, it can only repeat itself, "a cancerous cell producing nothing other than repetition and tautology" (LR 152). Not only do specific events recur, but the fact of repetition is made thematic. The reflexivity that I earlier alleged to characterize unspeakability also can be attributed to repetition. Levinas cites a crucial passage: "They were always conversing about the instant when they would no longer be there, and while aware that they would always be there conversing about such an instant, they thought there was nothing more worthy of their eternity than to spend it evoking its end" (LR153).[5]

Anything can become a marker of repetition—persons, rooms, their furnishings—in that all are exiled from any organizing nexus. What is depicted through repetition is "the panting of nothingness, and so to speak, its way of laboring, struggling and 'coming to pass' and departing from its identity as void" (LR 154).

Although this comment refers to *Waiting Forgetting*, it is likely that Levinas also has in mind the well-known passage from Blanchot's *The Space of Literature* in which Blanchot declares that writing exhibits language as negation: "In the [language of writing] what denies affirms. For this language speaks as absence. The language of negation therefore does not cease with silence but continues because silence speaks. But if language is the speech of silence, it cannot be heard. The poet then is 'he who hears a language that makes nothing heard'"(SL 51).

Blanchot's silences, Levinas claims, are not stillness but "a rustling." For Blanchot, ordinary language is punctuated by silences because it is purposeful: it communicates meaning and stops when this purpose is fulfilled. But literary language is always already silence and therefore it cannot cease. Divested of its referential function, this language is, Blanchot says, "an essentially errant word, for it is always cast out of itself" (SL 51), a word that designates an "infinitely distended outside which takes the place of the spoken word's intimacy" (SL 51). Levinas notes that in Blanchot language speaks from the other side of walls; perhaps—for Blanchot it is always perhaps—language merely replicates the enclosed linguistic space of the listener, not an outside but the same, over and over again. "It resembles the echo," Blanchot writes, "when the echo does not simply say out loud what first is indistinctly murmured, but merges with the whispering immensity and is silence become reverberating space, all words' exterior" (SL 51-52). One suffocates inside language for which there is no discernible outside just as Blanchot's characters stifle inside the bleak rooms in which they are locked.

It is not hard to equate this locked-in space with the enclosure of Levinas's separated self, the individual within the same, the world of cognition, work, play, and habitation. To be sure, for Levinas, the same is not the joyless terrain of Blanchot's walled-in spaces, but it is still the locus of the absence of meaning. And yet Blanchot's topos of repetition is magnetized by alterity just as the structural articulation of what Levinas calls the same is fissured by its obsession with the Other. Joseph Libertson, in his study of Bataille, Blanchot, and Levinas, sums up this situation when he writes: "Totalization is possible only because identity, relation, comprehension and action are moments of an insatiability in being: the exigency of the Other.... The time of the Same... is its eternal return and its metamorphosis: a time in which the Same is never entirely the Same, the 'world' is never entirely the 'world', because Time is the element of the Other's approach."[6]

Blanchot's language cannot speak alterity, Levinas maintains, cannot grasp it in a concept, simply because alterity resists conceptual grasp. But the errant word "gives sign," a giving that is a nonpurposive relation with another. Such signs are not referential, not transparent with respect to a content. Instead what is bestowed on the Other is "'the voice that has been imparted and entrusted to you and not what it says.'" For Blanchot, Levinas writes, "poetry transforms words into unfettered signs," signs let loose that can seep into the enclosed world of immanence, "go from the Same to the other (*Autre*) from Self to Other (*Autrui*),... give sign to undo the structure of language."[7]

Still, the poetic word can misfire in its errancy. Blanchot, Levinas contends, catches the word just "before" its fall into the process of totalization and after its "origination" in exteriority. As such, the poetic word, like the idea of the infinite, has no objective content that can fulfill it but instead "preserves the movement located between seeing and saying, that language of pure transcendence without correlative, ... noesis without noema."[8]

I argued earlier that in Levinas the strategies of aesthetic language seemingly abandoned at a higher level find their place in this author's conception of ethics and religious language. Nowhere are aesthetics and ethics more interwoven than in Levinas's comments on Blanchot, comments that exhibit totality as the plane of the always already broken and incomplete infiltration by alterity.

Conclusion: Levinas, Kierkegaard, and the Poetry of the Ethical

Despite Levinas's critique of art and literature, I have argued that Proust, Leiris, and Blanchot are for Levinas artists of alterity in different ways and in varying degrees. Each has, in his unique fashion, found out how to release into language the immediacy of the experience of the Other as Other. (In fact, for Levinas their greatness lies in just this discovery.) I have also maintained that the relation of art and literature to ethics in Levinas's sense roughly replicates Kierkegaard's strategy of importing the immediacy of the aesthetic into the religious despite Kierkegaard's critique of the aesthetic personality. The analogy must be seen against the backdrop of Levinas's linking transcendent meaning with ethics.

Yet Levinas explicitly rejects the idea that the ethical in the Kierkegaardian sense could be countermanded by God's word spoken to the faithful one. Ethics precludes violence, so that a conflict between ethics in the transcendent and in the sense of the moral law would not occur. This position is made explicit by Blanchot in a text that could be mistaken for the work of Levinas. Comparing Kafka with Kierkegaard and siding with Kafka, Blanchot writes: "Kierkegaard can renounce Regine; he can renounce the ethical level. Access to the religious level is not thereby compromised; rather it is made possible. But Kafka, if he abandons the earthly happiness of a normal life, also abandons the steadiness of a just life. He makes himself an outlaw, deprives himself of the ground ... he needs in order to be" (SL 61).

Yet, Blanchot continues, "for Kafka everything is more unclear because he seeks to fuse the work's demand [writing] with the demand which could pertain to his salvation" (SL 62). On this reading, poetry is not didactic in the narrow sense but a discourse touched by transcendence; it cannot, as such, remain a mere means deployed in the interest of salvation: such poetry becomes an ethics.

Notes

1. For some suggestive remarks about nonconceptual ethics see Jean Greisch, "The Face and Reading," trans. Simon Critchley, in RL 72-73.
2. Michel Leiris, *Manhood*, trans. Richard Howard (San Francisco: North Point Press, 1984), 42.
3. Ibid., 43.
4. Emmanuel Levinas, *Sur Maurice Blanchot* (Montpellier: Fata Morgana, 1975).
5. Levinas cites from *L'attente l'oubli* (Paris: Gallimard, 1962), 35.
6. Joseph Libertson, *Proximity, Levinas, Blanchot, Bataille, and Communication* (The Hague: Martinus Nijhoff, 1982), 343.
7. Levinas quoted in ibid., 156.
8. Levinas quoted in ibid., 157.

Part Five: Religion

14

Levinas's Teleological Suspension of the Religious

Merold Westphal

> Everyone will readily agree that it is of the highest importance to know whether we are not duped by morality.
> —*Totality and Infinity*

> Philosophy, for me, derives from religion. It is called into being by a religion adrift, and probably religion is always adrift.
> —*Nine Talmudic Readings*

Unlike the positivists, postmodernists have not taken their critique of metaphysics to mean the end of ethics. They act as if philosophy continues to play a morally significant critical role in a postmodern world and even say things like, "Nothing seems to me less outdated than the classical emancipatory ideal."[1] They have not been very eager, however, to give an account of how this is possible, and what little they have had to say has not seemed entirely satisfactory. For this reason, the first passage cited here in epigraph seems to many more urgent than when Levinas used it in 1961 to open *Totality and Infinity*.

No doubt the most conspicuous difference between Levinas and such thinkers as Derrida, Foucault, and Lyotard is that Levinas accompanies his powerful critique of ontology as the sustained attempt to reduce the other to the same with an at least equally developed account of how ethics is possible after the collapse of the Enlightenment project. At first he sounds very much like his secular contemporaries (whose critique of metaphysics, incidentally, comes after his). But then he goes decisively beyond anything they have offered as an account of how ethics is possible.

The other passage cited in epigraph points to a second difference between Levinas and Derrida et al. They are all more or less united in their irreverence toward the Greek *logos*; but in place of the secular irreverence (à la Aristophanes) that has been the hallmark of French poststructuralism, Levinas offers a prophetic irreverence (à la Amos) rooted in "a tradition at least as ancient" as the Greece to which Heidegger appeals (CP 53), going back to Parmenides (TO 42-43, 85; see also TaI 269). Or, as Derrida puts it, Levinas offers us a thought "for which the entirety of the Greek logos has already erupted, and is now a quiet topsoil deposited not over bedrock, but around a more ancient volcano" (WaD 82). Levinas's assault on Athens comes from the direction of Jerusalem, or, to be more precise, from the direction of Sinai.

"Philosophy," he tells us, "derives from religion." But anyone turning to Levinas with the expectation of finding a theological foundation for ethics to replace the philosophical foundations whose cracks have been found to be irreparable will be immediately and permanently disappointed. There is no direct appeal to Sinai, and Levinas is no Jewish version of Karl Barth. At the same time he tells us that philosophy derives from religion, Levinas forswears such a direct appeal. For how could theology be the foundation of ethics if "religion is always adrift"?

So what, then, is the relation between religion and "Ethics as First Philosophy"(see LR 76-87)? When speaking about ethics Levinas employs a vocabulary so deeply religious as to awaken even the sleepiest reader to the fact that something unusual is going on. But at the same time he seems to be as allergic (in his "Greek" writings) to describing God as a distinct reality as traditional ontology is allergic, in his view, to radical alterity in any form. At times it almost seems as if he wants to reduce religion to ethics.

Some readers of Levinas would welcome such a gesture, while others would think it a great loss. But in either case it is important to be as clear as possible about the role God plays in Levinas's thought. How are we to interpret such statements as these? "It is only man who could be absolutely foreign to me" (TaI 73); "God commands only through the men for whom one must act" (CP 59); "'Going towards God' is meaningless unless seen in terms of my primary going towards the other person" (FFL 23); "the invisible but personal God is not approached outside of all human presenc.... There can be no 'knowledge' of God separated from relationship with men.... It is our relations with men ... that give to theological concepts the sole signification they admit of.... Without the signification they draw from ethics theological concepts remain empty and formal frameworks" (TaI 78-79).

In his Talmudic writings Levinas contextualizes claims of this sort with such qualifiers as "since Maimonides" and "at least for the Talmud" (NTR 14-15). Are we dealing here with a postbiblical Jewish reduction of religion to ethics, one that would rescue ethics from bankruptcy in a postmodern world by returning to Feuerbach and transferring all assets of the divine bank account to the human account? Or is this rather a Jewish antecedent to the Christian warning "Those who say, 'I love God,' and hate their brothers or sisters are liars; for those who do not love a brother or sister whom they have seen, cannot love God whom they have not seen. The commandment we have from him is this: those who love God must love their brothers and sisters also" (I John 4:20-21)?

I want to suggest that the primary relation between philosophy, conceived by Levinas as the metaphysics of transcendence or the ethical relation, and religion is

Levinas's Teleological Suspension of the Religious / 153

best expressed in Kierkegaardian language. The ethical is the teleological suspension of the religious. One advantage of this formula is that by appearing to be exactly the opposite movement to the one Kierkegaard presents, it invites comparison with the nineteenth century's most powerful critic of the philosophical reduction of the other to the same, a thinker whose relation to Hegel strongly resembles that of Levinas to Husserl and Heidegger.

A teleological suspension is not a reduction. It does not say that X is nothing but Y. It is rather an *Aufhebung*. It says that X can only be properly understood in relation to Y, that X is not a substance in Spinoza's sense, something that "is in itself and is conceived through itself" (*Ethics* I, Def. 3). Its being, and thus its comprehension (objective genitive) is relational. Thus a teleological suspension does not eliminate; it relativizes. The object of a teleological suspension is negated in its claim to autonomy, to self-sufficiency and completeness; but it is affirmed in relation to that which is higher, that which draws it into a larger whole of which it is not the first principle. The highest card in its suit will take many tricks, but it can always be trumped.[2]

There is a triadic structure in *Totality and Infinity* that moves from enjoyment to dwelling to transcendence. Like the movement in Aristotle from the vegetative soul to the animal soul to the rational soul, this movement can be interpreted along the lines of Kierkegaard's movement from the aesthetic to the ethical to the religious, that is, as a sequence of teleological suspensions. In all three triads, Aristotle's, Kierkegaard's, and Levinas's, the second transition is the crucial one, the one that brings us to what each author views as the heart of what it means to be human. For Levinas the rationality and intelligibility that accompany enjoyment and dwelling (whose roots are in need) are to be teleologically suspended in the rationality and intelligibility of transcendence (whose roots are in desire). In his claim "The Other is the first intelligible" (Si 175-89; see also TaI 201-19), Levinas teleologically suspends a whole tradition that culminates, for him, in Husserl's account of intentionality and Heidegger's of disclosure, a tradition dominated by the metaphor of vision. He insists that his irreverence toward the *logos* of their phenomen*ologies* is not a flight into mysticism or a lapse into irrationalism but the ascent to a higher rationality.

Against the Enlightenment's claim that knowledge is corrupted by interest and can only truly be knowledge if it is objective in the sense of being disinterested, Levinas argues (1) that all knowledge is interested, (2) that desire (in his technical sense of the term as desire for the Infinite, for the Other) is a higher form of interest than is need, since "this desire for the non-desirable ... is the subjectivity and uniqueness of a subject" (OB 123), and (3) that the forms of knowledge rooted in need (and analyzed in terms of intentionality) are therefore not fully rational but need to be teleologically suspended in the genuinely rational knowledge rooted in desire, the knowledge that accompanies the ethical relation. The "object" of this "knowledge" is "the stranger in the neighbor" (OB 123).

This defense of desire has an immediate and very interesting correlate. If I want "to see things in themselves," I must transcend both "enjoyment and possession."

But this does not mean the suspension of interest in favor of a neutral (and neuter), impersonal objectivity. To know things as they truly are, "I must know how *to give* what I possess.... But for this I must encounter the indiscreet face of the Other that calls me into question. The Other—the absolutely other—paralyzes possession, which he contests by his epiphany in the face. He can contest my possession only because he approaches me not from the outside but from above"(TaI 171). It is only in the context of welcoming precisely this Other and opening myself to the teaching she addresses to me that I am able to fulfill philosophy's aspiration for the *Sache selbst* (ibid.). The ethical relation is the key to the meaning of the world. It is the philosopher's stone that changes opinion into Knowledge and understanding into Reason. Of course, these traditional ways of speaking will be misleading unless we notice that when the Other becomes the philosopher's stone, the highest goal of thought ceases to be *episteme* or *Wissenschaft* as traditionally conceived.

This account of knowing means that contemplative rationality, which belongs to the order of enjoyment, and instrumental rationality, which belongs to the order of possession, represent Reason adrift unless and until they are teleologically suspended in the welcoming, teachable, infinitely responsible rationality that belongs to the order of transcendence.

A similar movement, I believe, relates the religious to the ethical in Levinas's thought. Religion is no exception to the claim that we are never disinterested. It follows that the religious life is in the service either of the egoism of need or of the decentering transcendence of desire. For this reason both religious orthodoxy and religious orthopraxy must submit to interrogation by the ethical, which stands above them as it stands above enjoyment and dwelling (including its extension in labor and possession), refusing to accept their rationality and their intelligibility at face value and asking insistently, Yes, but is it good for the widow, the orphan, and the stranger? Just as Levinas has no respect for "that Reason which is capable of considering as ordered a world in which the poor man is sold for a pair of sandals" (LR 238; see also Amos 2:6), so he opposes any religion capable of considering such a world sacred.

Levinas is more than nervous about any theology understood as "an indication or a monstration of the signified in the signifier, according to the *facile* itinerary in which pious thought *too quickly* deduces theological realities" (CP 124, emphasis added). Part of the reason why he seeks to replace, or perhaps supplement, semiotics with talk about the trace is to make the move to theological realities at once less facile and less quick. "The trace in which a face is ordered is not reducible to a sign for the simple reason that a sign and its relationship with the signified are already thematized. But an approach is not the thematization of any relationship; it is this very relationship" (CP 124). Structuralism and poststructuralism think all but exclusively in terms of the relation of signifier and signified and for this reason can neither diagnose nor prescribe adequately in the present crisis.

If the face is not to be construed as a sign, then "the crisis of meaning, which is evident in the dissemination of verbal signs that the signified no longer dominates,... is opposed by the meaning that is prior to the 'sayings,' which spurns words and is unimpeachable in the nudity of its visage, which is felt in the proletarian destitution of another and in the offense he suffers" (LR 246). In other words, the decentering of the subject that occurs in structuralist and poststructuralist semiotics is teleologically suspended in the decentering of the subject that occurs in the ethical relation.

In the Talmud this meaning is expressed in the claim that some prayers "cannot penetrate to heaven, because all the heavenly gates are closed except those through which the tears of the sufferers may pass" (LR 246). For Levinas it becomes the claim that the semantic crisis of our time, including its religious version (the crisis in theology), is, to use Hegelian language, partly *Schein* and partly *Erscheinung*, whose *Wesen* in either case is a crisis in welcoming the Other. Is it possible that Levinas's closest kin are the liberation theologians of Latin America and South Africa rather than either the Jewish or secular intellectuals of Paris?

There is no mystery about how Levinas intends to resist "the *facile* itinerary in which pious thought *too quickly* deduces theological realities." Since it is the directness of the movement from signifier, whether it be the world or the data of biblical revelation and religious tradition, to deity as the signified that renders that movement both too easy and too fast, Levinas will insist on making it indirect. He will interpose the human Other into the middle of any situation in which I purport to find God, forbidding the sign to be a direct link, however hermeneutically hesitant, between myself and the absolute. "I approach the infinite insofar as I forget myself for my neighbor who looks at me.... [The infinite] solicits across a face, the term of my generosity and my sacrifice. A you is inserted between the I and the absolute He" (CP 72-73).[3]

In a polemical state of mind, he puts the point this way: "The direct encounter with God, *this* is a Christian concept. As Jews, we are always a threesome: I and you and the Third who is in our midst. And only as a Third does He reveal Himself" (LR 247).

Levinas appears to compromise this "trinitarian" moment in his thought when he tells us elsewhere that "the absolute is a person," because only that which supports justice could be absolute and such an absolute would have "the absolute status of the interlocutor." He immediately insists, "This is not at all a theological thesis; yet God could not be God without first having been this interlocutor" (CP 33). The argument would go like this:

1. Levinas makes it clear that this interlocutor is the human Other.
2. But he also identifies this interlocutor with God.
3. Therefore, he collapses the difference between the divine and the human and thereby reduces religion to ethics. The apparent threesome is an actual twosome.

But this would be a wooden and uncharitable reading. In other texts Levinas makes it clear that he intends no simple identification of the human and the divine. "The Other is *the very locus* of metaphysical truth, and is indispensable for my relation with God. He does not play the role of mediator. The other is not the incarnation of God, but precisely by his face, in which he is disincarnate, is the manifestation of *the height in which God is revealed*" (TaI 78-79, emphasis added).

The point is that the ethical relation is the scene, the clearing, the only horizon within which the true God is truly revealed.[4] "It is in this ethical perspective that God must be thought, and not in the ontological perspective of our being-there ... it is only in the infinite relation with the other that God passes (*se passe*), that traces of God are to be found" (FFL 20, 31). We might put it this way: the only horizon in which I can be truly open to the true God is the horizon in which all my horizons are relativized by the ethical claim of the Other.

This is not to say that humans do not think they find God elsewhere. Nor is it to say that concepts of deity originating elsewhere are vague, formal, and empty. Levinas himself seems to suggest the latter when he says, "It is our relations with men ... that give to theological concepts the sole signification they admit of.... Without the signification they draw from ethics theological concepts remain empty and formal frameworks" (TaI 78-79). But it is clear from the larger context of his writings that this emptiness is not final, but a standing invitation to evil. We are reminded of the situation Jesus describes of an unclean spirit, having left a person but having found no new home. "Then it says, 'I will return to my house from which I came.' When it comes, it finds it empty, swept, and put in order. Then it goes and brings along seven other spirits more evil than itself, and they enter and live there; and the last state of that person is worse than the first" (Matthew 12:44-45).

Religion that is not bound to the scene of the ethical relation consists of "empty and formal frameworks" in just this sense. However rich it may be in images, narratives, concepts, theories, practices, and institutions, it is utterly devoid of anything that would prevent it from being the home, the shelter, the base, the legitimizer of the various evils that deface the Other. Thus when Levinas speaks of "the very name 'God' [as] ... subject to every abuse" (NTR 14), when he suggests that the "degeneration" of religion is more dangerous than its disappearance (NTR 152, 159), when he joins Plato in the struggle against "tyrannical religion" (CP 23), when he warns of the danger of the move from the Other to divinity (LR 246), and when he distinguishes the holy from the sacred (NTR 140-46), in short, when he speaks of religion being always adrift (NTR 182), he is echoing Freud, who writes, "It is doubtful whether men were in general happier at a time when religious doctrines held unrestricted sway; more moral they certainly were not."[5]

The teleological suspension of the religious in the ethical provides, in the perceptive words of Derrida, "the premises for a non-Marxist reading of philosophy [including philosophical theology] as ideology" (WaD 97).[6] Religious representation easily becomes the "alibi" for historical oppression of every sort (WaD 83, 92). If Levinas is willing at times to risk sounding as if he wants to reduce religion to ethics, it is because he knows how easily religion drifts into defacement.

Levinas offers something of a catalog of dangerous, degenerate religion. It suggests some strange bedfellows. First, he expresses a strong mistrust "of everything in the texts studied that could pass for a piece of information about God's life ... these apparent news items about the beyond ... a pretentious familiarity with the 'psychology' of God and with his 'behavior'" (NTR 14, 32). This project of knowing the inner secrets of God without any linkage to our infinite responsibility in the face of the human Other he calls theosophy, alluding no doubt to certain forms of both Jewish and Christian mystical metaphysics.

Secondly, it is not easy to distinguish theosophy from more "sober" forms of philosophical theology. Levinas treats discussions of God as the Supreme Being or the creator or cause of nature as if they were theosophy (NTR 14; FFL 24, 32). He is equally hard on discourses that thematize the divine in terms of attributes (TaI 78; FFL 31), as if the content of theology did not come from the "dimension of height" that constitutes the ethical relation (LR 70) but belonged to the realm of that which is objectifiable and representable in terms of consciousness as intentionality (LR 77, 228). The genius of Kant's Copernican revolution consists in the fact "that immortality and theology could not determine the categorical imperative"; rather, the movement of rational thought goes in just the opposite direction (OB 129; see also LR 206 and IOF 128). In these contexts Levinas makes no distinction between natural and revealed theology. The question concerns the form and the content of discourse about God, not the mode of its justification.

Finally, if the assimilation of traditional discussions of the "metaphysical attributes" of God to theosophy causes distress in certain theological quarters, as it is intended to, and signals the disruption of many familiar modes of theological discourse, the same is true of Levinas's critique of the myth of participation. This is his name for those religious contexts, so powerfully described by Mircea Eliade, in which human society and human action are but microcosmic imitations of a macrocosmic order that is, as sacred, the epitome of a totality immune to any interrupting infinity.[7] When Levinas calls for a "break with participation" and a "faith purged of myths" (TaI 58, 77), many will no doubt congratulate their own discourse on the divine for effecting a sufficient linkage between Athens and Jerusalem to have made a decisive move from *mythos* to *logos* and to deserve the name theo*logy*.

Levinas does not deny this move, only its significance in the present context. In his view the ancient move from *mythos* to *logos* in Plato and Aristotle and its modern, Enlightenment and Hegelian reenactments serve to distinguish logocentric philosophical theologies from the myths of participation only as two species of the same problem, religion adrift in a discourse that at best marginalizes the discourse in which I and we are decentered by the face of the Other, who commands, judges, and takes us hostage from on high.

In short, the philosophical theologies that purport to be the triumph of the concept over primitive myth and esoteric theosophy are indeed just that. But unless the shadow of the Other dramatically dims even the uncreated light in which God would shine as directly present to my intellect, Levinas suspects that my theology is adrift; and even if I have a humble theology that identifies neither representation with sheer presence nor theology with the beatific vision, if the grounds for my caveat are the finitude of my intellect rather than the face of the Other, I will end up abusing "the very name 'God'" (NTR 14) or, to speak biblically, taking the name of the Lord my God in vain.

Derrida suggests that Levinas's true target is "the complicity of theoretical objectivity and mystical communion" (WaD 87). This is true but incomplete, for Levinas applies the same teleological suspension to religious practices as to religious representations. Thus he condemns "the impure stratagem of sorcery" or magic as the reduction of the sacred to a power in the service of profit (NTR 141-42). Then, in a move now familiar to us, he describes what takes itself to be quite different from such instrumental religion as being only superficially different. Just as traditional forms of philosophical theology were assimilated to theosophy and myth, here private personal piety is assimilated to sorcery. Levinas has in mind the devotional life in which God is "the correlate of the ego in an amorous and exclusive intimacy" (CP 32). He finds in the prophet Ezekiel a critique of "the righteousness of the righteous who save their own selves, who think of their own selves and their own salvation. The existence of evil people by their side attests, in fact, to the defect in their righteousness. They are responsible for the evil that remains.... Saints, monks, and intellectuals in their ivory tower are the righteous subject to punishment. They are the Pharisees, in the non-noble meaning of the term, which the Jewish tradition is the first to denounce" (NTR 188). "Watch out," he warns, "for the peace of private worship! ... the artificial peace of synagogues and churches!" (NTR 193).

From the point of view of the suffering it matters little whether religion becomes the magical pursuit of private material benefits or the liturgical and devotional pursuit of private spiritual benefits. In either case, the faithful have ears to hear but do not hear the cries of human anguish. *When the Other does not get in the way of my seeing God, God will end up getting in the way of my hearing the Other. That is what the teleological suspension of the religious is all about.*

The disparity between this view and the one presented in Kierkegaard's *Fear and Trembling* does not just consist in the reversed positions of the ethical and the religious; it also involves the different evaluations of mediation. Johannes de Silentio protests that the human relation with God is too mediated and looks for that mediation to be suspended in a direct encounter. Levinas protests that the human relation with God is too direct and looks for that directness to be suspended in a mediated encounter. "As Jews, we are always a threesome."

Before we conclude, however, that we are dealing with a simple contradiction and begin to ask whether we have located some fundamental difference between Judaism and Christianity, we need to notice the massive equivocation that confronts us regarding the term "ethical." The difference between what Levinas means by the term and what Johannes means could hardly be greater. For Levinas it signifies the direct experience of unconditional and infinite obligation that one human being is subject to in the presence of another, independent of any social mediations that may place limits or conditions on that responsibility.[8] For Johannes it does not signify the closely related Kantian theme of unconditional obligation grounded in the abstract universal of pure reason, and thus prior to any social mediation; rather, it signifies Hegelian *Sittlichkeit*, the ethos, the laws and customs of a particular social order.[9] It may contain obligation, but only as this has been interpreted by some historically particular "morality of mores." For just that reason obligation may be unconditional, but it will never be infinite.

The most extensive presentation of "the ethical" in the Kierkegaardian corpus is found in the letters of Judge William in volume II of *Either/Or*, a text filled with references to God. The pious worldview Judge William presents is precisely what constitutes Christendom as Christendom. It is, in Kierkegaard's view but in Levinas's language, religion adrift. It expresses a social totality humanly constructed so as to be immune to the intrusions of any infinite.

For Kierkegaard, then, as for Levinas, philosophy "is called into being by a religion adrift, and probably religion is always adrift" (NTR 182). The same prophetic sense that there is no sacrilege as dreadful as that of the "faithful" motivates the hermeneutics of suspicion both philosophers practice, a hermeneutics dramatically different from that of Marx, Nietzsche, and Freud just because of its different motivation.

There remains, of course, this difference. Both thinkers call for revelation (the expression καθ' αὐτό an infinite that will puncture the ontological and sociological totality in which the same prevails over every other. But for Levinas this infinity is human, while for Kierkegaard it is divine. The import of this difference deserves the most careful attention. For the present, I only want to note that the two positions need not be mutually exclusive. Is it not possible that the voice of the visible human face and the voice of the invisible God are in agreement? Is that not exactly what we should expect if, as the Genesis story found in both Jewish and Christian Bibles tells us, the Other is created in the image of God? Indeed, would it not be the deepest grace of all if in our violent world we could learn to hear the harmony of Kierkegaard and Levinas's hope for the widow, the orphan, and the refugee in the commandment *"You shall not commit murder"*?

Notes

1. Jacques Derrida, "Force of Law: The 'Mystical Foundation of Authority,'" in *Deconstruction and the Possibility of Justice*, ed. Drucilla Cornell, Michael Rosenfeld, and David Gray Carlson (New York: Routledge, 1992), 28.

2. For a fuller account of teleological suspension as *Aufhebung*, see my essay, "Kierkegaard's Teleological Suspension of Religiousness B," in *Foundations of Kierkegaard's Vision of Community*, ed. George B. Connell and C. Stephen Evans (New Jersey: Humanities Press, 1992), 111-14.

3. In this passage and a related one at FFL 31, Levinas argues that it is precisely this Other between myself and God that keeps God from ever being simply present.

4. We must not let this phenomenological language obscure the antiphenomenological insistence that to be revealed is to express oneself in seeing and speaking

rather than in being seen. For God to be revealed is not for God to be seen. "God thus reveals himself as a trace, not as an ontological presence" (FFL 31).

5. Sigmund Freud, *The Future of an Illusion*, chapter 7.

6. I have argued that Kierkegaard also opens the way for a non-Marxist practice of ideology critique. See Merold Westphal, *Kierkegaard's Critique of Reason and Society* (University Park: Penn State Press, 1991), especially chapters 5 and 7.

7. For a brief account of this kind of religion as *mimesis*, see Merold Westphal, *God, Guilt, and Death: An Existential Phenomenology of Religion* (Bloomington: Indiana University Press, 1984), chapter 10.

8. This independence is the point of Levinas's claim that the face-to-face relation is immediate (TaI 51-52) and that the Other manifests itself "καθ' αυτό. It *expresses itself*" (TaI 50-51). For a fuller treatment of this crucial theme, see Merold Westphal, "Levinas and the Immediacy of the Face," *Faith and Philosophy* 10, no. 4 (October 1993): 486-502.

9. For this reading see chapter 5 of Westphal, *Kierkegaard's Critique*.

15
Theology and the Philosophy of Religion according to Levinas

Theo de Boer

Levinas is one of the few French philosophers whose work sometimes features God. In *Totality and Infinity* this happens sporadically and more or less by chance. He may capitalize Transcendence and the Other, but his elaboration on the idea of God is so limited that commentators could think that he had replaced God with man. His later works, however, feature a well developed philosophy of religion. In the foreword to *Otherwise Than Being* he even states that the goal of this work is "to understand a God that is uncontaminated by being" ("entendre un Dieu non contaminé par l'être").

Another striking aspect of these later works is that Levinas's rejection of theology as a science seems to have become even more strict. Theology "thematicizes" and thus "destroys the religious situation." Speaking *about* God sounds false (AE 155). The question this raises, however, is, Can one maintain that a philosophy of religion does not thematicize? How can a philosophy of religion claim something that is being denied to theology? Why would not theology be capable of thinking a God uncontaminated by being? Does Levinas perhaps consider traditional theology as superfluous and only the philosophy of religion as qualified to speak about God? In the remainder of this article I will try to shed some light on this problem by paying attention to his development.

The Breaking of the Evidence—The Way Down

It is striking that when Levinas compares his own philosophy (which he calls "prophetical eschatology" or "eschatology of the Messianic peace") in the foreword of *Totality and Infinity* to current philosophy or the dominant philosophical discourse, he defines the latter in completely classical terms. One gets the impression nothing has changed in philosophy since Parmenides. The philosophy which Jewish wisdom is facing here is the philosophy which pits evidence against opinion. It is the opposition with which philosophy more or less started. Philosophy represents knowledge or *episteme*. In the classical tradition, evident knowledge of unchanging being was thus opposed to opinion concerning changing being. This opinion or *doxa* cannot contain truth. In the confrontation between Greek philosophy and Christianity, this judgment was also passed on to faith. From the beginning the opposition between reason and faith was formulated within this frame of reference, and it remained there for ages. The fact that theology accepted the classical Greek concept of science as a standard is also evident from the definitions of science that theologians were formulating. I will confine myself to only a few examples here: Duns Scotus defines science as knowledge that is certain, necessary, and evident. Another example, one from the period of the Enlightenment (which brought no change in this respect) is that of Reimarus. He describes science as insight into the interrelationship between truths demonstrated by irrefutable deductions from evident axioms. All this fits in with Aristotle's definition of science as the ability of the human soul to prove certain truths about the universal and the essential.[1] Today, no book on the methodology or philosophy of science would put forth these definitions, nor would they be applied in the field of philosophy.

Compared to "knowledge," faith is tantamount to opinion. Naturally, Christian theology could not resign itself to this judgment and has had a twofold response to this challenge. The first answer was a bold claim or strong bid: theology itself too wanted to be *episteme*, as a form of natural theology. This theology sought, as did Aristotle, to be the crown to ontology. God as a supreme immutable being is the ultimate object of science as *episteme*. Secondly, Christian theology has posited a supernatural theology for which religious truths indeed had to be accepted as a basis, truths that were not irrational but superrational.

The extent to which this classical tradition has remained dominant can, as I pointed out earlier, be seen in the foreword to *Totality and Infinity*. Here again wisdom, in this case Jewish wisdom, is pitted against the evidences of philosophy. It seems as though nothing had changed, although, in fact, a true revolution took place in philosophy after the mid nineteenth century. Dilthey introduced the concept of philosophy-of-life. Heidegger viewed this concept of philosophy already so self-evident that he considered the expression "philosophy-of-life" to be a pleonasm. The fact that we find no traces of this concept in Levinas might, I suppose, be due to the fact that Levinas was a student of Husserl, who, with his doctrine of the intuition of essences and his concept of philosophy as "strict science," can be considered the last representative of Greek tradition. Husserl sharply denounced Dilthey's worldview philosophy as a renunciation, even a denial, of reason. Philosophy-of-life would merely provide unscientific, provisional solutions for the problems of life and thus "bequeath to posterity need upon need as an ultimately ineradicable evil."[2]

Levinas actually said once of his method that he joined Husserl's phenomenology in order to overcome it.[3] Husserl was his point of orientation in the same way the classical philosophy of being was. From this formulation it appears that the way Levinas seeks to evade the monopoly of philosophy with its evidence is negative. He tries to find openings in the thinking that he embraces in order to escape its claims. He takes the evidence of philosophy as his starting point but then tries to break out, so that the evidence loses its totalitarian grasp. There are situations in which ontology "breaks" (TeI xiii). If we were to take the evidence of philosophy as a basis, we would find it inadequate sometimes. Levinas in his terminology refers to these insights as "metaphysical," because they express a dimension beyond, a "meta" ontology. The search for truth in science and philosophy, for instance, presupposes a pretheoretical feeling of obligation to the truth that is beyond the grasp of transcendental philosophy. We cannot prove with evidence that such a sense of obligation necessarily exists the way we can with postulates of science.

In natural science, as Kant argued, we have no choice but to make certain assumptions. For instance, we have to assume that nature is uniform, and that causality shows no gaps. In discussion we have, as Apel contends, to assume that the participants are intentional and rational, or discussion is futile. Apel, however, has to concede that there is one thing that we can never force a potential discussion partner to do, and that is to participate in the discussion. If the individual wills not to be rational, there is nothing we can do.[4] The evident transcendental way of reasoning has no grasp on this. Here, as Levinas would say, totality "breaks" where comprehensive thinking fails. If a discussion takes place anyway, it means that something is happening or has happened in a preceding domain that transcendental thinking has no hold on, a pre-original experience, a "dialogue before dialogue" that happens to us like an incident or a gift. Its existence cannot be proven, and as such, is an object of *doxa*, opinion. We cannot get further than what Husserl called assertoric evidence. That which obtains may also fail to obtain. The same principle applies to social philosophy, where obligating conclusions can be drawn from the existence of a social contract. This contract theory, too, has a flaw: it cannot force anyone to enter into the contract. How can it appeal to reason before the drawing of the contract, if it is this contract that produces rationality? How does the good faith originate with which one concludes the contract? Coexistence according to the contract presupposes an ethical disposition that precedes the contract and has to accompany and readjust life in society permanently if one wants to prevent it from degenerating into a mechanical adherence to rules. Without the ethical ferment of the origin, every society would get stuck in the deadlock of a machinery.

I call Levinas's approach in *Totality and Infinity* a negative or defensive strategy because the traditional classical notion of philosophy forms the framework and starting point of his approach to philosophy. His own ethical view lies at the end of it, outside of philosophy. One could also call it a way down: beneath the supposed foundations lies an even deeper foundation: the ethical experience. In an earlier publication I called it an "ethical transcendental philosophy" because "tracing back" is, formally speaking, a transcendental method.[5] Levinas also uses transcendental terminology, but in more radical terms: the origin is pre-original, involves a preliminary dialogue, is a condition on this side of every condition. In a certain sense we are touching a deeper fundament here. The rules of the game carry the game. The individual decisions to participate in the game carry the rules of the game.

Obviously, breaking out of traditional ontology also means a break with natural theology. We can also say of natural theology that it has a totalitarian claim, for God as a supreme Being is the basis of every temporary and finite being. Of the doctrine of participation, Levinas says that it "keeps us imprisoned in invisible nets" (TeI 19, 49, 61, 202, 269). Opposite the grasp of this theology he posits man as a free, independent, atheistic being who can refuse a relationship with God. Can we contend here too that there are experiences that break totality, experiences on which totality has no hold? The answer is, yes! It is the experience of the very independence of human existence. This experience starts with the enjoyment of the elements, continues in the cultivation of the earth and the building of a house, and finds its culmination in the experience of responsibility for a stranger. There is a way to God, but it is not the way of the classical line of reasoning, the arguing of the proof of God's existence. Man is separated from the Creator, frees himself, absolves himself of the relationship to an absolute ground. These are the situations in which totality "breaks up." And with that, natural theology loses every hold on us. If there is a return to or a trend toward speaking of "God"—if there are situations in which that word comes to our mind—it happens by way of a completely different course, beyond every ontology ("par delà toute ontologie," TeI 61).

Before I continue to show that in his later works, Levinas tends toward a more positive method, I would like to argue that Levinas also seems to be bound in another way to a classical, Greek way of thinking, one which plays a role in his concept of theology: his concept of thematization.

In his article "Philosophy and the Idea of Infinity" (1957) Levinas says that ontology as a philosophy of the Same makes its way to the other through an abstract essence that dissolves the otherness of the other. The stranger becomes theme and object and is made subordinate to the concept. "Knowledge is grasping the individual—not however in its singularity, because this no longer counts, but in its universality, because only of the universal is science possible" (DEHH 168; my translation). It is clear that Levinas conceived thematization as generalization. In the philosophy-of-life since Dilthey, however, we know a way of understanding that is directed toward the individual. The neo-Kantian school spoke in terms of ideography (Windelband) and of an "individualizing method" (Rickert). In general, it could be said that the concept of interpretation in hermeneutics is directed toward knowledge of the individual, whether this involves the individual psyche or an individual work of art or object of culture in general. This development seems also to have left Levinas completely unaffected.

What is true for the other is also true for the I. The I, too, is more than the individualization in time and space. From this, Levinas concludes in "The Ego and the Totality" (1954) that no concept corresponds to the I as being. He embraces the classical view that the individual, and thus the I, is inexpressible, ineffable. The I, however, does speak. More so, Levinas paradoxically states: "The I is inexpressible pre-eminently because it is speaking" (EN 38-39). I would like to remark here that when the I is speaking, it also expresses itself. In that case it is effable. In a conversation with others, the other can understand and interpret the speech. He then has a certain understanding of the I, and the reverse is also true. Levinas admits this himself when he says that one cannot separate the understanding of the other from the fact that one addresses him. "The other is not first an object of understanding and subsequently someone with whom we speak. Both relations coincide or, more specifically, in meeting the other I offer him the understanding I have of him" (EN 18-19). This last view breaks through the idea that thematization means generalization. Still, Levinas adheres to that notion in *Totality and Infinity* and also later. The other to whom I speak cannot become a theme or object of knowledge. Time and again, the nonthematizable other rises behind that theme. Of the other as a being that speaks we have no understanding. We can only invoke, or appeal to, him or her.

The notion that thematization is always generalizing in his earlier work also leads to a misinterpretation of Heidegger. He claims there that the relationship with the other is a greeting or invocation and not, as Heidegger would have it, an understanding. The other cannot be incorporated into a horizon but is a gap in the horizon. It seems that Levinas even interprets the hermeneutical concept of horizon or guideline as something universal, a universal idea to which the other as the other is subordinated. The understanding-of-being is a knowledge of the universal, and thus Heidegger's philosophy ties in with the main tradition of Western philosophy. Like Plato, he would subordinate perception of the particular to knowledge of the universal (EN 17-19; DEHH 170; TeI 61).

It should be remarked, however that "being" according to Heidegger always means the being of beings ("Sein des Seienden"), of individual beings, and thus cannot be identified with the universal. If the invocation appeals to the particular, to which Heidegger would surely assent, then this invocation, too, is a form of understanding-of-being. The understanding-of-being applies equally to the world, myself, and my fellowmen.

Philosophy of Life—The Way Up

Although Levinas says somewhere that methodology is not his main concern and that in the time one spends writing books on method, other more interesting books could have been written (DVI 143), we can find a number of remarks in *Otherwise Than Being* which show us that he no longer sees the classical Platonic-Aristotelian framework as the only description of what philosophy is doing. He now says of the ethical language he employs—a language including expressions such as substitution, responsibility, selflessness, expiation—that it stems from nonphilosophical experiences, and from the meaning of these experiences (AE 86, 154). He refers here to the Louvain philosopher de Waelhens, who, in his book *La philosophie et les expériences naturelles*, defends a view of philosophy wherein philosophy does not, as in the rationalist tradition, develop its truth on its own and then impose it on the facts. Philosophy has a more moderate task. It makes explicit the rationality that is already at work in the facts, in the actions of people in ordinary life, in work, culture, and communication. The disregarded facts thus would contain an inherent rationality. Levinas now claims that phenomenology is capable of reaching beyond the phenomenon as a theme. It can "follow in a description of the approach the inversion of the thematization in anarchy" (AE 155). The ethical language is capable of expressing the paradox. Here, therefore, we can speak of description and expression, even of phenomenology, of those experiences that go beyond thematization.

De Waelhens's ideas do not stand on their own. They must be regarded against the background of the revolution in philosophy which philosophy-of-life set into motion and which I mentioned earlier. One has to realize that philosophy-of-life is not hostile to comprehension. At most, such a hostility obtains with some philosophers, such as Klages and, in a sense, Bergson, philosophers who should be regarded more as vitalists. This thinking still depends on the rationalist tradition, insofar as it reverses the relationships. Blind facts would dominate over reason, life would be impenetrable to comprehension. This can justly be called irrationalism. According to Dilthey, however, life asks for reflection and a development of awareness through language and comprehension. There is a desire for expression that can be understood by others. Life, expression, and understanding (*Leben, Ausdruck, Verstehen*) to him are the three key concepts. Dilthey regarded thinking not as the subsumption of the individual under abstract concepts but as an articulation and clarification of the phenomena of life: a transfiguration of life in thought, "its transfiguration into flame and light," to use an expression of Nietzsche. Heidegger's thinking has taken over Dilthey's concept of philosophy. Every ontological formation of ideas according to Heidegger is anchored in ontic, factual experiences. Thus in the analysis of fear, for instance, he tries to show that what is involved is always fear for oneself.

It seems to me that we can find this same kind of reflection on the experiences of life in Levinas's works. When he mentions the experiences of substitution and responsibility before freedom, he often repeats the same sentence: "Il faut la penser." It's something we have to think. This thinking cannot be the generalizing thematization he condemns in his earlier writings. Obviously, there is a kind of comprehension or understanding that reaches beyond thematization and can grasp the sense of factual experiences which are utopian and "out of place" in this world but still factual and historical.

This comprehension differs in two respects from the classical, rationalistic tradition: there is a ratio within the facts and this ratio can be grasped. From this moment on it is possible to speak of a "hermeneutics of facticity" as does Heidegger, although Heidegger makes no mention of an occurrence like substitution in his discussion of these facts.

The importance of this breakthrough is evident from Levinas's view that it made it possible to adopt a positive strategy. In *Otherwise Than Being* it appears to be possible to analyze "phenomena" which were formerly only posited or postulated beyond phenomenology. In other words, where *Totality and Infinity* stops, after the description of interiority and economy—in short, after the phenomena of ontology—*Otherwise Than Being* begins: namely with the confrontation with the face of the other. In *Otherwise Than Being* a number of concepts are developed—such as substitution, obsession, proximity, hostage, subjectivity, vulnerability—in opposition to the central concepts of (existential-phenomenological) ontology such as intentionality, openness, dialogue, subject, coexistence. In addition to the method of working back from the phenomena of ontology to the depth level of metaphysics, in addition to an "intentional analysis" that penetrates the horizons of given phenomena (which I called his "ethical-transcendental method"), Levinas now uses new positive methods borrowed from rhetorics: iteration and exaltation. Both of them are techniques of exaggeration, of *emphase*, of emphasis. This placement of emphasis transforms ontological concepts into metaphysical concepts. The concepts of ontology acquire an ethical meaning by means of which they can express a dimension beyond ontology. In ontology we encounter a kind of passivity in the receptivity of the mind, but the passivity more passive than every passivity (plus passive que toute passivité) is the vulnerability or susceptibility of the self (*le soi*). In ontology, the phenomena pose themselves (*se posent*), but the ultimate exposition is the exposure of the hostage (*s'exposer*).

The disclosure of this metaphysical depth level makes a movement in two directions possible from ontology to metaphysics and vice versa. Besides the transcendental method, which is a reduction, a descent to the sources, there is also a way up from metaphysics to ontology; not a reductive method but a productive one. The original metaphysical relationship is a dual one, but the neighbor appears to have a neighbor too. In practice it is impossible and even immoral to limit oneself to one neighbor. Therefore you have to compare and divide your time. Distributive justice is necessary. The entrance onto the scene of the third party makes weighing of responsibility necessary and reckoning—and by implication also theorizing and thematizing. Ontology thus returns, not as a starting point but as the terminus of the reasoning.

Before I elaborate on the consequences of this turn for the philosophy of religion, I should draw attention to the fact that this development in Levinas's position is a natural one. The incitement to reflect on one's own standpoint is the confrontation with the alien. Jewish wisdom meets Greek philosophy. The first reaction to this contact will be an attempt to look for holes in this system of thought with totalitarian pretensions. When prophetic thought has found its own expression, however, and has articulated its view on life, it will make an attempt to integrate the Greek ontological way of thinking into its own philosophy.

It is obvious from his important article on the philosophy of religion, "God and Philosophy," that Levinas has developed his own positive philosophy and thus overcome the classical dilemma of science (*episteme*) and opinion (*doxa*). It is not true that we have to choose between the rationality of philosophy and the opinions of belief. There is a third possibility. Faith has its own rationality. According to Levinas a rational discourse is possible which is "neither ontology nor the language of faith." Levinas speaks of the "rationality of transcendence" and even of the "rationalism of transcendence" ("la rationalité et le rationalisme de la transcendance," DVI 96). Levinas now combats the alternative of the God of the philosophers and the God of the fathers Abraham, Isaac, and Jacob if this opposition is to be understood as an opposition between rational thinking and irrational belief. The prophetic wisdom has its own intelligibility or understandability. It represents experiences that can be "thought." The prereflexive attitudes of substitution and responsibility, the relationship of the-one-for-the-other can be expressed in philosophical terms. In other words, it is possible to be a philosopher without leaving your religion or to remain true to your prophetic tradition without rejecting philosophy.

From the Supreme Being to the Infinity beyond Being

The new view does not reject the Greek way of thinking. Everything that was excellent in Greece comes back, says Levinas in an interview in *Le Monde*, and he mentions the thinking about order and harmony, about distributive justice, democracy, and the state.[6] But what about the Greek natural theology, the crown of Greek ontology? Does it return too?

Of course, this seems to be impossible. When Greek philosophy is integrated into the Jewish tradition you could say that it has been turned upside down, which really means that it has lost its theological crown. The transcendental method, the way down from ontology to metaphysics, just means a decentralization, that is, a secularization. Ontology proves to have its center outside itself, which means that the beings of ontology no longer need an ultimate foundation in a Supreme Being. This is true a fortiori for the way up. Why look for a new center of gravity when the relationship of the-one-for-the-other has been discovered as the true ultimate sense of the world? This "intrigue" reveals the ultimate sense that is vainly looked for in ontology.

It is perhaps clarifying to formulate this state of affairs in terms of Husserl's reduction in *Ideas I*. We have seen that Levinas is looking for a concept of a God "not contaminated by being." Husserl's transcendental reduction is also a manner of putting being between brackets: the being of a supposedly independently existing world. In chapter 1 of his *Fundamental Consideration* in *Ideas I*, this being is "put out of action" by a voluntary act of the will. The positing of existence is simply canceled by a Cartesian attempt to doubt. This method of ruling out the existence of the reality of the world can be compared with the elimination of the reality of God in *Totality and Infinity*. God as a Supreme Being is simply removed by the ideas of separation and atheism. You can compare this with the Cartesian way of Husserl's reductions. The natural attitude and its correlate, an absolutely existing world, is thus ruled out "in one stroke." In his later development, Husserl regarded this Cartesian method as unsatisfactory because its operation is too immediate and abrupt. It is not enough to convince the adherents of the natural attitude. It appears that a positive, concrete analysis of consciousness and its correlates can prove that it is possible to put the whole natural world between brackets.[7]

In the careful and painstaking analysis in the second chapter of the *Fundamental Consideration* in *Ideas I*, Husserl demonstrates that this is possible. The negative operation of the *epoché*, or inhibition, is supplemented by a concrete proof that the idea of an absolute independently existing world is self-contradictory.

Levinas's more detailed analysis in *Otherwise Than Being* of the "phenomena" of substitution, hostage, responsibility and of the relationship to Infinity (in a metaphysical sense, see below) can, in the same manner, be considered a concrete, material demonstration that the idea of a Supreme Being is not necessary. The elimination "in one stroke" of the God of the philosophers (by the idea of separation), is replaced by an elaborate analysis of the categories of an "uncontaminated" religion (sometimes called a reduction as well) (DVI 126).

So the idea of a Supreme Being (an *ipsum esse subsistens*, or an *ens causa sui* in Levinas's own words [FFL 31]) seems to be radically denied, which would be the end of natural theology. One could, however, maintain that the natural theology *returns* … in the form of the philosophy of religion. In the last part of my paper I will draw attention to two aspects of this return to theology. The first is methodological, the second involves content.

In the first place, we notice that in a certain sense Levinas has overcome the philosophically laden concept of thematization. He has not replaced it with a more subtle concept of comprehension. He tries to neutralize the generalizing and ontologizing effect of this activity by alternating thematization and dethematization or saying and undoing what one has said (*dire et dédire*). This denial of course should not be understood as a denial of the content of what was said: it is a means of purifying the operation of thematization, of liberating it from ontological "contaminations" in order to understand (*entendre*) something that is not, at the same moment of this comprehension, conceived of as something general and ontological. In this respect it can be compared with Husserl's inhibition or disconnection (*Ausschaltung*) of naive ontological claims (*Seinsgeltung*) in his phenomenological reduction.

In the second place, we could say that in a material respect as well, the natural theology which is eliminated in a first move returns when we look at some of the important concepts of philosophical theology. This is a second point of formal correspondence with Husserl's transcendental reduction. The world, first put between brackets, returns "under another sign." The only thing we lose in the *epoché* is an illusion: the contradictory idea of an independently existing world.

Take, for instance, the idea of Transcendence. This concept returns, but in a radical transformation, "uncontaminated by being." Instead of the highest being, the Transcendence is "beyond being." The traditional concept of transcendence, according to Levinas, is actually a concept of immanence. The predicate of highness (*hauteur*) is borrowed from ontology. The adjective "eminent" and the adverb "eminently" are derived from the highness of the heaven above our head. They don't transcend ontology (DVI 95, 104). It is the Transcendence beyond being that ordains the other, my fellowman, to the Other with a capital O and gives him the "power" to stop my egoistic energy and change it into hospitality. The Transcendence, the absolute distance from God, is thus converted or reverted to my responsibility (DVI 115).

The concept of infinity also comes back but not as the infinity of a Supreme Being that cannot be encompassed by a finite being. The infinity of the Infinite, his differing from the finite is his nonindifference regarding the finite (DVI 109). The finite being is not overwhelmed or overpowered by the infinite but disowned, unseated, and directed to the other. In this respect, subjectivity is the ambiguous temple or theater of the Transcendent and of his Glory (DVI 115, 124).

This theology in the form of a philosophy of religion has in common with the classical natural theology that it is based on experience and reason and not on revelation. But it is not founded in "the quicksand of religious experiences" as Levinas contends (DVI 124). It is not a restoration of opinion that is at stake here. Opinion, the opposite of evidence in philosophy, is also speaking the language of being. "Nothing offers less resistance to ontology than opinion and belief" (DVI 96). Very specific experiences are at stake here: the being shaken out of its enchantment with being, the awakening of conscience. It is a philosophy of religion in the time of the suspicion of ideologies. This suspicion has its origin in a cry of protest against injustice, in prophesy (DVI 125-27). This is the modernity of this philosophy of religion (or perhaps its postmodernity). It is an appropriate philosophy in the time of the death of God. I called the natural theology in the classical sense a strong bid in the beginning of my paper, but it has proven to be, in the course of history, a weak bid, an admission of weakness. In our time, the philosophers themselves do not believe in the God of the philosophers.

At this point of my exposition, one could make the objection that the experiences at the basis of this philosophy of religion are so specific, so tied up with one specific religious tradition based on revelation, that the reflection on these experiences coincides with a specific theology or a dogmatic theology, bound to a particular group or denomination. First of all, my answer to this objection is that the particularity of Jewish tradition according to Levinas is always directed toward the universal.

A more important observation, however, is that there is no longer any difference between so-called supranatural or revelational theology and natural theology, or between theology and the philosophy of religion under postmodern conditions. When natural theology can no longer attempt to reduce factual, historical truths to eternal rational truths (the program of the Enlightenment according to Lessing), and no longer seeks to construct a natural, rational religion as the suprahistorical common core of all historical religions; when it has lost its self-evident foundation in a commonly held theistic belief; when natural theology is, to the contrary, a reflection—in the sense of the philosophy-of-life—on religious experiences as described by Levinas; and when it is an explication and interpretation of certain local and temporal "sensemaking" events, this distinction loses its significance.

Every tradition that says something about the meaning of life is a "proposition de sens" in the sense in which Ricoeur uses the expression.[8] Every proposition of sense has its own right. All traditions are equal and no tradition is more equal than others in making an exclusive claim to reason. But there is—perhaps somebody will object—still the claim to the truth of hard science. Indeed, there is still a "rigorous science," but in a totally different sense than that which Husserl hoped for, not as a guide for life. Modern science is no participant in this competition of traditions. Science is out of the running because it has eliminated itself. Science refuses in principle to raise and to answer questions of sense.

In modern times—this is our postmodern predicament—we are, to use an expression of Sartre's, "condemned" to dialogue, to a dialogue between different narrative traditions. In this situation, the principal difference between theology (natural or dogmatic) and the philosophy of religion has evaporated.

Notes

1. H. J. Adriaanse et al., *Het verschijnsel theologie* (Amsterdam/Meppel: Boom, 1987), 15, 21, 27.
2. Edmund Husserl, "Philosophie als strenge Wissenschaft," *Logos* 1 (1910-11), 289-341, "Philosophy as Rigorous Science" in *Edmund Husserl, Phenomenology and the Crisis of Philosophy*, ed. Quentin Lauer (New York: Harper and Row, 1965), 69-147.
3. Letter to R. Bakker from July 1971.
4. K. O. Apel, *Transformation der Philosophie*, vol. 2 (Frankfurt am Main: Suhrkamp, 1976), 413.
5. Theo de Boer, "An Ethical Transcendental Philosophy," FFL 102.
6. *Le Monde*, 2 June 1992.
7. See Theodore de Boer, *The Development of Husserl's Thought* (The Hague: Martinus Nijhoff, 1978), 434.
8. Paul Ricoeur, *Temps et récit*, vol. 3 (Paris: Du Seuil, 1985), 322, 328.

16
Tracing Responsibility in Levinas's Ethical Thought

Jill Robbins

Absolutely toward the Future

In the final sentences of "The Trace of the Other," Levinas writes: "The revealed God of our Judeo-Christian spirituality maintains all the infinity of his absence, which is in the personal order itself. He shows himself only by his trace, as in Exodus 33. To go toward Him is not to follow this trace which is not a sign; it is to go toward the others who stand in the trace" (TTO 359). These sentences are the culmination of an argument that has proposed "trace"—namely, the mark of the effacement of a mark—as the specific manner in which the other signifies. In contrast to other forms of signification, such as the sign, which is constituted by referrals within immanence, "trace" denotes a referral to transcendence, a relationship with a certain absence not reducible to the opposition presence/absence and belonging to an immemorial past. The term "trace," here introduced in an essay written two years after the publication of *Totality and Infinity*, announces the distinctive emphases and departures—stylistic and conceptual—that come to characterize all of Levinas's subsequent work. It is central to his thinking about ethics. The aim of this paper is to consider the consequences, for ethics and theology respectively, of thinking responsibility to the other as a relation to the trace. I will pursue in particular the intertwining of the question of God and the question of the other that these enigmatic sentences suggest. I will focus on Levinas's presentation of the conceptual figure of the trace in the 1965 essay "Enigma and Phenomenon" as well as in "The Trace of the Other," from 1963.

In the latter essay, as in each of his works, Levinas asserts that the habitual mode of philosophical thought is one of an "allergy" to the other that remains other (TTO 346). Philosophy in its essential project is an adventure, or a would-be adventure, that in the end discovers only itself, returns to itself, "like Odysseus, who through all his peregrinations is only on the way to his native land" (TTO 346). There is an "imperialism" of the philosophy that unfolds within this homecoming paradigm, an indiscretion about a philosophical enterprise which, in its relentless orientation toward what shows itself, insists on bringing everything into the light. Yet there has also been, in the history of Western philosophy, a movement of transcendence, or "something as contradictory in its terms as a heteronomous experience" (TTO 348). It was prefigured by the Platonic good beyond being, the Cartesian thought of infinity—exceptional moments that Levinas invokes frequently—and, as he states singularly in "Enigma and Phenomenon," "a God always absent from perception" (CP 62). The heteronomous experience is an irreversible movement that goes out unto the other, a departure without return which he associates with the biblical Abraham: "To the myth of Odysseus returning to Ithaca, we wish to oppose the story of Abraham leaving his fatherland forever for a land yet unknown, and forbidding his servant to bring even his son to the point of departure" (TTO 348). The one-way movement is exemplified by *goodness* and the *work*, according to the particular inflection he gives these terms.

The work requires a *radical generosity*. It is a gift that demands consequently the radical ingratitude of the other, as opposed to the cyclical movement of warm thanks, recognition, and gratitude, "return to origin" (TTO 349). It also requires, and here Levinas introduces another key term that is very close to generosity, *patience*:

> The departure without return...would lose its absolute goodness if the work sought for its recompense in the immediacy of its triumph, if it impatiently awaited the triumph of its cause. The one-way movement would be inverted into a reciprocity. The work, confronting its departure and its end, would be absorbed again in calculations of deficits and compensations, in accountable operations. It would be subordinated to thought. The one-way action is possible only in patience, which, pushed to the limit, means for the agent to renounce being the contemporary of its outcome, to act without entering the promised land (TTO 349).

The allusion is covert, at least compared to Levinas's naming of Abraham. The paradigmatic figure for patience is Moses, who, in Deuteronomy 32, sees but does not pass over into the promised land. Moses is denied the reciprocity, the compensation implied in the law that he himself taught, namely, "in the same day thou shalt give him his hire" (Deuteronomy 24:15), the principle of daily remuneration for labor.[1] Moreover, this denial of recompense is necessary. For the radicality of the one-way movement risks—fault of language, fault of what Levinas here refers to simply as "thought"—being reappropriated in a calculation, a reciprocity. Moses' not getting into the promised land thus *affirms* the one-way movement. It makes him the very figure for the non-self-contemporaneity, the non-self-coincidence that is patience.

To be patient means to be given over to the future—absolutely toward the future, a future that always belongs to the other. Levinas will also call it "liturgy," in the sense of "a profitless investment" (TTO 349-50). Not to be confused with the time of personal immortality—to be patient is to go beyond the horizon of *my* time, beyond the being unto death. It is "passage to the time of the other" (TTO 349). In its ordinary sense, patience refers to the capacity for calm endurance or for bearing delay. But as Levinas renews the term, there is nothing psychological or existential about it. "I" cannot "be patient." Blanchot glosses the word: "patience has already withdrawn me...from my power [*pouvoir*] to be patient: if I *can* be patient then patience has not worn out in me that me to which I cling for self-preservation" (WoD 13). To be patient then is not a *pouvoir*: not *my* possibility, it is not an ability, nor is it anything that the subject could initiate. It is in a certain sense *impossible*. Yet the absolutely patient action is ethics itself.

The Face

"The relationship with the Other," says Levinas, "puts me into question, empties me of myself.... The I loses its sovereign coincidence with itself" (TTO 350-53). For Levinas, ethics is this putting into question of the self, the interruption *of* self arising in the encounter with the face of the other (*le visage d'Autrui*). The face is the concrete figure for alterity. Just as the definition of face in *Totality and Infinity* emphasized its nonadequating, infinitizing mode, "the way in which the other presents himself, exceeding the idea of the other in me, we [...] name face" (TaI 50), so too, here, the face's mode of presentation is described as an exceeding. In the terms that Levinas uses, the other is given first in a context, in a totality, in the light, in a world. But while the other is given in a world, he is also out of world. Signifying *in* a context, with its totalizing explanatory power, the other also signifies out of context. The other is given as a *phenomenon*, but also as a *face*.

Note that in Levinas's descriptions, the face is not hypostatized in any way. It is defined precisely as a disturbance between world and that which exceeds world, a shaking up of the mundane, a collision between two orders. The significance of facing is approach; it is the other's coming toward me, a mobile orientation, an interpellation. The face is an active surplus over the plastic image that would enclose it. Inherent in manifestation is the threat of rendering the face "captive" or "mute," negating its life, which is its mobility. The face is by definition always on the move: it "divests itself of its form," "breaks through its own plastic essence" (TTO 351-52).

How indeed does this extraordinary event called *face* conserve its significance? How can the face *appear* without renouncing its alterity? In *Totality and Infinity* and in the works preceding it Levinas answered these questions by means of the conceptual figure of facial expression. Expression, a combination of glance and speech, is the concrete way in which the face accomplishes its breakthrough or divestiture of form. Moreover, the face's expression signifies in a distinctive manner, καθ' αὐτό, "according to itself": it signifies only with reference to itself and thereby escapes the referrals inherent in sign systems. As Levinas had described the face's autosignification in "Freedom and Command," "A face has a meaning not by virtue of the relationships in which it is found, but out of itself" (CP 20). That is to say, in contradistinction to other forms of signification, facial expressions signify only themselves. They do not refer to something else, either to states of mind or feeling. Like the nonadequating relationship to the face that Levinas had called "discourse" in *Totality and Infinity*, the language of facial expression is conative and interlocutionary in its orientation, performative in its speech. Not denotative, not a bit of information, it is a command, or a greeting. It is prior to communication as an exchange of signs. There is also a technical sense of expression καθ' αὐτό, namely, the other signifies "without qualities or attributes"—by himself (TaI 65-66, 74, 296). He does not even signify as himself; he signifies without benefit of the "as" structure. In the writings subsequent to *Totality and Infinity*, the other is also said to signify "by himself"—again, without context, without mediation, and with a distinctive autosignification: "the beyond from which a face comes…signifies as a trace" (TTO 355).

Tracing an Absolute Past

Levinas proposes the trace in contrast to dissimulation and disclosure, revelation and unveiling. Dissimulation and disclosure are modes proper to the phenomenon and being: they would absorb the other's alterity. The model of revelation—invariably conceived as a dialectic between hidden and manifest—would convert transcendence into immanence. The conceptual figure of the trace allows Levinas to think a relationship to the other which does not convert the other into the same, and a relationship to transcendence which is not convertible into immanence.

For the face's presentation is, in Levinas's terms, "enigmatic," namely, a "way the other has of seeking my recognition while preserving his incognito,…a way of manifesting himself without manifesting himself" (CP 66). Levinas evokes the absolute disturbance produced by the approach of the other, by "an expression, a face facing and interpellating, coming from the depths, cutting the threads of the context" (CP 64). The face disturbs absolutely, but—as one might say in the singular syntax that is reminiscent of the Blanchotian diction—it disturbs *without* disturbing. Levinas asserts that "disturbance…is a movement that already carries away the signification it brought: disturbance disturbs the order without troubling it seriously. It enters in so subtle a way that unless we retain it, it has already withdrawn. It insinuates itself, withdraws before entering. It remains only for him who would like to follow it up" (CP 66). Hence disturbance is a movement that is already in retreat; withdrawal is built into its presentation. Moreover, Levinas says, it withdraws *before* entering. In similar formulations Levinas says: "the hand was thrown in before the game began; the disconnection took place before the connection" (CP 65); the other "has left before having come" (CP 68). Note the impossibility of ever coinciding with the other; with the other there is no recognition, no simultaneity, no meeting. This structure, which Levinas calls "anachronism," is necessary because the disturbing alterity is not a difference visible to the gaze, which always synchronizes the same and the other. In disturbance what is required is a present that "destructures itself in its very punctuality" (CP 68). Hence alterity occurs as a past that is not available to any present, an absolute past, as "the trace of an irreversible past." Levinas asks, "How refer to an irreversible past that is a past which the very reference would not bring back.... like memory which retrieves the past, like signs which recapture the signified? What would be needed would be an indication that would reveal the withdrawal of the indicated instead of a reference that rejoins it. Such is the trace" (CP 65).

Ordinarily a trace is conceived as a residual phenomenon—the examples that Levinas gives are the fingerprints left by a criminal, the tracks of an animal, the vestiges of ancient civilizations. In each of these examples, the trace is the *mark* of an absence of what previously was present, and is derivative of full presence. This kind of trace is a mark *in* the world, the *effect* of a cause *in* the same world. Moreover, ordinary traces can be taken as signs, as signifiers relating to signifieds, accessible to an interpreter who would decode them. As indicative signs they are for Levinas synchronous; "they reestablish a conjuncture, a simultaneity, between the indicating and indicated terms, thus *abolishing* depth" (CP 65). All of Levinas's examples of trace-signs are the empirical signs of an absence; they are signs of a departure. Because they mark the absence of something that was previously present, they remain within the phenomenal order, in a world.[2]

But the trace as Levinas understands it, the trace of the other, is otherwise. *This* trace escapes not only phenomenal presence but the very conceptual opposition between presence and absence. Neither "presence" nor "indication" nor even "an indicated presence" (CP 66) will be adequate for understanding the trace. For this enigmatic trace is simultaneous with its effacing. Says Levinas: "Its original signifyingness is sketched out in, for example, the fingerprints left by someone who wanted to wipe away his traces and commit a perfect crime. He who left traces in effacing his traces did not mean to say or do anything by the traces he left. He disturbed the order in an irreparable way. He has passed absolutely. To *be* qua *leaving a trace* is to pass, to depart, to absolve oneself" (TTO 357).

The trace, as Levinas defines it, leaves a trace by effacing its traces. Such a trace is not the mark of an absence (which could be conceived in relation to a past or modified presence). Rather, it is the mark of the effacement of a mark. As it is the mark of the effacement of a mark that was already the mark of an absence, it is a double effacement, a double erasure, a re-mark and a re-tracing [*un re-trait*]. That is why Levinas says, "it occurs by overprinting [*sur-impression*]" (TTO 357). Belonging to an immemorial past and accessible to no present, this trace is outside the presence/absence dyad. It is, as Levinas puts it, "the presence of that which properly speaking has never been there" (TTO 358). It is an irreversible past; its presence is "the very passage toward a past more remote than any past" (TTO 358). That is why when the trace leaves a trace, it leaves.

There is indeed a close relation between the trace as Levinas exposits it and what Derrida calls the arche-trace, between Levinas's destructuring and Derrida's deconstruction of pure punctuality, whereby "an interval must separate the present from what it is not in order for the present to be itself, but this interval that constitutes it as present must, by the same token, divide the present in and of itself, thereby also dividing, along with the present, everything that is thought on the basis of the present."[3] Another point of intersection would be Levinas's description of the structure of the trace as "overprinting" and Derrida's as tracing-erasure, that is, as an erasure that is the "same" as the tracing of the trace.[4] It is worthwhile here to recall Derrida's assessment of the "inversion" that is produced by such a structure of tracing-erasure, a structure constitutive of presence: "the present becomes the sign of the sign, the trace of the trace."[5] For if every metaphysical concept retains the mark of what it has set aside—is traced by a structure of generalized reference to Other— this mark also divides and deconstitutes presence. What are ordinarily the terms of plenitude within metaphysics—for example, presence, self, God—become a function, an *effect* of the structure of generalized reference to other, a function or effect of the trace.

The consequences of the convergence between Derrida's and Levinas's thinking of the trace are decisive and can be summarized as follows. If the Derridean trace can be understood as "a minimal structure of a relation to alterity" without which no self could be self and because of which no self can be itself,[6] then there is an always possible commerce between Derrida's general Other, *Autre*, and *the* Other, the specific otherness of the other, Levinas's *Autrui*. The interruptions and the alterities with which Derrida's work is concerned may be shown to have an ethical force.[7] Reciprocally, Levinas's thought takes on a deconstructive potential, for in identifying something like an internal division or border within the same that opens the same to the other, it achieves as it were a deconstruction of self, and of self-coincidence, by the relation to the other. Levinas's descriptions would indeed seem to offer a way of thinking about ethics that is, as Derrida would understand it, nonmetaphysical, nonlogocentric, not oriented toward the subject, consciousness, or any of the philosophemes of traditional ethics.

But what are the implications of such a nonmetaphysical, nonhumanistic ethics? What are the consequences of thinking responsibility to the other as a relation to the trace? First, the other to whom I am responsible cannot be said to *be there*. The trace by which the face of the other signifies is outside the presence-and-absence dyad, and thus the other cannot be conceived in terms of the metaphysics of presence (that is, as another presence or as a subject). In fact, to claim the other in terms of the metaphysics of presence, with its phenomenalizing and adequating forms, as when, for example, I see, know, recognize, or comprehend the other, would be to deny and enclose the other. It would be another instance of the economy of the same. It is the interruption of all such closed systems that lets alterity be glimpsed.

A second consequence of thinking of responsibility as a relation to the trace concerns the status of the interruption, the disturbance. The ethical event has an ontological insecurity because withdrawal is built into the trace's presentation. But such a structure is, as Derrida puts it, menaced "by its very rigor" (RL 37). Will the ethical event have happened? Can it be said to happen? Strictly speaking, it does not happen; nothing forces us to take up the obligation, the imperative of responsibility that the face delivers; the imposition is altogether without force. But such is the risk, the necessary risk of a thought that does not claim the other in advance, does not merely reconstitute the economy of the same. Without this risk, the alterity of the other drops out altogether. And this is the risk that Levinas's *theology* is willing to run when he asks whether religions do not come to us from a past that has never been present and when he asserts that "the trace...is the proximity of God in the face of the other."[8]

The Trace of God

To what extent can the God of Exodus be said to reveal himself as a trace? In "Enigma and Phenomenon," Levinas will propose a very condensed reading of two scriptural passages that recount a theophany, and the exegetical emphases and consequences of his reading need to be spelled out. The first scriptural passage concerns the call of Moses in Exod. 3:2. Moses is tending his flock when he comes to the mountain of Horeb, and "the angel of the Lord appeared to him as a flame of fire from the midst of a bush." (This fire is a figure for God's presence here and at the Sinaitic revelation as well.) "And Moses said, 'I must turn aside that I may see this marvelous sight, why the bush does not burn up.' When the Lord saw that he turned aside to see, God called to him from the midst of the bush saying, 'Moses, Moses.' He answered, 'Here I am.' He said, 'Do not come any closer; take off your sandals from your feet, for the place where you are standing is holy ground.' Then he said, 'I am the God of your father, the God of Abraham, the God of Isaac, and the God of Jacob.' And Moses hid his face, for he was afraid to look at God" (Exod. 3:3-6).

In the words of commentator Brevard Childs, "What began as just another day doing the same old thing, turned out to be an absolutely new experience for Moses."[9] Called to his prophetic office, Moses puts himself at God's service with the words, "Here I am," words which echo those of pious ancestors and which, in Levinas's later work, are the paradigmatic response of responsibility. After hearing the name formula that effectively renews a promise, Moses—in his inexperience, in his timidity—hides his face.

Levinas comments: "The great 'experiences' of our life have, properly speaking, never been lived.... To the voice that calls from the burning bush Moses answers 'Here I am' but does not dare to lift up his eyes. The glorious theophany which makes so much humility possible will be missed because of the very humility which lowers the eyes. Later, on the rock of Horeb, the prophet ventures to know but glory is refused to the boldness that seeks it. As transcendence, as pure passage, it shows itself as past. It is trace" (CP 68-69).

Levinas juxtaposes (in midrashic fashion) Moses' humility in Exod. 3—he hides his face, "afraid to look at God"—with his boldness in Exod. 33, where he seems precisely to want to look at God. Or at least he asks to see God's glory (*kabod*). This term, sometimes rendered as "Presence," appears to denote "that side of the divine nature that can be perceived by man through revelation."[10] It becomes associated with "face" when God refuses to comply in full with Moses' request, saying, "'You cannot see my face, for no mortal man can see me and live.' And the Lord said, 'Look, there is a place beside me. Station yourself on the rock, and, as my glory passes by I will place you in a crevice of the rock, and shield you with my hand until I have passed by. Then I will remove my hand and you will see my back, but my face shall not be seen'" (Exod. 33:20-33).

What is the meaning of this request and its refusal? The request to see—the glory or the face of God—is a desire to know God. (Note how Levinas assimilates this particular project to the indiscretion of the mode of knowing in general, saying simply, "on the rock of Horeb the prophet ventures *to know*.") But God will not be known in his essence. In an anthropomorphic image, scripture asserts that Moses sees not God's face but his back—his hinderparts—after he has passed by. The image, as it has been interpreted by Jewish and Christian commentators alike, suggests the limits of man's knowledge of God. God will not be seen with a totalizing view but glimpsed partially in his passing from the back. He will not be known in his essence but (for medieval interpreters) through his attributes and through his works.[11] God's denial of Moses' request recalls his denial of Moses' earlier request in Exodus 3:14 to know God's name, another "vehicle of his essential nature."[12] There God's paronomastic answer is more like the evasion of an answer, with its circular *idem per idem* formula, *'ehyeh asher 'ehyeh* "I am that I am."[13] Both in Exod. 3 and Exod. 33 God is a *deus absconditus*.

But is not the scriptural statement that Moses saw God's back in contradiction with other places in scripture—e.g. "The Lord would speak to Moses face to face, as a man speaks to his friend" (Exodus 33:11)—all of which assert, by means of the anthropomorphic image of facing, Moses' special intimacy with God. What *did* Moses see? One rabbinic reading, *Berakhot* 7b (cited by Levinas in "Revelation in the Jewish Tradition"), says in effect: He saw neither face *nor* back. He saw the *knot* of the *tephillin*, the phylacteries at the back of God's neck. In the manner of the most negative of negative theologies, the rabbinic comment proposes that Moses saw nothing (corporeal) of God. The whole question of seeing (or knowing) God is displaced, even by means of the anthropomorphic image of God praying. As Levinas understands it, the theophany is referred to the centrality of the prescriptive in Judaism, the ritual observance that teaches obligation to the neighbor.

Let us come back to the scriptural text and to God's phrase to Moses, "you will see my back." If face or facing suggests approach, back suggests departure, would seem to be a sign of departure. The back of God would be like one of the ordinary traces to which Levinas refers, the sign-traces exemplified by footprints, fingerprints, animal tracks, indicative signs that mark the absence of something which was previously present. For example, the back of God denoting his works is a sign-trace, an effect of God within the phenomenal order. But what if the back of God were not a sign-trace but a veritable trace, another kind of absence? Moses sees God leaving, but what he sees is not a sign of departure. He sees a God who disappears *in* his appearance: "it [the theophany] shows itself as past. It is a trace." This God is pure passage, and has never been present. "The term present," says Levinas, "suggests both the idea of a privileged position in the temporal series and the idea of manifestation" (CP 61). To think God as a trace is to think the invisibility of God outside the opposition manifestation/nonmanifestation. For Levinas this means an *enigmatic* mode of presentation whose retreat is inscribed in advance. Within this logic, the Sinaitic theophany (in Exod. 19 and 20) is rigorously indistinguishable from a thunderstorm.[14]

In summary, at the theophany at the bush, Moses hides his face, afraid to look at God, and he sees nothing. Later, he asks to see, "Pray, let me see thy glory." He requests it, not quite in the manner in which he *pleaded* with God to let him into the promised land (Deut. 3:23-25),[15] but this time he wants to see. God answers: "You cannot not see my face" (Exod. 33:20). The rabbinic comment on this verse from *Berakhot* 7a, to which Levinas refers, in a footnote, but which he does not cite, emphasizes this persistent noncoincidence. "A Tanna taught in the name of R. Joshua v. Korhah: The Holy One, blessed be He, spoke thus to Moses: When I wanted, you did not want [to see my face], now that you want, I do not want."[16]

Perhaps this is an instance of what Harold Bloom calls the Hebrew Bible's rhetoric of the double bind, a rhetorical pattern of cruel power, in which "everything is given to us, and then what matters most is taken away from us."[17] But in the rabbinic interpolation, is there not also a *structure* that, beyond psychological and existential despair and frustration, characterizes what Levinas understands as the *enigma* of the revelation of the other: missed recognition, nonreciprocity, non-self-presence? The theophany at the bush is the radical incognito of transcendence. Precisely because it *is* an experience of transcendence, it is missed; the experience is not one.

How, then, are we to understand Levinas's repeated suggestions that the trace is the proximity of God in the face of the other or, in the passage with which we began, that to go toward the (trace of) God is to go toward the trace of the other? These statements could be said to continue—albeit in a less anthropological form—an emphasis which has been present from Levinas's earliest work, namely, that the relationship with the divine does not accomplish itself outside the interhuman. Certainly they do not mean that God is an ontological guarantor of ethical responsibility to the other, or that God left his mark on the interhuman, because God [is] (nothing) but trace. God *is* not, apart from trace. The trace *of* God means the trace that is God. "And if God were an effect of the trace?" Derrida asks. "If the idea of divine presence (life, existence, parousia, etc.), if the name of God was but the movement of this erasure of the trace in presence?" (WaD 108). That is, the self-presentation of God would be the illusory halting of the chain of referrals of the arche-trace, the figure of the one unerasable presence.[18] But (and the qualifier is enormous) a God conceived within ontotheology as first being, presence, *causa sui*, and so on. If God can be understood as "not contaminated by being," as Levinas puts it, that is, in accordance with what can be called a "Judaic"[19] *non*ontotheological theology, then perhaps the nonmanifestation of the revelation of God can be understood otherwise, as a differential constitution of (textual) traces, as the other-trace. Then perhaps we can begin to think God, in Levinas's work, as the *name*—unpronounceable if you like—for the difficult way in which we are responsible *to* traces.

Notes

1. Deuteronomy Rabbah 11:10.
2. On the precise manner in which the trace escapes phenomenology, see Edward Casey, "Levinas on Memory and the Trace," in *The Collegium Phaenomenologicum*, ed. J. C. Sallis, G. Moneta, and J. Taminiaux (Boston: Kluwer Academic Publishers, 1988), 243.
3. Jacques Derrida, "Differance," in *Margins of Philosophy*, trans. Alan Bass (Chicago: University of Chicago Press, 1982), 13.
4. There is not the space here to discuss the way in which the Derridean conception of trace, modeled on the Heideggerian motif of the forgetting of the ontico-ontological difference, is specifically oriented toward the Heideggerian undermining of the determination of being as presence in a way that Levinas's is not. See Robert Bernasconi, "The Trace of Levinas in Derrida," in *Derrida and Differance*, ed. David Wood and Robert Bernasconi (Evanston: Northwestern University Press, 1988), 13-29.
5. Derrida, "Differance," 13.
6. Rodolphe Gasché, *The Tain of the Mirror: Derrida and the Philosophy of Reflection* (Cambridge: Harvard University Press, 1986), 186-94.
7. See Jacques Derrida and Pierre-Jean Labarrière, *Altérités* (Paris: Osiris, 1986), 76-77, and Simon Critchley, *The Ethics of Deconstruction: Derrida and Levinas* (Oxford: Blackwell, 1992), 30.
8. Levinas, "Énigme et Phénomène" (DEHH 211), and "Un Dieu homme?" in *Exercices de la patience* 1 (1980), 72.
9. Brevard S. Childs, *The Book of Exodus: A Critical, Theological Commentary* (Philadelphia: Westminster Press, 1974), 72.
10. Childs, *The Book of Exodus*, 597.
11. This is one of the interpretations attached to the phrase in Exod. 33:19, "I will make all my goodness to pass before you."
12. Childs, *The Book of Exodus*, 591.
13. The interpretation of this verse poses enormous questions in the history of exegesis. Suffice it to recall for our purposes that the formula was often interpreted as a statement of being by the church fathers.

14. It is as if the predominance of naturalistic images of God's presence in scripture confirms the enigma of biblical revelation. See CP 62 and 66.
15. The many midrashim on Deut. 3:23-25 ("I pleaded with the Lord at that time, saying, 'Let me, I pray, cross over'") extend and offer a narrative expansion of this pleading. For example:

    Moses: "Lord of the world! Let me, I pray, enter into the Land, live there two or three years, and then die."

    God: "I have resolved that thou shalt not go there."

    Moses: "If I may not enter it in my lifetime, let me reach it after my death."

    God: "Nay, neither dead nor alive shalt thou go into the land."

    Louis Ginzberg, *The Legends of the Jews*, vol. 3 (Philadelphia: Jewish Publication Society, 1911), 424.
16. *Babylonian Talmud*, trans. Isadore Epstein (London: Soncino Press, 1948).
17. Harold Bloom and David Rosenberg, *The Book of J* (New York: Grove Weidenfeld, 1990), 268-69.
18. See Rodolphe Gasché, "God for Example," in *Phenomenology and the Numinous*, The Fifth Annual Symposium of the Simon Silverman Phenomenology Center (Pittsburgh: Duquesne University Press, 1988), 43-66.
19. Here we can no longer take for granted that we know what we mean by "Judaic," since the "Judaism" in question is arrived at only after such a detour through ontotheology and the Greco-Christian conceptuality.

17
Transcendence

Adriaan T. Peperzak

The question of transcendence has been dominant in two philosophical contexts: (1) the epistemological and ontological context of human subjectivity in its theoretical and practical relations to the world and (2) the context of philosophical theology. Socrates' pointing to the Good as that which, from "beyond the *ousia*," grants being, light, and truth gave orientation to Plotinus, Pseudo-Dionysius, and Saint Bonaventure in both areas, and they were not the only ones who were grateful for his suggestions.

In our century, Heidegger and Levinas have drawn inspiration from Socrates' hint, and both of them—though Levinas more than Heidegger—have asked whether and how that hint could be used to translate another, older inspiration about goodness, being, and truth into philosophy. In this paper I would like to show how Levinas has retrieved Plato's enigmatic phrase about the Good's goodness beyond Being.

"Beyond Being"

If the translation of *to agathon* as "the Good" (*le Bien*) and of *epekeina tés ousias* as "beyond Being" (*au-delà de l'essence*) is correct, the paradoxes contained in this phrase are obvious. How can we speak about the Good, or about any X, that is neither a being, nor Being itself? Is Being enclosed within the limits of a horizon? Is it separated from another dimension, a beyond? Would this beyond then be and not be at the same time? If the Good were inaccessible to ontology—and, a fortiori, to phenomenology—shouldn't we be silent about it, rather than stammer on in a pseudological manner? The fact that such paradoxes as these and others also threaten the logic of Aristotelian, Thomist, or Heideggerian ontologies cannot console us once we are entangled in the paralogical difficulties of a Platonizing meditation. For some practitioners of philosophy, "metaphysical" paradoxes are reason enough to drop these questions altogether, at least within philosophy; other thinkers, and not insignificant ones, see them as the unavoidable consequences of thinking that approaches the limits of human thought. When human thinking reaches out beyond its own dimensions, it produces contradictions: but this is not a good reason to withdraw to easier terrain. Thinking through and beyond the unfolding of *ousia* and *physis*, meta-physics or meta-ontology, seems to be the task that philosophy must achieve, today as yesterday.

Transcendence and Transgression

While Plato characterized the human relation to the Good-and-Beautiful as an ascent or a "transascendence" (TeI 5; TaI 35), modern secularization has leveled the dimensions of heaven, earth, and hell. Still, even in today's enthusiasm for "transgression" we hear echoes of the ancient desire to reach beyond the order of a world ruled by the laws of equivalence, exchange, coherence, and logic. The fact that a certain violence is inherent to all kinds of transgression shows the finite character of its passing beyond the limits, for violence is possible only between limited realities: the Infinite does not compete with anything. As philosophers from Plato to Hegel knew, God is not jealous.

But does transcendence not cause suffering? Yes, but not in a violent way; that is, not at the cost of a loss in human worth or dignity, and not at the price of sickness or slavery. How then must transcendence be lived and thought, if it exceeds the possibilities of human existence without repression or violence? It must be in accordance with or even coincide with the deepest of human desires.

Desire

The first part of *Totality and Infinity* opens with a chapter entitled "Metaphysics and Transcendence"; and the first section of this chapter is entitled "Desire for the Invisible" ("Désir de l'invisible," TeI 3; TaI 33). Transcendence, as movement toward the Other, is identified here as a desire, and the text seems to start with a phenomenology of eros that makes obvious allusion to Plato's metaphysics. I would like to spend a few moments on a careful reading of its first lines.

What does desire for "the invisible" announce? Does Levinas champion a theory of nonempirical, nonphenomenological realities, a kind of *Hinterwelt* from which we thought Marx and Nietzsche had finally delivered us? Or does he, like Heidegger and Nietzsche, aim to show that transcendence leads away from a false reality and thought in order to discover and achieve a truer loyalty to body and earth? All thinking—and not only thinking—is situated; an explanation of any possible thought demands the reconstruction of its context, an interpretation of the material and cultural network, the customs and traditions from which it emerges. However, hermeneutics as (re)contextualization is not enough, because all thinking—and not only thinking—turns to something or someone which is completely new, and which cannot be contained in the text or context that is already there. Thinking addresses some other that is elsewhere and different, some other beyond the parts or elements of a context or an economy in which the thinker feels at home. To think is to leave the familiarity of one's home country for a foreign place, which is "elsewhere" (*ailleurs*), *alibi*, "there" (*là-bas*), as Levinas, alluding to Plato, writes.[1] By abandoning the closure of "being-at-home-with-oneself" (*Beisichselbstsein*), one enters a dangerous kind of existence. Unrest but also passion are the consequences of a desire that precedes all choices and decisions.

The urgency of an exodus manifests the post- or meta-physical character of human existence. This exodus does not lead to the heights of heaven or the depths of a netherworld; it is not even a synthesis of ascent (*anabasis*) and descent (*katabasis*), as Plato's *Politeia* would have it. Exodus leads to others who share the earth with me. For "we are in the world." This world is more than a space to dwell in and more than the general condition of a common ethos; as universe it embraces all possibilities of exodus and wandering. The only way to leave the world is to die, and all attempts to get in touch with gods or God are earthly modulations of worldly possibilities. And yet "true life is absent," as Rimbaud declares in the passage quoted by Levinas from *A Season in Hell*.[2] Of course, in a secularized world hell is no longer below or out there; it is an infernal mode of existence whose description is given in the outcry "What a life! The true life is absent. We are not in the world." In this complaint, a certain form of existence—or, in fact, a form of coexistence (the coexistence of Verlaine and Rimbaud)—is revealed as inhuman, devilish, extramundane. Desire is frustrated. But can it be satisfied? Does the desired other open a possibility of escape from suffering, boredom, violence?

The Other awakens us to new possibilities, but how can we wake up if we are not already moved by a desire for the surprising new? Exteriority and otherness do not destroy all elements of anamnesis, but they respond to what we already are before we know it. Desire is oriented before one can discover it. In trying to say what and how we desire, we thus try to reach back to that which precedes our consciousness.

Economy

In prevailing interpretations human praxis is caught in a web of needs, desires, values, the rational use of means toward chosen ends, exchanges on the basis of calculated equivalence, and so on, that is, in an *economy*. The law (*nomos*) of the house (*oikos*), the law of being at home in the world, is constituted by a combination of natural needs and rational choices. Human beings are rational—that is, reasoning and choosing—animals, looking for satisfaction. Since isolated individuals cannot satisfy their own needs, they group together, creating social, political, and cultural conventions to achieve their ends, the "norms and values" of their communities. Sociality rests on individual hunger and fear, although reason implies the possibility of distance, choice, delay, and the preference for some "values" or "satisfactions" over others. The most popular explanation of the ethos that belongs to this economy is utilitarian. By distinguishing quantitative and qualitative differences of satisfaction and dimensions of satisfaction, such an explanation tries to maintain all human ends and actions within the limits of an economy. Not only entertainment but also science, art, philosophy, and religion are seen as values, and the fulfillment of these values has a place on the overall scale of human contentment and happiness.

The global picture given here shows the decadence of a long philosophical tradition: the Aristotelian tradition of *eudaimonia*, perfection, and self-realization, which is much more respectable than both its trivialized caricature in eighteenth-century *Glückseligkeitslehre* and twentieth-century utilitarianism. All these doctrines share a common presupposition, however. Like Plato and Aristotle, they understand the fundamental desire to be a lack, a privation, a want that must be filled or fulfilled. All behavior, including all choice, is motivated by a felt emptiness that urges the feeling subject to search for fulfillment. All action is self-realization; all feeling is, in the end, self-affection; and all consciousness is self-consciousness. The elsewhere and all otherness are forms of a return of the self to itself. Beauty, the Good, truth, the gods, and God are valuable only insofar as they promise someone's satisfaction. All kinds of want and desire, then, fit perfectly into the structure of intentionality, as defined by Husserl: the dynamic emptiness of the "erotic" intention is the exact correlate *in negativo* of the desired satisfaction. Both have the same width and identity. "True life" might still be absent, but the measurement of desire reveals the exact contours of the desired and beloved who would still our hunger. It is obvious, then, that the beloved cannot be infinite, unless the depth of our heart is as infinite as the beloved. In any case, the first principle of ethics, according to this interpretation of human *economy*, is: "Fulfill, accomplish, realize what you are!"

Levinas does not deny the importance of human needs and the part they necessarily and rightly play in politics, culture, and history; but his interpretation of their economy differs from the prevailing theories. First, Levinas grounds the economy of needs in a wider and more elementary phenomenology of human life as spontaneous assimilation and enjoyment (TeI 82-90; TaI 110-17). Second, this phenomenology permits him to see all human activity, including art, science, philosophy and religion, as an attempt to enjoy the world's wealth. Third—and this is the most decisive move—Levinas reinterprets the characteristics of economy as emerging from Being itself. In *Otherwise Than Being*, the connections between economy and Being are analyzed through a phenomenological ontology in which Levinas explicitly expresses his debt to Heidegger (AE 49 n. 28; OB 189 n. 28).

Whereas the chapter on "Interiority and Economy" in *Totality and Infinity* reinterprets our being-in-the-world as the vital enjoyment of a dwelling place and nourishment on an earth bathed in water, air, and light, *Otherwise Than Being* deepens those analyses by showing that Being itself has an economical (or "pre-economical") character. Levinas's phenomenology of Being describes the way of Being's being—its mode of happening, arriving, and coming to the fore, its behavior and its course (*la geste d'être*)—as an active and transitive "Essence" (*essance* in the sense of Heidegger's *Wesen und Walten*) that is essentially interested—an "interessence," or a being-linked of all entities, whose interrelations are determined by each being's endeavor to maintain and expand its own existence. *Esse* is *interesse*; essence is being-interested, "inter-est-ing," *interessence*. Levinas appeals to Spinoza's *conatus essendi* and Pascal's analysis of *concupiscence*[3] as key elements of his phenomenology of Being, and his entire effort is oriented by the desire to evade[4] the realm of general interestedness without exception, that is, by the desire to escape Being as such.

This conception of Being's essence explains why Levinas can think of the Good only as surpassing the limits of Being. Yet is his phenomenology of Being really an ontology, or does it show only a *mode* of Being? Do not goodness, generosity, giving, and substitution exist? Are they not other faces or powers of Being? Hasn't Levinas made his task too difficult by separating the Good from Being? He is not at all convinced of the generosity that other thinkers hear in *es gibt*, and prefers to stress the dark, threatening, and chaotic side of the indeterminate *il y a*: but how can there be a place for goodness if Being fills all the gaps? And if it does not need a place, how can it have its time?

Desire and Need

In *Totality and Infinity*, Levinas's phenomenological critique of economy starts with a radical distinction between needs (*besoins*) and desire (*désir*); in *Otherwise than Being*, the ontological structure of economical existence is analyzed. Desire, thematized in the beginning of the first book, transcends economy, just as the Good, in the second, is shown to transcend ontology. Desire is not interested in satisfaction or exchange; it does not assimilate or integrate, because it is not oriented toward enrichment or expansion. As desire for the Other, it accords with the surprising strangeness and distance without which there would be no otherness, and thus no relation between the Other and the Same. Proximity does not diminish but rather intensifies desire. If it is a hunger, this hunger grows by coming into contact with the desired one.

The formal analysis of desire with which *Totality and Infinity* begins does not immediately focus on a concrete figure of the Other. Shortly thereafter, however, Levinas does declare that in desire, the otherness of the desired one is "understood as otherness of the human other (*autrui*) *and* as otherness of the Most High" (TeI 4; TaI 34, emphasis added). The remainder of the book concentrates on the other human's face. In later publications, the difference between *autrui* and God is thematized, but the affirmation that the encounter with another human coincides with one's relation to God remains constant in Levinas's work. *How* do they coincide, since it is obvious that God and *autrui* are neither wholly nor partially identical?

Desire transcends economy by desiring the other—not for satisfaction or consolation, not as a partner in love, but as the one whose face orients my life and thereby grants it significance. In desire I discover that I am not enclosed within myself, because I am "always already" to and for the Other, responsible, hostage, substitute.

Transcendence surpasses and sacrifices but also presupposes the economy of enjoyment, for how could I give without having experienced the pleasure of fulfillment? How could I live for others (which also involves—at least some—dying for them) without myself enjoying the goods of the earth I want them to enjoy? Levinas is not a preacher of austerity; transcendence does not condemn the joys of life, but it prevents them from becoming absolute; it despises idolatry.

Transcendence, responsibility, substitution are there before we discover them. Consciousness and self-consciousness, the possibility of initiatives and choices comes afterwards. I am "always already" dedicated to the Other, chosen before I can agree or accept what I desire, transcend—and *am*! My own transcendence has started before my time, in a strange sort of "before," in a strange quasi time that does not belong to human history. Levinas calls it the diachrony or the anachrony by which an immemorial past is inserted into the time of history. "A past that was never present," a past more and otherwise past than any preceding time period— should we degrade these expressions by calling them "mere metaphors" for a timeless eternity? Are we, then, able to think of such an eternity without narrowing it down to a kind of presence without past or future, which would then constitute a finite presence? And what shall we propose as a nonmetaphysical translation of the "before" by which our always-already-being-responsible has become an inescapable "given"? Perhaps the temporal "metaphors" of "before," "past," the "pre-original," "diachrony," and "anachrony" can be neither translated nor dropped when we try to speak about transcendence—no more than the spatial metaphors of height and depth more frequently used in classical philosophy.

In any case, transcendence constitutes our ultimate passivity. Not being able to choose or reject my responsibility, I am therefore not free either to be or not to be responsible. The Good that chose me created me as already oriented, listening, looking up to the Other, obedient to the "law" of substitution. In this sense everybody begins by already being good. Of course, when I become conscious of the enormous burden responsibility puts on me, I can decide to refuse further obedience. The passivity and the patience of responsibility demands and presupposes the freedom of decision and initiative, as celebrated in modern philosophy, but it rejects the arrogance of an autonomy that begins with itself. Freedom cannot be originary in the strongest sense of the word; it is released by the "pre-original" compassion that comes from the anachronic Good.

Indeed, passivity is a passion. The subject's being possessed and obsessed by transcendence is concrete in sensibility and affection. Levinas breaks with a long tradition according to which what is ethical and truly human stems from an immaterial spirit that conquers or saves or informs the natural tendencies of corporeality. To be for the Other is neither a fight of the spirit against temptations of the body nor obedience to a purely formal law of reason in ordering the chaotic material of emotions and drives. The human subject is first of all an animated and inspired body, the incarnate, affective spirituality of a passion for the Other.

Subjectivity is being sensitive, being touched, affected, already wounded by the Other's proximity. It is passion and affection, vulnerability and suffering. The classical duality of spirit and matter has been replaced by the duality of two affective modes of existence. Economy and transcendence, enjoyment and living for the Other need one another to be human, but the passion of responsibility governs their ethical concretization.

Passion is more than passivity; it is also suffering. Levinas's ethics does not promote heroic actions or loudly celebrated tragedies. The transcendence of "pre-original" passivity is lived in the humility of a devotion that is not planned but undergone. It both burdens and wears one out. The life of a hostage is tiresome and exhausting; one grows old by obedience. To live for others is to suffer, and even to suffer gratuitously, without meaning, for nothing, because only such a passion unquestioningly realizes the unchosen, entirely disinterested character of transcendent passivity.

The figure of the silent "servant of God" thus emerges from Levinas's phenomenology of sensibility and affection. That is the other possibility of human existence, over against the satisfied and boasting ego, whose sin is not hedonism but the attempted infinity of a monopoly.

Transcendence is no longer the ascent to a heaven of the ideal or the sublime but the humble endurance of everyday life, touched, affected, burdened, wounded, obsessed, and exhausted. A human subject is an inspired body. It is moved by a breath that comes from an immemorial past. As respiration between this inspiration and the expiration of tiredness, old age, and death, a human life is breathing for others, the repetition of obedience to the Good's command. The Good itself can be neither chosen nor contemplated but can be loved only by accepting the responsibility for goodness in the world. This is at least a partial answer to the question asked above, How does my relation to *autrui* coincide with my relation to the Good?

This answer becomes more complex, however, when we bring in Levinas's distinction between the immediate Other (*you*) and the third (*they*). You and I are related through a double asymmetry, in which you are the highest for me, while I am the highest for you.[5] At the same time, all others are present with and among you and me, as those to and with whom we ought to achieve justice in reciprocity. The triad of you, me, and the third, contains the human universe *in nucleo*. It could and should be developed in a theory of the intertwinings of intersubjectivity and sociality in ethics, politics, and history. For theology, Levinas's indications about the diachronic past that was never present and about the trace in which we live are precious but difficult. He uses many words that traditionally were reserved for God to describe the human Other. Terms like "invisible," "absolute" and "absolution," "epiphany," "revelation," "separation," "liturgy," "height," and "highness" name the transcendent "character" of *autrui* and his or her proximity to God. For

God, not much more than "*Il*" or "*ille*" is left over, but the abyss that separates God's "glory" from all powers of Anonymity is immense. The Name is never pronounced, but always remembered. As inspired by the Good, we are in the trace of its passage. To live this inspiration is spirituality.[6]

Notes

1. See the beginning of "La philosophie et l'ideé de l'Infini" in DEHH 165-67 and my commentary in Peperzak, *To the Other: An Introduction to the Philosophy of Emmanuel Levinas* (West Lafayette, Ind.: Purdue University Press, 1993), 89-90.
2. See Arthur Rimbaud, *Une saison en enfer*, in *Oeuvres complètes* (Paris: Gallimard, Bibliothèque de la Pléiade, 1963), 229.
3. See the fourth and fifth quotes on the second page of *Autrement qu'être* (AE vi-vii).
4. In this respect, the early essay *De l'évasion* already expresses a constant concern of Levinas's later work, notwithstanding the distance expressed in his letter of December 1981, which takes the place of a preface to the second edition of *De l'évasion*, with an introduction and notes by Jacques Rolland (Montpellier: Fata Morgana, 1982).
5. Although Levinas insists on the nonreciprocity of the relationship between the Other and me, the asymmetry of this relation does not seem to exclude a double asymmetry in which I am as "high" for the Other as the Other is for me. See TO 135-36, 171, 173-74.
6. Thanks to Aron Reppmann and Beth Spina, who typed and retyped this text, and to Catriona Hanley, who revised my English.

18
Response to Adriaan Peperzak on Transcendence

David Tracy

Adriaan Peperzak's concise paper, at once exact in expression and exacting of genuine thought in the philosophical in the work of Levinas, puts us once again in his debt. Since I find myself fundamentally not only instructed but also persuaded by Peperzak's interpretation of Levinas's complex position on transcendence, I shall confine my response to two points. First, I shall reflect on some further implications of Peperzak's reading of Levinas on transcendence from the viewpoint of the role of such philosophy in theology—mainly Christian theology but also, in passing, Jewish theology. Second, I shall question some possible limitations of Levinas's notion(s) of transcendence for theology and for the philosophy of religion.

Reflection

My reflections may be read as a parenthesis on two passages from Professor Peperzak's succinct and evocative paper. As it happens, one passage appears at the very beginning of his paper and one at the very end.

The first passage admirably states the clarity of the aim of the paper and its principal claim:

> The question of transcendence has been dominant in two philosophical contexts: (1) the epistemological and ontological context of human subjectivity in its theoretical and practical relations to the world and (2) the context of philosophical theology. Socrates' pointing to the Good as

that which, from "beyond the *ousia*," grants being, light, and truth gave orientation to Plotinus, Pseudo-Dionysius, and Saint Bonaventure in both areas, and they were not the only ones who were grateful for his suggestions.

In our century, Heidegger and Levinas have drawn inspiration from Socrates' hint, and both of them—though Levinas more than Heidegger—have asked whether and how that hint could be used to translate another, older inspiration about goodness, being, and truth into philosophy. In this paper I would like to show how Levinas has retrieved Plato's enigmatic phrase about the Good's goodness beyond Being.

The second passage is aphoristic, suggestive and, I suggest, brilliant in its evocation of the thoughtfulness in Levinas's work and in Peperzak's own study of that work, a study nicely entitled "Transcendence": "The Name is never pronounced, but always remembered. As inspired by the Good, we are in the trace of its passage. To live this inspiration is spirituality."

Between the clarity of the beginning and the aphoristic suggestiveness of the end of Peperzak's reflections one finds his analysis of the key relevant elements in Levinas's thought: in *Totality and Infinity*, transcendence and objectivity, enjoyment, desire and transcendence, and economy and transcendence; in *Otherwise Than Being*, "essence" as "interesesse," the Good transcending ontology, and the ontological structure of economical existence.

In relationship to religion and theology, Peperzak's interpretation of Levinas shows the clarity and consistency of Levinas's insistence on the priority of the ethical for any proper understanding of transcendence and thereby the use of the philosophical categories of the Infinite and the other for naming and not naming the absolutely transcendent Other, God. With Peperzak's reading here (including his criticism of Levinas's relative profligacy with adjectives for the human "other" and perhaps excessive parsimony on descriptive adjectives for the absolutely other), I am in substantial agreement: surely, on the central question of transcendence, this ethical route to the Absolute Other only by way of the interrelationships of human others is Levinas's most original, and daring, and for Jewish and Christian theology, both promising and, as we shall see below, controversial move.

Indeed what is most striking in Levinas's appropriation of Plato on the Good is how novel this interpretation actually is in relationship at least to the history of Christian Platonism. (It may be less so—although here I am not informed enough to be sure either way—in the history of Jewish Platonism.) What Levinas develops out of the famous *to agathon* and *epikeina tés ousias* of Plato is developed in this ethical direction for transcendence in neither Plato nor Plotinus, neither Philo nor Pseudo-Dionysius. Indeed, with the partial exception of Bonaventure's Platonic and Augustinian reinterpretation of what might be named the spirituality of other-directedness of Francis of Assisi (whose "others," unlike those of Levinas, included, of course, not only human others but all living creatures of the Absolute

Other as the site of transcendence), there is, in my judgment, nothing in the Christian Platonic tradition on the centrality of an ethics of the other in the understanding (ethical and theological) of the Good beyond Being. Even Pseudo-Dionysius' insistence on "The Good" as the primary cataphatic name for God in *The Divine Names* is, after all, making an ontological-theological rather than an ethical-theological point.

In Levinas one finds a reading of the Platonic Good beyond Being united to a new reading of the Hebrew Bible, especially of the Book of Exodus.

This singular Levinasian reading of the ethical, other-directed, neighbor-directed character of the Good as illustrated by Exodus differs notably from two other famous Christian Platonic readings of Exodus: the patristic emphasis (e.g., in Gregory of Nyssa) on Moses' journey up Sinai as a paradigm of the Christian apophatic mystical journey and, especially in its most famous medieval version in that brilliant semi-Platonist, Thomas Aquinas, what Gilson nicely named the "metaphysics of Exodus 3:14," that is, the Vulgate translation "Ego sum qui sum" become the Thomist understanding of God as the one being whose very being it is to be (*ipsum esse subsistens*).

Levinas surely knows these former views even as he turns instead to a Jewish prophetic, wandering Rosenzweigian understanding of ethical transcendence in Exodus as the key to the ethical relationship to the other. That relationship is both "first philosophy" and the site (the interhuman site) where alone (as *Totality and Infinity* insists) God as the Absolute Other is genuinely to be found: not, note, in either the naming of God (*ipsum esse subsistens*) provided by the "metaphysics of Exodus 3:14" or the classical journey of apophatic mystical theology well represented by Gregory of Nyssa's *Life of Moses*.

The closest analogue in Christian theology to Levinas's reading of Exodus is neither Christian Platonist nor Aristotelian. It is, perhaps surprisingly, the readings of Exodus of much contemporary Christian liberation theology, both Latin American, like Gustavo Gutierrez's reading of Exodus, and African American, like that of James Cone.

For these contemporary Christian theologies Exodus 3:14 or Moses' ascent of Sinai or any other single incident in the Book of Exodus should be read as incidents in the larger "total liberation" narrative of Exodus—that is, as the story of God's liberation of the oppressed Jewish people from Egyptian bondage become the prophetic paradigm of God's continuing involvement in the liberation of all oppressed peoples.

These contemporary Christian theologians retrieve the centrality of Exodus for Christian theological self-understanding (even as necessary for reading and "deprivatizing" other Christian readings of "salvation," e.g., for any reading of the Passion narrative: the Passion cannot be told without recalling the liberation narrative of Exodus). It is perhaps not so surprising after all that Levinas is so powerful an influence on Christian and not only Jewish thought: above all on many European and Latin American political and liberation theologies.

Professor Peperzak interprets Levinas on Exodus as follows: "The urgency of an exodus manifests the post- or meta-physical character of human existence. This exodus does not lead to the heights of heaven or the depths of a netherworld; it is not even a synthesis of ascent (*anabasis*) and descent (*katabasis*), as Plato's *Politeia* would have it. Exodus leads to others who share the earth with me. For 'we are in the world.' This world is more than a space to dwell in and more than the general condition of a common ethos; as universe it embraces all possibilities of exodus and wandering."

Levinas's reading of Exodus helps political and Christian liberation theology, and perhaps also philosophy, to clarify the human situation as one of exodus and wandering as well as to clarify his reading of the goodness of the Good beyond Being. God may be named the Good beyond Being because God's goodness consists in God's wanting neither the Good nor Being for God's self. God simply gives freely; recall here Levinas's brilliant reading in *Totality and Infinity* of creation ex nihilo as preferable for understanding the same-other relation to the "pagan Platonists'" choice of emanation—where "otherness" becomes for Levinas really "the same."

Therefore—and here is the peculiar and, for political and liberation theology, emancipatory insight of Levinas—the God of Exodus is not primarily the God of apophaticism or of the metaphysics of Exodus 3:14. He is rather the Absolutely Other Transcendent One of the Bible, whose very Otherness demands that all who know the God of Exodus know God by accepting responsibility for all others in exodus and wandering: all with whom we share the earth, that is—the other, the neighbor, and not only, notice, the "friend" as in Nietzsche's Zarathustra and Nietzsche's Greeks.

In the history of Christian theological (usually Platonic or, as in Aquinas, semi-Platonic and Aristotelian) readings of Exodus, this Levinasian reading is absent—except perhaps, by implication, in the Franciscan Bonaventure and, by ethical demand, in liberation and political theology. This Levinasian reading of Exodus, in sum, may prove a crucial influence not only in contemporary postmetaphysical philosophy but also in postexistentialist and posttranscendental Christian political and liberation theology. It is true of course that political and liberation theologies are not only ethical but, as their names show, political as well—and therefore involved with "justice" more than Levinas usually is (i.e., beyond his well-known general and cautious comments on justice and on "the third" and the "ontological" structures of justice). Christian political and liberation theologians (like many of the prophets) also tend, more than Levinas characteristically does, to puzzle over the "preferred other" of the oppressed and the marginal as well as over the power disparities between oppressed and oppressor in the face-to-face relationship. These are significant differences. But they do not negate the central affinities between Levinas and these theologies of ethical transcendence, nor do they prevent Levinas's philosophical reflections from informing the latter, for example, with regard to the Absolutely Other character of the God of Exodus as expressed (not disclosed) in the face of the other.

A Further Question

My principal question is one from the viewpoint of theology, the philosophy of religion, and the history of religions. On the one hand, I am convinced that Levinas's contribution to clarifying the relationship of the ethical to transcendence and thereby the character of prophetic religion is unequaled in contemporary thought: hence, Levinas's amazing influence not only on Jewish thought but also, as noted above, on Christian liberation and political theologies. On the other hand, I am unpersuaded by Levinas's consistent polemic against the religious phenomena he variously names mysticism, the violence of the sacred, and paganism.

I realize that the latter are difficult, subtle, and often analogical categories in Levinas's thought. Nevertheless, if I may presume to say so, Levinas nowhere, to my knowledge, phenomenologically studies these categories with the care and subtlety he accords other phenomena in his rich thought. This is strange given the importance these categories have in the other relevant disciplinary studies of religious phenomena. Among many other examples (especially in the phenomenology of religion) consider the following: in the history of religions, Mircea Eliade's morphological studies of "the dialectic of the sacred and the profane" and how that dialectic functions in different ways in the archaic ("pagan") and prophetic ("ethical") traditions; in the study of Judaism, the groundbreaking work of Gershom Scholem (developed and partly corrected by Moshe Idel and others) attempting to show how cabalistic readings of the rabbinic traditions are neither betrayals of nor simply alternatives to the ethical-prophetic traditions. In the wake of such work, is it really possible simply to use the categories "paganism," "the violence of the sacred," and "mysticism" without far more phenomenological nuance than Levinas has thus far accorded them?

Nor is this issue related only to the history of religions and theologies. In the phenomenology of religion Paul Ricoeur's development of the dialectic of "religions of manifestation and religions of disruptive prophetic proclamation" is representative of the many efforts, within philosophy, to show the dialectical character of religion without the loss of the ethical "center" of the prophetic, proclamation traditions. In a similar manner Jean-Luc Marion can affirm Levinas's understanding of "infinity" (and thereby the "ethics of the face") while also developing the religious phenomenon of the "icon" (a manifestation phenomenon) dialectically in opposition not to "mysticism" or "the sacred" or "paganism" but, more exactly, in opposition to the "idol"—which is ultimately the real (and here, I affirm, entirely correct) target of Levinas's analysis. Until Levinas shows phenomenologically (instead of simply asserting) that "mysticism," "the sacred," and "paganism" are synonymous with idolatry, I shall remain unconvinced by his curiously undialectical analysis of these complex religious phenomena.

But my comments on religion and on Levinas's position on religion remain, until a further and necessarily lengthy phenomenological analysis, more critical questions than anything like final judgments even on this aspect of Levinas's crucial work. For in Levinas one finds dialectically developed what is often deemed impossible: what Nietzsche did not foresee—a defense of the love of the "neighbor" (as other) without *ressentiment*; what many Platonists did not envisage—an exposition of desire beyond need and lack; what much Western thought has not achieved—a defense of spirit without denigrating body as well as an insistence on the philosophical primacy of ethics without moralism but with a true enjoyment of the earth. This is indeed an achievement, at once singular and emancipatory, both genuinely Jewish and fully philosophical. I agree fully with Adriaan Peperzak's brilliant final summary: "The Name is never pronounced, but always remembered. As inspired by the Good, we are in the trace of its passage. To live this inspiration is spirituality."

19
Amen

John Llewelyn

> I can no other, God help me!
> Amen.
>
> —Nietzsche, *Thus Spoke Zarathustra*

At the beginning of the first chapter of *Otherwise Than Being* Levinas refers to "strange rumors about the death of God or the emptiness of the heavens" (AE 5; OB 5). That his book purports to say Amen to that rumor is evident from his making precise in the very next paragraph and in the very last paragraph of the book that the death here rumored, the death rumored by Nietzsche's Zarathustra, is the death of a certain God inhabiting a world behind the scenes. But what is it to say Amen?

In *The Star of Redemption*, the work of which Levinas says in the Preface of *Totality and Infinity* that it is too often present in its text to be cited there, Franz Rosenzweig writes that God is neither dead nor living. "To say the one or the other of him, with the old [philosopher] that 'God is life,' or with the new one that 'God is dead,' reveals the same pagan bias. The only thing which does not resist verbal designation is that neither/nor of dead and alive."[1] The resistance to designation of what is other than this neither/nor referred to in the last book of the *Star* mirrors a similar resistance to designation referred to in the first book of the *Star*, where Rosenzweig writes of a word that is often considered to be the last word but is in fact the first, or rather is before the fact and before the law, before the distinction between the de facto and the de jure. This word is Amen, the first tremendous and unlimited Yes of a "positive theology." In the light of Levinas's acknowledgment of Rosenzweig as his guide, I propose to consider a few paragraphs in which Rosenzweig treats of the words Yes and God, in the hope that this may help to articulate together two allusions in Levinas's two main philosophical writings: first, his allusion in *Totality and Infinity* to the plane on which Yes is opposed to No, neither of these opposed words being that which institutes language (TeI 11-12; TaI 41-42) and second, his allusion in *Otherwise Than Being* to an unconditioned and critical Yes (AE 156; OB 122). Because Rosenzweig's "grammatical thinking" of the word Yes is at the same time a grammatical thinking of the word "God," in pursuing my exegetical aim it is my hope also that we may make some progress toward either allaying or deepening what for some of Levinas's readers may be more a disquietude than a question of exegesis.

Having endorsed Nietzsche's proclamation of the death of the God of ontotheology, why is Levinas either unable or unwilling to eliminate the word "God" from the lexicon in which he expounds what he himself describes as a humanism of the other man? Would the appropriateness of that description of Levinas's account of ethics not be increased if the description could be conducted without that word, at least once it had, for the reasons Levinas gives in the first section of *Totality and Infinity*, said good-bye, as Dante bade farewell to Virgil, to the gods of paganism? In other words, although Levinas is seeking to show in *Otherwise Than Being* that, as he writes there, "the problem of transcendence and of God and the problem of subjectivity irreducible to essence—irreducible to essential immanence—go together" (AE 20; OB 17), could he show that the problem of transcendence and the problem of subjectivity go together without showing that these two problems go together with the problem of God? Is it possible that in this sentence of *Otherwise Than Being* and in other sentences of that book the name of God is traced only with a view to its own effacement?

Bearing in mind these questions as well as their place within what, remembering Levinas's reference to the need to get away from the climate of Heidegger's philosophy (DE 19; EE 19), might be called the wider question of philosophical meteorology as to whether it is possible to breathe freely both in the atmosphere of Levinas's thinking and in that of Nietzsche's, let us now read a few paragraphs of Rosenzweig's "grammar of assent."

Having called Amen the first word of a "positive theology," Rosenzweig writes that the point of departure of negative theology is a Something from which by the negation of predicates it moves to a Nothing or a Nought, a *Nicht*, where, he says, mysticism and atheism shake hands. Rosenzweig's method is the reverse. Putting the Nothing behind it, even before the Yes and the No, it aims at a Something or at an Aught, as the English translation renders the *Icht* Rosenzweig prefers to *Etwas* in order to keep at arms length the Hegelian definition of the latter as a definitely qualified existing being whose moments are being in itself and being for another reflected into each other through the negation of negation. The *Nicht* that Rosenzweig here distinguishes from this *Icht*, although not defined, is yet not the uncircumscribed universal (*allgemein*) Nothing of Nothing at all. It is the Nothing of God. That alone is presupposed, the Nothing of a fragmentary all, not the Nothing of the one and universal totality. Rosenzweig, who is readier to write of methodology than Levinas is, contrasts his method with the method of decomposition, destruction, or deconstruction of essence, *Verwesung*, which is the method of atheism, and the method or way of *Entwesung*, which is the mystic way and which takes essence away. The dissolution or deportation of the essence of something leads to a formless night of nothing, a *Nacht des Nichts* that, notwithstanding Rosenzweig's concern to distance himself from Hegel, is a close relation of the night in which all cows are black of Hegel's innuendo toward Schelling. The method of annihilation, *Vernichtung*, the method of Mephistopheles, the method in which atheism and mysticism shake hands, affirms the Nothing. As against these methods, Rosenzweig's method is to ask hypothetico-positively, if God exists, what can be truly affirmed of his Nothing? This is not an affirmation either of Nothing in general or of the Nothing of God. Nor is it a negation of Nothing. Distinguishing the beginning from the point of departure, which is at most the beginning of our knowledge, as Descartes does in the *Third Meditation* and as Levinas will do in his meditation on that *Meditation*, Rosenzweig argues that No cannot be the beginning because it would have to be the negation of a presupposed positive Yes. But both Yes and No presuppose a Nothing that is no more than a positionless posit for the posing of a problem. "It is no 'dark ground' or anything else that can be named with the words of Eckhart, Boehme or Schelling. It does not exist in the beginning. *Es ist nicht im Anfang*." In the beginning is the Yes. But, as already explained, this Yes is not the Yes opposed to the No but the Yes presupposed by the No. Before the neither/nor, it is before the either/or, before the *enten...eller*: *Ent-Scheidung* before *Entscheidung*, *avant toute décision*, prior to *every* decision (AE 153; OB 120).

It might reasonably be objected that this archetypal Yes presupposes an archetypal No, the No of the presupposed Nothing. And Rosenzweig himself admits an archetypal and, as he describes it, tremendous (*gewaltiges*) No. He even says that the No is as original as the Yes and does not presuppose it. A derived No may presuppose the archetypal No, but the original archetypal No presupposes nothing but the Nothing. However, although it does not presuppose a Yes, a *Ja*, it does presuppose an affirmation, a *Bejahung*: in Nietzsche's words, the "highest form of affirmation that can ever be reached."[2] For the Nothing it presupposes is, as we have seen, not the utter Nothing of Mephistophelian meontological annihilation, of the "dark ground" or of the "abyss of divinity," but the Nothing only of the cloud of unknowing as a problematic point of departure from which affirmation concerning the divine essence would come. On the basis of this fine distinction Rosenzweig asserts that the archetypal word No is younger than the archetypal word Yes.

God's essence is infinite yessence. Here Rosenzweig's notion of the infinite appears to be derived from the sense in which a judgment is defined as infinite, for example by Kant, when it affirms that S is non-P. So although, following Rosenzweig's method, only the Nothing of God is given, and since the Yes cannot refer to the Nothing because that would be to exceed the merely heuristic positing of the Nothing as a point of departure for knowledge, the Yes must relate to the non-Nothing: "Therefore the affirmation of the non-Nothing circumscribes as inner limit the infinity of all that is not Nothing. An infinity is affirmed: God's infinite essence, his infinite actuality, his *phusis*."[3]

That Rosenzweig is aware how difficult these sentences will be found by his reader is indicated by his warning that they state only purely formal preliminaries. An obvious source of difficulty for the reader following the *Star* as a guide to the interpretation of the words "God" and "Infinity" as understood by Levinas is Rosenzweig's reference to God's infinite essence. How can that be anything but a hindrance to interpreting the "beyond essence" referred to in the title of Levinas's book? This would be one reason for agreeing with the statement made by Robert Gibbs in his admirable study *Correlations in Rosenzweig and Levinas* that in the sense intended in this title Levinas and Rosenzweig are not in correlation—to which statement it can be added that in Levinas's sense of that word no two human beings are ultimately in correlation. Rather, "Levinas creates a *drash*," Gibbs says, and the verb here is carefully chosen; "he makes an adaptation of Rosenzweig."[4] However, it can be added also perhaps that Levinas creates a *drash*—a Hebrew-Greek chiasmic *drash*, perhaps one could say—of essence, as at least in *Totality and Infinity* he creates a *drash* of being. He exalts, emphasizes, creatively exaggerates these words beyond their ontological sense, or discovers that they exaggerate and produce themselves, as with scores of others, not least the word "ontological" and, to return to our immediate worry, the words "Amen" or "Yes" and "God."

Yes, Rosenzweig writes, "is the arche-word of language, one of those which first make possible, not sentences, but any kind of sentence-forming words at all, words as parts of a sentence. Yes is not a part of a sentence, but neither is it a shorthand symbol for a sentence, although it can be employed as such. Rather it is the silent accompaniment of all parts of a sentence, the confirmation, the 'sic!', the 'Amen' behind every word. It gives every word in the sentence its right to exist, it supplies the seat on which it may take its place, it 'posits.' The first Yes in God establishes the divine essence for all infinity. And this first Yes 'is in the beginning'" (*Stern* 36, *Star* 27).

Why does Yes make words but not sentences possible? Rosenzweig's answer to this question both anticipates and qualifies the Saussurian structuralist doctrine that the meaning of a word is more negative than positive. While recognizing the reason for saying this, Rosenzweig says almost the opposite. Having associated position with the position of a word, he goes on to grant that what is posited depends not only on the other words in a given sentence but on words in other sentences in which that word might figure. The meaning of a word is the class of its sentence frames. But this relation of a word in one sentence to words in the same and other sentences is expressed by the arche-word No. This No expresses opposition rather than position. However, since the identity of what is posited is a function of the alterity of what is opposed and vice versa, a third original word has to be posited, the word And. This primordial And expresses the systematicity of language as *langue* on which every speech act of language as *langage* or *parole* depends. The question of the relative priority between Yes and No thus raises the question of the relative priority between system and act of speech, and this question raises the question or pseudoquestion of the relative priority between historical and logical priority.

Saussure says that while the linguistic system and some mastery of it are logically presupposed by the performance of acts of speech, the latter are historically prior.[5] There are problems with this claim that can only be mentioned here in passing. For example, can even locutory acts, let alone illocutory acts be performed without presupposing competence in finding one's way about a system of grammar? Are not *langue* and *parole* conditions of each other? Are they not equiprimordial? The same answer would seem to be called for when the analogous question is raised with regard to systematicity and sincerity as treated by Levinas. Yet Levinas sometimes says that the giving of my word to the Other is not equiprimordial with the grasp of a grammatical or conceptual system but prior to it. In what sense can it be prior? In the sense of a priority that is presumably prior both to the priority of the formally logical system and to that of historical events. So the priority of neither, a priority that is constitutive and at the same time deconstitutive of the continuum of time and of the order of logical implication and presupposition: the priority of a certain primary "position," of a *Setzen* before *Gesetz*.

In trying to sort out Rosenzweig's answer to these questions concerning the order of priority of Yes and No and of the historical and logical, his distinction between originality and age must be recalled. When he says that the original *Non* is not *propter sic* but *post sic*, that is, not on account of but after the Thus affirmed by Yes, it sounds as though he is saying that although Yes and No, and we now conjoin And, are all original, Yes is in some sense historically older. But when he says that No is not on account of Yes, can he be denying that it is logically dependent on it? And has his quasi-Saussurian and quasi-Hegelian argument not shown that the reverse holds equally? It would seem that he is arguing both for systematicity and for its delimitation. If No is more immediately connected with the infinity of non-Ps affirmed of the Nothing of God from which Rosenzweig's argument departs, and if No is more directly connected, as he also maintains, with God's freedom, God's essence is, as we put it, his Yessence, because No itself is a word that must be affirmed. We must distinguish, on the one hand, the rhetorical opposition between the Yes and No of affirmation and denial, as well as the nonparallel semantic opposition of True and False, from, on the other hand, the affirmation that appends a speaker's signature, *firma*, or mark to what he says, whether what he says, the word that is marked by it, is positive or negative, and whether what he says is true or false.

We must distinguish truth from truthfulness or, as Levinas variously writes, from veracity or sincerity, meaning not the veracity that is opposed to the deceit or insincerity with which I may address myself to another or to myself but the veracity in the name of which even such deceitfulness must be practiced. A No may masquerade as a Yes. One may be suspicious whether what appears to be a Yes is a No, but one's suspicion is always backed by a Yes. However far back one retreats, what one moves toward is not a No behind a Yes but a Yes behind a Yes or a No. Even the double denial, Nay Nay, of Nietzsche's ass is doubled by an Amen Amen posited in the beginning, however remotely the beginning is postponed, however immemorial its past, the past quasi-performative Thereby to which every Hereby owes its force.[6]

The difficult phrase "past quasi-performative Thereby" marks the difficult time and place of the tacit contract that any explicit contract presupposes. Rosenzweig's primal Amen is also tacit. He says, you will recall, that it is the silent accompaniment or companion (*der stille Begleiter*) of all parts of a sentence. This absolute reticence is required also by Levinas when he says that the Saying of witness without words, but not with empty hands ("Dire sans paroles, mais non pas les mains vides"), precedes the Said (DVI 122; CP 170). In saying this he runs the risk, fine or otherwise, of implying a primal speechless scene behind the scenes, a postontotheological version of the theological transcendentalism with which he and Nietzsche try to break. It is all too easy to slip into thinking of the unrememberable past on analogy with the myth of an age before the ages of the world. Perhaps this idea is fostered by reading Levinas through an oversimple reading of Rosenzweig and of a book that is too often present to be cited in the text of *The Star of Redemption*, Schelling's *Ages of the World*. Such a reading of Levinas cannot be correct for it makes use of a naive continuist notion of time that would be at best appropriate only to the Said. Nor are matters much improved when Levinas's many references to the unrepresentable past are taken together with his less frequent references to the unrepresentable future and that future is pictured as a messianic promised land on which we have not yet set foot. The chances of interpreting in this way Levinas's assertion of the precedence of Saying to the Said are dashed and drashed by his apparently contradictory assertion that something must be said, *dit*, about how things are before saying only pure saying, *dire* (AE 183-84 n. 7; OB 198 n. 7). This appearance of contradiction is the pivot of Levinas's appeal to the return of skepticism despite skepticism's apparent self-refutation. Rather than repeat here what he says about that, let me draw your attention to the apparent carelessness with which, in *Otherwise Than Being* at least, Levinas employs the expressions "on this side" (*en deçà*) and "on the other side" (*au-delà*). There seems to be no consistent pattern in his uses of these expressions. To mention only a few of these uses: "on this side of" is prefixed to references to nature and its states (AE 106; OB 83), to being, to the said, to the free and unfree (AE 94; OB 75), to ontology (AE 59; OB 46); the Self is said to be on this side of coincidence with itself (AE 143 n. 17; OB 195 n. 17); responsibility is said to be on this side of memorable time. "On the other side" or "beyond" is prefixed to essence, but in one and the same paragraph, when writing of the reduction of the said to the saying, Levinas says that this is a reduction to what is on the other side of Logos, and when explaining that it is not to an entity that the reduction of being leads, he writes disjunctively of what is "on this side or on that side of being" (AE 57, cf. 121; OB 45, cf. 95). It is as though his title could just as well have been *Autrement qu'être ou en deçà de l'essence* or *Autrement qu'être ou Au-delà ou en deçà de l'essence*. Either prepositional phrase is correct, depending on your point of view, and there are two points of view. However, to speak of points of view is to speak representationally and so to misrepresent the saying as a said. One moment of discourse is translated, but the other moment of discourse is betrayed (AE 31, 88; OB 24, 70). Betrayed, however, in both senses of the word. The point is made early in *Otherwise Than Being* when Levinas distinguishes the verbal infinite to-be from nominalized essence but notes that the verbality of the propositional to-be "makes essence resound without entirely deadening the echo of the to-say that bears it and brings it to light" (AE 60; CP ix; OB 47; CP xli). Perhaps there is a reecho of this echo in John Austin's discovery that his original attempt to distinguish constative from performative speech acts ends in defeat, because on the hither and thither side of what is stated there resounds the "hereby," the "hear hear," or Amen of ratification performing constation, perforating the message.[7] But the defeat of the moment of pure constation is not the triumph of the moment of the pure to-say. The to-say must suffer the defeat of the attempt to constate it. Only thus, through struggle and the pain of mourning (*lutte et douleur*), is confirmed the "thus," the *sic* of the saying that confirms or ratifies; only by contestation does it receive attestation (AE 148 n.; OB 195-96 n. 19). Only if the not entirely deadened echo of the to-say is an absolutely passive suffering in the activity of speech. Only if in this not entirely deadened echo resounds the death knell of a certain God, as Levinas says.

But, to return to our point of departure, why does his ethics within the bounds of ratification alone not also say Amen, Finis, End of History, to the word "God"? Why does his critique of pure religion say only À-*Dieu*, Good-bye, God-be-with-you, notwithstanding that the extraordinary word "God" will be a scandal to many potential readers of *Otherwise Than Being*? One reason perhaps is that the God you don't know is better than the God you think you do. If "God" is a word in the life of those to whom one is addressing in "Greek" the claim that ethics is *protéphilosophia*, then it is a word from which it would be dangerous to avert one's eyes. Ignored, it could hardly fail to be a stumbling block. This is a lesson Levinas teaches more insistently than do Heidegger and Derrida, the lesson that the old words cannot simply be abandoned in creating the new, that one cannot take leave without ceremony, the lesson, embalmed in the phrase *faire son deuil*, that to take one's leave may be to take on the difficulty of mourning. If, with some risk of oversimplification, it can be said that *Totality and Infinity* rises beyond being and fundamental ontology by demonstrating how being and ontology rise emphatically above their selves to what is "more ontological than ontology" (DVI 143), it can perhaps be said that *Otherwise Than Being* performs a similar feat for the word "God." "I pronounce the word God," Levinas writes in that book, "without suppressing the intermediaries that lead me to this word, and, if I may say so, the anarchy of its entry into discourse, just as phenomenology states concepts without ever destroying the scaffoldings that permit one to climb up to them" (AE 165; OB 128). Indeed, maybe this hyperbolization of the word "God" leans on the hyperbolization of "being"—and of another word whose power *Totality and Infinity* would interrupt: the word "power" itself, or *pouvoir*, to be able. For the de- and reconstrual without destruction of the word "God" that *Otherwise Than Being* would effect is modified by the adverb *peut-être*, "could-be." The essay entitled "The Name of God according to Certain Talmudic Texts" is collected in the volume entitled *L'au-delà du verset*. Although the subtitle of this volume is *Lectures et discours talmudiques*, that does not make them purely confessional texts. For when Levinas seeks to get beyond the verse it is in order to teach a philosophical lesson, and to do so in "Greek" (TrI 47). The essay in question is grouped with other readings Levinas calls "Theologies" in the plural, meaning by this not that any dogmatic theology is propounded in them but that they seek to speak in a rational way about God. And it is in a subsection entitled "Philosophy" of the essay on the name of God that he writes: "But the language of thematization that we are using at this very same moment has maybe been rendered only possible [*a peut-être été rendu seulement possible*] by this Relation and is only ancillary" (ADV 157). The Relation here referred to is that of the animating responsibility of which Levinas has said a moment before that "before discourse bearing on the said," it is "probably the essence of language." Here, meeting the difficulty for our "correlation" of Rosenzweig and Levinas presented by the fact that the latter wishes to pronounce the word "God" without letting divinity be said (AE 206; OB 162), the word "essence" wears the invisible shudder quotes with which Rosenzweig might have invested the word in the sentence I cited earlier which declares that "The first Yes in God establishes the divine essence for all infinity." Maybe the same should be said about the "maybe" in the sentence just cited from Levinas, even though he says in it that at that very same moment he is using the language of thematization. Does not the very same word in the moment of its thematization resound with the diachronically re-, pro- but not in-tended moment of the echoing Amen? And must not the same be said of those other modal words here encountered, "possible," "probably," and of the "maybe" as it is said once again in Levinas's statement that the word "illeity," a nominalized pronoun, marking the excluded third beyond being and nonbeing, beyond the modalities that are *Seinsweisen, manières d'être*, beyond skepticism and its self-refutation, marks maybe what is said also by the name or pronoun "God"?

This "maybe" is said, but still very unstraightforwardly, when Levinas refers to "the Revelation of the beyond being which is certainly maybe only a word [sic: *qui certes n'est peut-être qu'un mot* (!)]," adding "but this 'maybe' belongs to an ambiguity where the anarchy of the Infinite resists the univocity of an origin or principle; to an ambiguity or ambivalence and an inversion that is enunciated precisely in the word God" (AE 199; OB 156). This "maybe" does not belong to Heideggerian belonging. It is not from the meaning of being that the meaning of maybeing is drawn. Its *peut-être* draws its breath in a climate other than that of *Seinkönnen*. However, Levinas's claim that ethics is protophilosophy is not a simple inversion of the claim Heidegger made at Zurich in 1951 that "the experience of God and his revelation (so far as this comes man's way) takes place in the dimension of being."[8] It would have been necessary to speak of the shudder-producing things "the 'experience' of God" means for Levinas—*schauderhaft* things, we might say, following his citation from Goethe's *Faust* by way of epigraph to the final chapter of *Otherwise Than Being*, where the last thing which that citation invokes is sacramental fear and trembling—if we were to have tried to get to the bottom of the worry which has motivated this essay. That worry is a disquietude in the sense of the *Besorgnis* which Heidegger distinguishes from and subordinates to *Sorge*, existential care or concern, and its existential modes (BT 192). It is the worry over what *more* might be said except "illeity" and that anagram of "name," "Amen," by the exceptional name or pro-name "God." It would have been necessary to try to speak of the tests, trials, or ordeals, *épreuves*, Levinas is remembering when he says that phenomenology must be concrete, among them the events that took place between 1933 and 1945, of which he says that they contributed to his break with the later phenomenology of Husserl (EN 142), events which overflowed any idea of concrete experience Rosenzweig and Schelling could have invoked to explain what they meant when they described their philosophy or theology as "positive."[9] If Levinas is not caricaturing his teaching when he writes in *Entre nous* that human being is not only being-in-the-world, so not only being toward one's own death, but being toward the Book, *zum-Buch-sein* (EN 127), it may well be that the lay reader of that Book will have to make an effort to learn the ancient languages in which it was written, for "one cannot reject the Scriptures without knowing how to read them" (DL 77; DF 53). That is a responsibility and risk to which he may be called. However, if the *cri de cœur* of that reader after the death of God is to receive a response—and how, consistently with Levinas's doctrine, could the responsibility to give a response be denied?—it is important that that Book should be able to untie one's tongue from a shibboleth. It is important to see therefore that notwithstanding the oblique references on so many of Levinas's pages to the unpronounceable Name of God, notwithstanding his reference to the word "God" as a *hapax legomenon* (AE 199; OB 156), he insists that the relation to God is presented nonmetaphorically in the relation to the transcendence of the face of the other human being.

It so happens that the transcendence of the face is traced through the transcendence of a word in an exegesis recorded by Levinas of an incident commented on in *Sôta* 53b. According to Numbers 5 a woman suspected by her husband of adultery must be taken to the Temple where the pontiff exclaims, "If a man had intercourse with you, may you be cursed by the Eternal [written as Tetragram]." And the woman responds, "Amen, amen."[10] The pontiff's words containing the Tetragram are then written in ink on a parchment from which they are effaced by being immersed in the bitter water. In this way, Levinas notes, the ancient prohibition against the effacement of the Name is superseded for the sake of the reconciliation of human beings (ADV 152-53).

Another, though inevitably still not unenigmatic clue to the way an entry into the Book may be an entry into a humanism that is neither specifically Jewish nor specifically Christian is provided by Levinas's citation of the New Testament in support of his claim that although the Other is not to be identified with God, the Word of God is heard in the Other's face (*visage*), that is to say, in his or her looking to me (EN 128). According to Matthew 25, when those on the Lord's right hand and on his left protest that they have neither given nor refused food, drink, or shelter to Him, they are told, "Inasmuch as ye have done it unto one of the least of my brethren ye have done it unto me."

So in this humanism of the other human being in which atheism is defined as the restriction of thinking to intentional representation where the thinking and what is represented may in principle be mutually adequate (EN 145, 246) and, precisely by being so defined, allows of subversion by the nonintentionality of ethical "experience" that accompanies every intentional experience (EN 146) as the pre-original *responsio* Amen accompanies (*begleitet*) every word, maybe that experience, although expressed by the word God, is not dependent on that word for its expression; maybe that word does not have to be said when one says Amen. "'Me voici, au nom de Dieu'.... 'Me voici' tout court!" (AE 190; OB 149).

Or, reminding ourselves that hidden stumbling blocks are more dangerous than unhidden ones, lest the silent return of the God of a reality behind the scenes be facilitated by the obliteration of his name, should perhaps the iterated effacement of that name be effaced in turn by the eternal return of the name, forever coming and forever going, enigmatically on the hither side and on the thither side of the opposition between Yes and No, like the winking of a star? If so, although we may begin by reminding ourselves, as Léon Brunschvig reminds us, of the danger of worshipping the shadow of concepts we believe we have slain (DL 71; DF 48), and by realizing that a concept cannot be redefined without keeping the concept's old name, readers of Levinas must keep on reminding themselves that he is seeking neither to reinstate an old concept nor to introduce a new one in the manner of an astronomer scanning the heavens until his telescope comes to rest on a heavenly body so far overlooked. His writing is disastrous, a patient *écriture du dés-astre*. The frequentative trace in it of Rosenzweig's *Star* means precisely that the thinking beyond thinking which endures in it, its consideration beyond consideration, is not the tracking of a star, not *auf einen Stern zugehen*, even when that star is not a being but being, uniquely this, *nur dieses* (DMT 164).[11] On the hither and thither side of any star fixed in the firmament, susception before and after perception and conception, is the Amen, the pre-original Yes in which experience originates, affirmed by the Other in me (TeI 66; TaI 93), thanks to whom this me is never a me and no more, never a me *tout court*. If You, *Autrui*, the pronoun of the pronoun Me, has as its pronoun He, and He is the pronoun of God, otherwise other than *Autrui*, then, Yes, Amen, like Jonah, I cannot escape from God. But if (hereby to repeat Levinas's constation of contestation) voicing, the *en gage* of *langage*, is the fact (sic: *fait*) that "God" is the only word which always proffers itself as *Opfer* and is the very word which verily paroles transcendence, thereby suffering from an equivocity of which one moment is the contestation voiced by "It is maybe only a word" (AE 199; OB 156, NP 137), then it is maybe the only word that voices the worry with that word from which I cannot escape.

Notes

1. Franz Rosenzweig, *Der Stern der Erlösung*, 2nd. ed. (Frankfurt am Main: Kauffmann, 1930), 477; *The Star of Redemption*, trans. William W. Hallo (Notre Dame, Ind.: University of Notre Dame Press, 1985), 380.
2. Friedrich Nietzsche, *Ecce Homo, Kritische Gesamtausgabe*, ed. Giorgio Colli and Mazzino Montinari (Berlin: De Gruyter, 1967 ff), 6.3.333.

3. "...so umschreibt die Bejahung des Nichtnichts als innere Grenze die Unendlichkeit alles dessen, was nicht Nichts ist. Es wird ein Unendliches bejaht: Gottes unendliches Wesen, seine unendliche Tatsächlichkeit, seine Physis" (Rosenzweig, *Stern* 36, *Star* 26-27).
4. Robert Gibbs, *Correlations in Rosenzweig and Levinas* (Princeton: Princeton University Press, 1992), 32-33.
5. Ferdinand de Saussure, *Cours de linguistique générale* (Paris: Payot, 1971), 37; *Course in General Linguistics*, trans. Jonathan Culler (London: Fontana-Collins, 1974), 18-19.
6. Jacques Derrida, "En ce moment même dans cet ouvrage me voici," *Psyché* (Paris: Galilée, 1987), 187: "At this very moment in this work here I am," RL 34-35.
7. John Austin, *How to Do Things with Words* (Oxford: Clarendon Press, 1962), Lecture XI.
8. *Aussprache mit Martin Heidegger an 06/XI/1951*, Vortragsausschuss der Studentenschaft der Universität Zürich, Zürich, 1952. This is not, as far as I am aware, commercially available, but it is reproduced in part with acknowledgment to Jean Beaufret by Jean-Luc Marion, *Dieu sans l'être* (Paris: Communio/Fayard, 1982), 93, and translated by Jean Greisch in *Heidegger et la question de Dieu*, Richard Kearney and Joseph Stephen O'Leary, ed.(Paris: Grasset, 1980), 333-34, and by D. Saatdjian and F. Fédier in *Poésie* (Paris) 13 (1980), 60-61.
9. "I prefer the word *épreuve* to *expérience* because in the word *expérience* a knowing of which the self is master is always said. In the word *épreuve* there is at once the idea of life and of a critical 'verification' which overflows the self of which it is only the 'scene.'" Interview in Salomon Malka, *Lire Lévinas* (Paris: Cerf, 1984), 108.
10. "Yes," according to James Joyce, as well as being "the most positive word in the human language," is also "the female word." See Richard Ellmann, *James Joyce* (Oxford: Oxford University Press, 1983), 522, 501.
11. Maurice Blanchot, *L'écriture du désastre* (Paris: Gallimard, 1980). Martin Heidegger, *Aus der Erfahrung des Denkens* (Pfullingen: Neske, 1954), 7: "Auf einen Stern zugehen, nur dieses ..."

20
Adieu, à dieu, a-Dieu

Hent de Vries

At first glance, Levinas's intransigent critique of Kierkegaard's distinction of the ethical from the religious dimension seems to pose no major obstacle for the attempt to retrace what is at stake in the project of *Totality and Infinity*. Nor does it seem to pose a problem for the interpretation of the later works. What bothers Levinas in Kierkegaard ("Ce qui me gêne dans Kierkegaard…," he writes in the essay devoted to this author and reprinted in *Noms propres* [112]) is the fact that his notion of a subjective existence that in its irreducible interiority or secrecy retreats from the order of the general and universal and thereby "rejects all form," is—paradoxically—also in danger of adopting an "exhibitionist" and "violent" (NP 112) pathos. It is, Levinas claims, perhaps since Kierkegaard and not since Nietzsche that we have learned what it means to philosophize with a hammer and thus to become sensitive to a "new tone in philosophy" (NP 106). This new tone exalts in "a permanent scandal," in an "opposition to everything" and is in some regards the echo of, the prelude or the overture to the worse violence yet to come. For there is a certain resonance here, Levinas does not hesitate to suggest, with all the tremors brought about by National Socialism and all its intellectual and cultural allies (NP 112).

The violence and harshness (*dureté*) of Kierkegaard's writing would manifest itself precisely at that moment of the dialectical lyric at which personal existence, in passing beyond (*dépassant*) the aesthetic stage, also "transgresses [*dépasse*] the ethical" (NP 106, 112) in order to enter a religious realm of a faith which no longer lets itself be justified on external grounds. This transgression not only turns faith into an absolutely *singular* event in which sublime communication and utter solitude coincide; it also reduces the ethical to the *general*, to the rule of law applicable to all, in which the very secret of the self as well as of its innermost secret decisions will always be betrayed (NP 106).

But, Levinas asks, does the ethical really reside where Kierkegaard thinks it does, that is to say in some generality? Does it not consist in a responsibility toward another person (to *autrui*, that is) that, instead of absorbing me in the universal, precisely "*singularizes*" me by putting me in a "unique" (NP 113) and irreplaceable position? Does Kierkegaard's association of the ethical with the general not "prejudge" the interpretation, given in *Fear and Trembling*, of the story related in Genesis 22 of how God tempted Abraham by demanding him to take his son Isaac and present him as a burnt offering on the mountain Moriah? And is it an accident that Kierkegaard chooses to ignore that other story about Abraham, according to which he intervenes on behalf of those few just who might still be found in the idolatrous cities of Sodom and Gomorrah which are destined for destruction (see Genesis 18, 23-33)? Is it not precisely here, in Abraham's *ethical* gesture, that the very "preamble" [*le préalable*] to "every possible triumph of life over death" is formulated, as a "gift of sense," "in spite of death" (NP 113)? Is it not here, in the relation to the Infinite which emerges only *in* and *as* this responsibility for (other) mortals, that Abraham becomes aware of his own finitude or mortality? According to Levinas the exclamation "'I am cinders and dust' almost opens the encounter and the annihilating flame of the divine anger burns before Abraham's eyes at each of his interventions" (NP 109; MT 135).

Kierkegaard is wrong, Levinas argues, when he identifies the ethical that Abraham—in raising the knife—leaves behind with an abstract universal distinguished from the religious realm. For the most remarkable moment of the narrative is not so much the fact that through the encounter with the infinite God, the finite subject is said to "elevate itself to the religious level," as if God were to be found outside, above, beyond, in short, external to the ethical order. The decisive moment of the dramatic scene is, rather, the instant in which Abraham hears the voice which *calls and leads him back to the ethical order:* "That he had obeyed the first voice is astonishing; that he had kept with regard to this obedience sufficient distance to be able to hear the second voice—that, precisely, is essential" (NP 109).

But are the two voices that Levinas sets apart in his reading of Genesis 22 not in fact different intonations or modulations of "one and the same" voice, that of the "one" Other, that of the Other as "the One"? Does God speak in different tongues here? Are his dictates contradictory since he first promises Abraham will have descendants through Isaac, who is given to him in old age, and then makes the fulfillment of this promise impossible by demanding that he be sacrificed? Is the voice that calls Abraham to order, interrupts his sacrifice, and recalls him to the ethical God's genuine voice, whereas the first (the one that brings him to the point of committing the crime) is only a simulacrum, a *flatus vocis* open to misinterpretation? Is it the ruse of a demonic impostor or the—perhaps necessary—temptation of the ethical?

Kierkegaard's attempt to subtract the secret interiority of the subject both from the *aesthetic* stage of "sensible dispersion" (NP 100) and despair and from the *ethical* generality of the legal order, of social institution, and intersubjective communication is bound to fail. Only the continuously reiterated "salto mortale" of faith, a leap into the "solitude" of the "tête-à-tête" (NP 103) with God, would constitute in its very silence the true communication. But the *ipse* that Kierkegaard seems to adopt and to oppose here to the Hegelian dialectic remains, Levinas claims, a constitutive moment of the order of the Same—an *idem*—which ultimately cannot escape the speculative logic of Absolute Idealism. In its very *incommunicability*—in the *brûlure* of its *sin* and in the *thirst for salvation*, which can be neither expressed nor mitigated by any objective order—it retains the structure if not of self-*reflection*, then at least of a self-centeredness, of a tense self-concern (a *tension sur soi*) (NP 100). The Kierkegaardian self betrays here both its Christian and its pagan source. It is the modern existentialist form of a self-identification, not so much according to a formal tautological scheme—"the repetition of A is A"—but in harmony with the concrete phenomenological structure that describes the "identification of A as A" as "the anxiety of A for A" (NP 101). The quest of existence for its own redemption and pardon thus resembles the Hegelian struggle for *Anerkennung* as well as the Heideggerian *Sorge*, both of which, Levinas maintains, are nothing but translations of the sixth proposition of the third part of Spinoza's *Ethica*, of the *conatus essendi*. And it is precisely this premise, this presupposition (*Unaquaeque res, quantum in se est, in suo esse perseverare conatur*), that Levinas puts into question: "The human *esse* is not *conatus* but *désintéressement* and *adieu*" (MT 25). It does not emerge as a superstructure to Being but, on the contrary, marks a "for-nothingness" (*gratuité*) in which the perseverance of (and *in*) Being "undoes itself" (MT 32). Other "humanity," humanity more paradoxical than the anthropology of the West can even fathom, can only be thought responsibly as "the fact of suffering for the other and, in this very suffering, suffering for the suffering that my suffering inflicts upon the other" (SS 149-80, 167). The irreducibility of a responsible subjectivity, then, of the responsibility of the self as well as of the risks it has to run, should be understood in different terms from those of a philosophy of identity and/or of speculative totality, and, Levinas hastens to add, along very different lines from those sketched by the Kierkegaardian, existentialist, "nonphilosophy" (NP 102). The ethical moment cannot be identified with the usurpation of a purported, pure and silent interior by an exterior order or objectivity (NP 102).

Kierkegaard would have seen that the dialectical transition from the egocentric self to discourse, described by Hegel as "the *possibility to speak*," is only thinkable as the covering over of "a remote impossibility of discourse" (NP 101). The very notion of the persecuted truth would come to stand for the "insight" (although there is nothing to be seen here) that, dialectically or speculatively speaking, the very moment and momentum of the subject's decision is an inexplicable instant of "madness," a "moment of crisis," which is never given without *passion*.[1] Levinas raises doubts, however, as to whether the irreducibility of this "passionate decision" should be ascribed to the subject's interiority. It is not the secret of the individual ego that, in the final analysis, disrupts the totality and the political totalitarianism of the Hegelian system but, Levinas claims, only the Other (*l'Autre*) (TeI 10; TaI 39-

40). This other does not have the objectivity of a political or symbolic order, nor, for that matter, does it attain the generality and the relative stability of a logical category, of alterity as such. Rather, this other, whether as *autrui* or as the Infinite that leaves its trace in the other's face or visage, "is" always singular and indeed always contested, persecuted, threatened, haunted, shadowed, mirrored, and mimicked by the worst.

It is important to recall, at this point, that in Levinas's account of the ethical the "ethicity" of ethics is therefore not kept at a safe distance from *its* other, as if it could *calculate* or *wager* without being haunted by the specter of the immoral or, for that matter, the amoral. On the contrary, the premoral anonymity of the *there is*, of the *il y a*, the chaotic *tohu v'vohu* which is said to precede the divine act of creation but which at any given time can come to unsettle the world of beings forms and deforms the condition of possibility of every ethical intrigue. And the paraexperiences of the *exoticism* of modern art, of the phenomenological thought experiment of *world destruction*, of fatigue and sleeplessness would remind us of this (conceptually and experientially) impossible "possibility" of the possible.

The interminable passage, back and forth, from absolute obligation to the ethical order, mediated by reason and the state, as well as from this order back to the anarchy of responsibility and even further "down" into the depths of a trauma, and an absurdity of suffering for the other, *for nothing*—this alternation is precisely what constitutes the drama of an ethics which is neither that of neo-Aristotelean virtues nor that of Kantian pure duty but which, in a way to be described in further detail, takes place within the space opened up by Nietzsche, without, however, being confined to it. The *au-delà* (or, for that matter, the *en deçà*) of Levinasian "transcendence" is beyond the "beyond" of "beyond good and evil."

Levinas never forgets to inscribe "the other, oblique, face of the Other" in his description of the ethical situation: there is no ethical transcendence without trans-*descendence*, we read in *Totality and Infinity* (TeI 66; TaI 93). And the indifferent, yet radically different *il y a* to which this descent into—and beyond—the elements or the "elemental" of our experience leads us should in the final analysis, *Otherwise than Being* demonstrates, be considered as a "modality" (AE 208-9; OB 164)—perhaps as *the* modality—of the otherwise than being that disrupts the *conatus essendi*, the perseverance of each being in its own being, particularly in the face of its own death. It is as if only this "*il-y-a-*tic" modality of the relation to the ab-solute breaks away from the "Eleatic" God who, since Parmenides, has been "contaminated" (AE x; OB xlii) by Being. Moreover, the recurrence of—and of the return into—the *il y a* protects this ab-solute relation to the ab-solute from being misunderstood and perverted in a moralistic sense.

Only violent figures, figures which render one speechless, like that of a "catastrophic fire," of an "ignition," of "burning," of "the flame," of a "holocaust," and of "cinders," seem to suffice to evoke the passion of this responsibility, in which the "subject" does not simply eclipse but literally burns up, like a candle or a torch. Levinas speaks of the "gnawing away at oneself" (*se ronger*, AE 155; OB 121), thereby giving yet another meaning to the notion of *incarnation*, that of a *carnage in the flesh*;

that the *in*finite leaves this intrigue *in* the finite is just another way of saying that responsibility *eats its way in and through the flesh*, infinitely. Solely by hollowing "itself" out—only by turning "itself" "inside out"—is the self capable of *giving*. Responsibility "is" the consummation—the self-consummation—of the self. And yet this consummation *is* not, properly speaking: it signals an otherwise than being, an otherwise than whatever *is*. And to underscore the interminability of its movement, Levinas stresses that the Other, who can never be *incorporated* by me, precisely affects me without *absorbing* me. We are thus dealing with a relationship that, "while remaining one of *the more in the less*, is not transformed into the relationship in which, according to the mystics, the butterfly drawn by the fire is consumed in the fire" (CP 54). The relation does "not sink into participation, against which the *philosophy of the same* will have the immortal merit to have protested" (CP 54).

The passage from the self to the other, then, is a passing away in which the self becomes its "own" other in an endless, *infinite* incineration or *pure brûlure* (AE 150 n. 21; OB 196 n. 21). Not that there is any "magic" of "purification" at work here. The "pure burning" stands for a "surplus of non-sense over sense," indeed a "suffering for nothing," for an other who withdraws himself from the relation to the point of not even showing his face. It is precisely this withdrawal or *ab-solvere* of an absolute relation with the absolute, as *Fear and Trembling* formulates it, that keeps responsibility from ever being assumed in freedom or in good conscience.

How, then, should we understand the relationship between the Kierkegaardian displacement of ethics and that other ethics, that other ethics of the other, the ethics of that other other for which the name Levinas stands here? Why their common preoccupation, or rather obsession, with "the worst," with a certain suspension of the ethical, whether through the sacrifice of the ethical or through the haunting non-sense of the *il y a*? How to read the uncanny circumstance that the "binding" (*Akedah*) of Isaac on the altar of a holocaust entails a *double* or even *triple bind* in which the moral community, God, and the "demonic" are uncannily intertwined? And is it an accident that Levinas takes the utterance "Here I am!" (*me voici, hinneni*), which throughout his writings comes to stand for the *alpha* and *omega* of responsibility, from precisely this biblical passage, thereby giving it an almost paradigmatic stature?

One way of answering this question would be to take a closer look at yet another reading of Kierkegaard that sheds light on the aforementioned suspension of the ethical in the face of the totally other, indeed of the other-than-other, and helps us to better describe the movement and the implications of the *à Dieu*, whose semantic—and perhaps no longer simply semantic potential—the translation *to God* or *toward God* renders only in part.

Like Kierkegaard and Levinas, Derrida, in a recent text entitled "Donner la mort" ("Giving Death"), reads the story of the sacrifice of Isaac as the narrative ellipsis of the paradoxical logic of obligation, of absolute responsibility, and of decision that marks the ethical—and more than simply ethical—relation with the absolute Other for which "God" is also here the singular proper name, and perhaps the most proper name.

One is tempted to interpret this "exegesis" of Genesis (of this genesis of morals, mediated as it is through the reading of *Fear and Trembling*, much more than through, say, Nietzsche's *Genealogy*) as yet another supplementary note to the dossier of "Violence and Metaphysics" and "At this very moment in this work here I am." These texts at the heart of *L'écriture et la différence* and *Psychè* had marked the first two major instances of Derrida's encounter with the work of Levinas. But, as always, the supplement, in a sense, was already there, setting the tone for the very first text. For already in the first reading Derrida draws our attention to a certain injustice and an unresolved debate in Levinas's reading of Kierkegaard: "Let us add, in order to do him *justice*, that Kierkegaard had a sense of the relationship to the irreducibility of the totally-other, not in the egoistic and esthetic here and now, but in the religious beyond of the concept, in the direction of a certain Abraham." Not unlike Levinas, Derrida continues, Kierkegaard sees "in Ethics, as a moment of Category and Law, the forgetting, in anonymity, of the subjectivity of religion." It is precisely against this background, Derrida says, that for Kierkegaard "the ethical moment is Hegelianism itself, and he says so explicitly. Which does not prevent him from reaffirming ethics in repetition, and from reproaching Hegel for not having constituted a morality" (WaD 111; ED 163-64).

This "juxtaposition" of the names and the thought of Kierkegaard and Levinas, despite the latter's repeated admonition not to confuse the Christian thirst for personal salvation with the genuine desire for the other, should not make us forget, Derrida notes, that "as concerns the essential in its initial inspiration Levinas's protest against Hegelianism is foreign to Kierkegaard's protest" (WaD 111; ED 164). To be sure, if the Levinasian notion of ethics can be said to stand for "an Ethics without law and without concept, which maintains its *non-violent* purity only before being determined as concepts and laws" (WaD 111; ED 164, emphasis added), it should be noted that it is not without some violence of its own. Regardless of this resemblance, however, Levinas "often warns us against confusing—as one is so tempted to do—his anti-Hegelianism with a subjectivism, or with a Kierkegaardian type of existentialism, both of which would remain, according to Levinas, violent and premetaphysical egoisms" (WaD 110; ED 162).

And yet it should also be noted that notwithstanding his emphasis on the "peace of absolutes," Levinas does not shy away from describing the "shock" with which "the revelation of the infinite conquers my consciousness,"[2] gives it conscience and makes it responsible, in terms of another "violence," as a "violence" of the other. Here, of course, "violence" would be attributed—quite paradoxically—to the "welcoming of a being to which [consciousness] is inadequate" (TeI xiii; TaI 25). This "violence," therefore, would not be of the same order as the "violence" that it comes to judge or call to a halt. For the so-called "good violence"—the "violence" *with* and *as* which "the good" appears—would not be identical with the violations of identities attributed to terror and war. And yet in its very structure it would *somehow* seem to resemble nothing less than "the worst." Levinas would thus invite us to consider an unsentimental and at bottom unsettling account of the intrigue and the drama of responsibility and the testimony it provokes. If violence, in its most disturbing features, could be said to "aim" at the "face" of another, at a face, moreover, which is human, then it should not only be stressed, as Jean-Luc Nancy does, that violence "also originates from a face, on which wickedness can, occasionally, be read *as the devastation of this same face.*"[3] For even beyond this distinction of the good and the evil, another "violence"—the "violence" of another "other"—would continue to haunt.

According to Kierkegaard, Derrida elaborates in "Donner la mort," the testimony of obligation entails an anxiety in the face of a *given death,* or rather of a *giving of death,* of a *donner la mort,* that is also a monstrosity: the necessity to choose between one's love and the sacrifice of this love.[4] Abraham transgresses the order of the ethical, which for Kierkegaard stands for the validity of and the respect for a universal law or generality, not only or not primarily that of Kantian morality (*Moralität*) but also that of Hegelian ethical life (*Sittlichkeit*), as well as that of plain common sense; in short, of that which ties us not only to formal or abstract rules but also to family, neighbors, friends, and nation. By obeying what he takes to be God's command to go out and sacrifice his most beloved son, and by keeping his intentions secret, by speaking, of necessity, to no one, Abraham violates—indeed *sacrifices*—the basic principles that, *for good reasons,* that is, *rightfully,* govern every human community. Ethically speaking, Kierkegaard insists, Abraham commits a criminal act. Ethically speaking, the sacrifice is nothing but murder. From a religious perspective, however, from a perspective that can only be ascribed to God and the "knight of faith," Abraham's decision represents "the movement to infinity." And the latter is *at once, in the same instant* a movement of renunciation, of "infinite resignation" and a "grasping everything again by virtue of the absurd."[5]

In what sense, then, could what is called the religious relation here—that is, the sacrifice of what one loves in a movement of infinite resignation—be understood as the condition or the in-condition of possibility of what is called here the ethical?

Abraham, Derrida comments, is responsible "to God and before God" (*à Dieu et devant Dieu*[6]), face to face with a God who withdraws himself from this relation and shows, if anything, his hither, indeed ugly side. The face of the other is a Janus face. The bind (*Akedah* means, literally, binding) is double also in that it ties Abraham—and, for that matter, Isaac—to the apparition of a God who has at least the appearance of having, at least, two faces. And it is precisely this doubling of the good God who gives and his evil genius who takes away that accounts for the unsettling tension of this story, as well as of every "act."

What the suspension of all naturalistic, rational, or communicational ethics makes clear is that to speak *in* or *on* obligation comes down to speaking *of* and *to* "God." It is to speak *of* and *to* the *tout autre,* the *totally other,* but also *of* and *to* the *tout autre,* in the sense of *every other,* every other totally other, with a gesture in which the *address* and a certain *suspension*—an *à Dieu* and an *adieu,* a going toward God and a leave taking—coincide in an enigmatic way. The *a*—with and without *an accent grave,* separated from and linked to *Dieu/dieu*—in the ambiguity of the *à* and the *a,* would stand as much for a *turning toward* as for a *turning away from,* and only thus constitute the very enigma, the "duration," "inspiration," and "prophecy" of time. The turn of phrase it introduces into language would mark the distance from any linear movement stretched out in the direction of a goal, a *telos* or vision (TrI 36). And we could go one step further here. The address marked by the *a* would also say farewell to the omnipotent, omniscient, and benevolent God of ontotheology and with the same gesture face the oblique or nether flip side of God, the other—*un*- or *a-godly*—face of the other, the faceless face of *no god, Niemand, pas de dieu, a-dieu*, a "'transcendence to the point of absence'" (CP 166; cf. DVI 115).

Granted, neither Levinas nor Derrida *seems* to mention the possible privative interpretation of the *a-dieu* that, perhaps somewhat violently, can be distinguished from the *à Dieu* as address and the *adieu* as a gesture of leave taking or departure. Only Kierkegaard seems to explicitly thematize the fact that in the silent agony of Abraham both the *divine* and the *demonic* cast their shadow and, more uncanny still, *shadow—or haunt, if not mirror—each other*. While the "tragic hero," "the favorite of ethics," stands for the "purely human," the one who one can "understand," whose "undertakings are out in the open," the knight of faith belongs to a different category, to a category, that is, beyond all category. Here one would "run up against the paradox" that silence belongs to both the divine and the demonic: "Silence is the demon's trap, and the more that is silenced, the more terrible the demon, but silence is also divinity's mutual understanding with the single individual."[7]

Stretching his argument further, one could maintain that following the structure of a similar paradox, Levinas also describes how the ungenerous sonority of "the impersonal being: *il*" (EeI 37) at the bottom of the *il y a* is *as ab-solute* as its equally incommensurable counterpart, the so-called *illéité*. Moreover, the *il y a* could be said to form and de-form the condition and the possibility of the trace of this *illéité*. In a disturbing way the *illéité*, the "third person: He at the bottom of the Thou" (DVI 114), and the *il y a*—another *excluded third*, which 'is' beyond Being and not-Being but also without common measure with the Heideggerian *es gibt*—would thus constitute the two poles of one and the same elliptical "experience." *Il y a* and *illéité* would alternate and resonate to the point of becoming interchangeable as the comedy "enacted equivocally between temple and theater" and in which "the laughter sticks to one's throat when the neighbor approaches" (CP 166). To live face to face with the Other implies to face also the other than the Other, the absolutely other of the Other, and this to the point of "sacrilege." Even though Abraham embarks on his mission at the breaking of dawn, the nocturnal element is not left behind but filters through the daylight. Night casts its shadow *en plein jour* (SS 168).

The in-direct, im-mediate, ab-solute relation to the Ab-solute thus implies a relation to the other of the Other, to the oblique and nether side of God, to the haunting of the *il y a* in the trace—the echo or the shadow—of the *illéité*. And if it is true that one cannot describe the relation to God (*à Dieu*) without speaking of the relation to the neighbor, the other man (*autrui*), it must also be said—by implication or otherwise—that this relation finds the "condition of its possibility" in what always threatens to make it *im*possible, that is to say, the other of the Other, the Other Other, the other than other, the otherwise than other, the otherwise than otherwise than being, or rather the otherwise than being yet otherwise still.

"Being" nonteleological, nondialectical, nonintentional, nondialogical, noncommunicational, the *à Dieu* would address a *giving* of the one *to* the other, which—at the same time—would mean a *giving up* of oneself, that is to say, of being oneself—one's own self or, in other words, of *one* self—to the point of being invaded or hollowed out by the surplus of non-sense over sense that makes sense—as a genuine signal of and to the other—possible.

In *La mort et le temps*, Levinas describes this condition as follows: the impossibility of having oneself replaced in one's responsibility, that is, of one taking the place of, or substituting for, the other, is a passivity, indeed a "patience which must risk itself in the eventuality of non-sense and even face to face with the discovery of the arbitrary;" for if its meaning were that of an "inevitable obligation," if there were not the danger and the threat of a "madness," it would become "self-sufficient," an "institution" with a "statute" and an "enterprise" (MT 23). This necessary possibility of non-sense, then, is not only guaranteed by a deference with respect to a death which does not let itself be "situated" and cannot be "objectified"; it remains the "reverse side of a unthinkable dimension" (MT 23).

Only the possibility of the suspension of the ethical, then, is what makes the ethical possible. One does not have to speak here, with Kierkegaard in his first "Problema," of a *teleological* suspension of the ethical. It suffices to acknowledge that a structural similarity and always possible confusion between the *il y a* on the one hand and ethical transcendence on the other, between horror and the sublime, guarantees the very moment, movement, and momentum of responsibility. And the latter may well be "a deficit, waste, and foolishness in being" (DVI 114; CP 165),[8] an entering of the "divine comedy" in which there is no place for tragic heroes but only for the silent testimony of saints, the wordless gestures of the knights of faith.

Notes

1. S. Kierkegaard, *Fear and Trembling*, trans. Howard V. Hong and Edna H. Hong (Princeton: Princeton University Press, 1983), 42n.
2. Adriaan Peperzak, *To the Other: An Introduction to the Philosophy of Emmanuel Levinas* (West Lafayette, Ind.: Purdue University Press, 1993), 129.
3. Jean-Luc Nancy, *The Experience of Freedom*, trans. Bridget McDonald (Stanford: Stanford University Press, 1993), 204 n. 2.
4. Jacques Derrida, "Donner la mort," in *L'Éthique du don, Jacques Derrida et la pensée du don*, Colloque de Royaumont, Décembre 1990 (Paris: Métaillié-Transition, 1992), 11-18, 68.

5. Kierkegaard, *Fear and Trembling*, 40.
6. Derrida, "Donner la mort," 72.
7. Kierkegaard, *Fear and Trembling*, 88.
8. Translation modified.

Part Six: Levinas and Benjamin

21
Facies Hippocratica

Rebecca Comay

I wish to consider a certain "proximity" (all the more imperative for lack of contact) between Levinas and Benjamin. The point is not comparison—whether through a token gesture toward the residues of a poorly understood (at least by Benjamin) "Jewish" tradition or by way of specific historical confluences (Rozenzweig, Buber, Bloch)—an exercise that would be perverse and pointless insofar as such parallels would be trivialized by the performative contradiction inherent in the historicist effort to connect. Nor is it a question of using Benjamin to correct Levinas (and vice versa) according to a logic of complementarity. Tempting as such a dialectic might be—invoking Benjamin, say, to politicize Levinas (as if Levinas had forgotten something), enlisting Levinas to fill in Benjamin's elliptical and occasionally, it must be said, patchy theology (as if Benjamin had not got around to something)—that appropriation would be equally problematic.

So if I seem to lean on Benjamin to supply what is, in Levinas, if not lacking, at least (for essential reasons) attenuated—I mean the complex of history, politics, the "public space of appearances"—it is not a question of importing a missing theme. If Benjamin appears to offer the political supplement required to think the ethical in a non-"clandestine" fashion (thus to think the ethical *as such*), such supplement will have been initiated from within Levinas's own terms. Which is not that Benjamin has nothing to *add*.

If, then, I invoke Benjamin frequently—appear initially not to *face* Levinas directly—such "asymmetry" implies neither subjective preference nor objective dominance (obviously easily reversible) but signals the need to disengage an opposition running not only between both thinkers but within each insofar as both problematize the gap and thus the proximity at stake.

I am referring to the hyphen (properly a caesura) of the theological-political.

Part One

An obvious parallel and hypothesis: does not Benjamin's notion of "aura" exemplify Levinasian "proximity"? The classic formulation defines the former "as a unique appearance of a distance, however close it may be. If someone resting on a summer afternoon follows a mountain range on the horizon or a branch which casts its shadow over him, he breathes the aura of this mountain, this branch."[1]

Passing over the significance of this example from nature (and ignoring the residues of the Kantian sublime), I will only point to the motifs of height, inspiration (the Latin etymology of "aura" indicates breath or wind), singularity, deixis, asymmetry, and, finally, the discontinuously spatial "distance" characterizing this encounter with an alterity all the more radical for being non-anthropomorphic. Such distance operates not only despite phenomenal proximity but precisely because of it. Benjamin elsewhere invokes the "primal erotic relationship between nearness and distance"—I here ignore the complication arising from the introduction (and effacement) of the theme of sexual difference—characterized by an imbrication of attraction and withdrawal. "How the beloved [*die Geliebte*] becomes distant and gleaming [*blinkend*], how her minuteness and her glow withdraw" (II.1.362; R 268). Such attraction is epitomized by the "Platonic love of language" attributed to Karl Kraus: "The more closely you look at a word, the more distantly it looks back." In short, an *approach* is at stake.

The introduction of the theme of arrested vision, a gaze both prolonged and preempted by the "blinking" counterlook that draws insofar as it withdraws from visibility, a *Sehen* sustained and limited by a prior *Ziehen*, leads directly to the topic of the face.

Benjamin's second, slightly less familiar definition reads: "There is the expectation, when we look at someone, that the recipient of the glance will return [*erwidert*] our look. When this expectation is met... there is the experience of aura in its fullness. 'Perceptibility,' as Novalis puts it, 'is a kind of attentiveness.'... The experience of aura rests on the transfer [*Übertragung*] of a response common in human society to the relationship between the inanimate, or nature, and human beings. The person who is seen... returns the glance. To experience the aura of a phenomenon means to invest it [*belehnen*] with the ability to look at us in turn [*den Blick aufschlagen*] (I.2.646; CB 147-48).

I'll bypass the interesting complication implied by the notion of a "transfer" to the natural world (again the imbrication of trope and anthropomorphism) and emphasize the theme of "attention." Benjamin elaborates this as a "glance" (*Blick*) to be "returned" or "countered" in the sense of "contested," "resisted," and thus displaced *(erwidert)*. What initially presents itself as a recognition scene—symmetrical, recuperative, tautological—is immediately problematized insofar as the glance is tropically deflected, is reflected precisely in being refused, in a movement without totalization. If the look presents itself *economically*—as an "investment" assuming a returning dividend or surcharge (*Aufschlag*)—its logic exemplifies a sacrificial expenditure without return. Elsewhere Benjamin suggests that the circle of identification is ruptured by the very logic of mimesis otherwise implying empathy or conformism. The mimetic faculty yields affinities "opaque" (II.1.314; ILL 204) in their similarity, appearing evanescently, in a "flash," "flitting by" with the speed of reading (II.1.212-13; R 335-36). Briefly: these "nonsensuous" correspondences do not *appear*.

The final elaboration introduces the issue of desire. "The painting we look at reflects back at us that of which our eyes will never be sated. That which fulfills desire would be the very thing on which this desire incessantly feeds. What distinguishes painting from photography is therefore clear...: to the eyes that will never have their fill of a painting, photography is rather like food for the hungry or drink for the thirsty" (I.2.645; CB 146). Again, I slide over all the complications, here arising from Benjamin's introduction of the artwork as exemplary auratic object. I want to consider this notion of a desire beyond need, exceeding the restricted circle of self-preservation—*orexis*, *appetitus*, the representational calculus of *perceptio*—defining Marx's "realm of necessity." Such desire—Bloch's "other, transcendental hunger"—marks the limits of appeasement. In refusing the consolations of every finite, "culinary" satisfaction, it grows only stronger in being satisfied and thus resists accommodation to every present.

And so on. If I refrain from pursuing this set of parallels (the drift is obvious), it is because what concerns me is less aura per se than what Benjamin will characterize, in curiously naturalistic language, as its "withering," "unpeeling," "decay," or "decline"—*Verfall* (I.2.477-79; ILL 221-23), an event simultaneously mourned and celebrated, by Benjamin, as the 1930s pick up steam.

Part Two

It is not through inconsistency or bad faith that Benjamin will inflect the notion of aura in apparently opposed ways. What seems valorized (in Levinasian language) under the "holy" rubric of proximity will prove inseparable from its "sacred" manifestation—an event institutionalized as a form of privilege: noumenon congealed into numen, height into power, asymmetry into hierarchy, proximity congealed into an authoritarian distance all the more alluring for being unbreached. "Attention" will have crystallized into the "absorption" of the spectator within the consoling plenitude of *schöne Schein*. Singularity would be finitized as numerical self-identity within the totality of given ends. Transcendence would be reified as otherwordliness, enigma as the exclusive clandestinity marking the regime of private property, the deictic "me voici" as the "pagan" particularism of a Place. Thus Benjamin writes, referring to the artwork's reification of contingency, of "a unique existence in the place where it happens to be" (I.2.475; ILL 220). In short, idolatry. This is the "bad" aura (thaumaturgic, ultimately fascist) whose demystification Benjamin apparently celebrates in 1935 in the name of a radical *enlightenment*.

It is photography that is introduced as exemplar and occasion of the desacralizing movement challenging the authority of the occult. Photography signifies the ultimate effacement of auratic distance in effecting the homogenization of social space. As its name suggests, photography would be the supreme instance of writing (as described from Plato to Levinas): the displacement of original "expression" by "copies, signs and images," self-attestation by representation *in absentia*, enigma by phenomenon, "revelation" by the "disclosure"[2] characteristic of a visibilized world.

Photography is the convertibility of light and writing—the untethered universality of a heliology bespeaking the utter "betrayal" (to use Levinas's language) of the "plenitude" of oral speech (TeI 37, 69; TaI 66, 96). But photography does not violate an aura somehow pristine in its proximity. The camera's violence supervenes only on a previously occluded violence—initiating the "violent shattering" (I.2.477; ILL 221) of a tradition characterized by exclusivity or domination—such that this prior coercion comes to light. For photography exposes the aura to have been already implicated in its own self-betrayal, figuring in its own disfigurement: what is defaced is a face already defaced in having entered the regime of prestige and power. The "decay" of aura is the decay of an always already degenerated form of aura, the doubling or intensification (but equally the twisting and displacement) of an "originary" decline, the fall of a fall (*Ver-fall*).

Thus the fall into the faceless urban crowd. Benjamin enumerates the disfigured faces of a public realm characterized by the transparency of light: the dandy's tics and grimaces; Baudelaire's daily changes of mask, ephemeral as those of a "ham actor"; the fashionable hairdos designed to be seen in silhouette; the vacant stares of Simmel's streetcar passengers; the mirror-eyes of Baudelaire's prostitutes—"tes yeux illuminés ainsi que des boutiques." Such eyes fascinate because, in reflecting everything, they simultaneously crowd and evacuate the space of proximity, substituting for the distanced nearness of desire the claustrophobic remoteness that Benjamin calls "sex." "In eyes that mirror, the absence of the looker remains complete. It is precisely for this reason that such eyes know nothing of distance" (I.2.649-50; CB 150-51).

In such a disfigured world the face itself becomes the compensatory phantasm testifying to the immeasurable loss of transcendence—happy faces plastered onto a universe packaged as merchandise, whose inviting smiles ("look, don't touch") exemplify the "theological caprices" of which Marx speaks. According to Benjamin's articulation of the classic chapter on commodity fetishism, "things" acquire speech, glance, personality—the anthropomorphic features stripped from a reified humanity—in a chiastic transfer whereby man vicariously "saves face" and thus prolongs by dissimulating his deepest loss. In the "phantasmagoria" of the bourgeois *intérieur*—a "habitation" sealed off in the secure "economy" of its acquired "movables" (the vocabulary of *Totality and Infinity* is appropriate)—property is personified to the degree that humans are "encased" in plush like "dead fauna" fossilized in granite (I.2.549; CB 46). Trinkets are bedded in velvet "houses" symptomatic of the radical *Unheimlichkeit* of the home. Such a transfer would redeem by integrating humanity within the seamless imaginary of the "*tête-à-tête sombre et limpide* of the subject with itself" (I.2.659), reinforcing by aestheticizing the irreparable loss of face.

It is striking that Benjamin here introduces the overdetermined Blochian notion of the trace (*Spur*). The draperies cluttering the Second Empire apartment provide a sur-face within which tangible "tracks" (Peircean indices) can be preserved. Cocooned within the interior, the modern citydweller "cheerfully takes the impression of a host of objects" (I.2.548-49; CB 46-47), doubling the contours of each possession within the fuzzy outlines of the plush. Such imprinting both marks every object as inventory and blurs its edges to protect it from the "profane glance of non-owners," thus confirming the iron fist of private property beneath ornamentation's velvet glove. Corresponding to this phantasmagoric interior is a public sphere marked as a postal apparatus—letters stamped, houses numbered—an "extensive network" multiplying the marks of personal identity so as to erase the prior erasure of every trace of life. Napoleon's administrative project attempts to "compensate" for the utter "inconsequentiality" (*Spurlosigkeit*) of metropolitan existence: people now "disappear into the masses of the big cities without a trace" (ibid.).

Thus Benjamin cites Brecht's imperative—"Verwisch die Spuren!"—from the first poem of the *Handbook for Citydwellers*, a poem that continues, "Do not, oh, do not show your face." An infinitely apotropaic gesture would erase the reified (i.e. empirical, phenomenalized) traces that themselves both prolong and dissimulate the prior effacement of the "original" trace. For those who have become refugees in their homeland, such "crypto-emigration" is the only survival tactic left.

"Le visage est défait..." (DE 208; CP 65). The "unmaking" of the face is the only way of "saving" a face already defaced by its inscription in the world of visibility and measure—the world as such. Photography introduces the "inhuman, one might even say deadly" (I.2.646; CB 147) experience of staring into an apparatus which, in refusing to return the gaze, defaces to the degree that it targets the human face as object (Benjamin stresses the essential origin of photography in portraiture). Under such circumstances, it would be self-defeating to invoke the face (but equally to fetishize its absence) as the essential instance of transcendence, ethicality, or, therefore, the face. That would be to succumb to the physiognomic delusion denounced by Hegel—idealism's inherent blindness to its empiricist projections—and thus to commit the ultimate violence: anthropomorphism, idolatry, the absolutization of the finite.

Visibility thus takes on iconoclastic proportions. Phenomenality becomes the very principle of "expression." *Schein*, "beyond essence" (beyond every dialectic of ground-and-appearance and thus beyond the conciliations of *schöne Schein* as the harmonizing luster of appearances), becomes the infinite inconspicuousness of a mask.

"To go naked is the best disguise," says Congrève (*The Double Dealer*, xi). Thus Kierkegaard's incognito; the epic "nobody"; the "Confucian" sage; Kafka's Karl Rossman; the man without qualities; Baudelaire's *flâneur*; the man of the crowd, invisible in his visibility, hidden by the mass that in exposing him functions precisely as his "veil." Thus, equally, the face presented by Fewkoombey in the *Threepenny Novel*—victim, proletariat, falsely accused, and (therefore) judge of his accusers—"a new face, or rather, scarcely a face but 'transparent and faceless,' like the millions who fill barracks and basement apartments" (III.2.443; R 196). In Brecht's *Die Massnahme*, the faces of the revolutionaries are reduced to "empty pages on which the revolution may write its orders."[3] Stripped of mythical (exclusive or proprietary) singularity, the human face now assumes "new and immeasurable significance," legible in class terms—as a "type" (II.1.380; OWS 251). The "untragic hero" appears as a "trigonometric sign" (IV.1.397; R 302), devoid of empathic interiority, a "perfect setting" (II.2.534) for the exhibition of social forces. "Whether one is of the left or right, one will have to get used to being looked at in terms of one's provenance" (II.1.380; OWS 252).

So too the "nameless physiognomy" captured by both Russian film and surrealist photography, each consecrated to "the most impossible of renunciations"—the relinquishment of every anthropocentric "intimacy"—in exposing empty courtyards, "cleared out" cities, uninhabitable landscapes presented "without make-up," "at face value" (II.1.377-79; OWS 249-51). "Things" come to "put on their true—surrealistic—face" (V.1.579). This invokes neither pathetic fallacy nor anthropomorphism—the consoling tropes of consumer capitalism. If "no face is surrealistic to the same degree as the true face of a city" (II.1.300; R 182), this statement, in turn, expresses neither fetishism nor the corresponding ideology of compensation. The "face of modernity"—a "Medusa's gaze" (V.72)—deflects all recuperation along anthropomorphic lines. "One is already far from the continent of man" (II.1.419-20; ILL 122). Thus Kraus's dogs and Kafka's animals, allegorical ciphers of a humanity stripped of its "traditional supports"—spirit, soul, genius—a humanity that thus repels the mythical solidarities assumed by empathic identification. The familiar circle of reconciliation—the humanization of nature, the naturalization of man—twists into a chiasmus in which neither "man" nor "nature" remains intact. Benjamin's "real" (anti-essentialist, anti-idealist, anti-humanist) "humanism" contests precisely the "idol" of a "harmoniously and perfectly formed humanity": the "phantom of the unpolitical or 'natural' man." Only a "monster" emerges—"inhuman" [*Unmensch*]—the demonic messenger of the modern age (II.1.348-66; R 253-72).

This is Benjamin's version of "saving the phenomena"—Levinas's "'phenomenology' of the noumenon" (CP 21)—or, according to Benjamin's idiosyncratic revision of Kant, of finding the noumenal in the phenomenal (see I.1.214; OGT 33). Otherwise put, it is a matter of locating transcendence in an utterly disenchanted world. Thus we come to the familiar oxymorons—*heilignüchtern* (I.1.104), "profane illumination," the "dialectical convolution" of "the mystery" and "the everyday" (II.1.307; R 190). Such a chiasmus marks the chance of finding a "sabbatical existence" (see TeI 78; TaI 104) in a world marked by "porosity" (IV.1.311; R 168) or transparency. A world in which Sunday has been "dropped" from the calendar (I.2.643; CB 144) is one for which "the festival penetrates each and every working day" (IV.1.311; R 168). "Every second of time [is] the narrow gate through which the Messiah may enter" (I.2.704; ILL 264). Rosenzweig, never distant, writes of the world as "every inch" the kingdom coming, "mysterious in broad daylight."

Part Three

Levinas too insists on this. If "to destroy the sacred groves"—"pagan" numinosity—requires no less than a total "demystification of the universe," he stresses the "purity" underlying this "apparent vandalism." Gagarin, flying to heaven, wrenched humanity from its enthrallment to every local particularism (including its exilic obverse) fostering the exclusivity of "family, tribe and nation." "For one hour… a man existed in the absolute of homogeneous space" (DL 301-2; DF 232-33).

Thus Levinas correlates the "abstract universalism" attributed to Judaism with the modern regime of technology insofar as both relate iconoclastically to sacral fascination. The *Makom*, "absolute place," subverts every absolutization of contingency—thus Israel's peculiar status as the site of a nonparticularistic election (see ADV 152)—introducing, as in the Sanhedrin, a nonhierarchical classification "in which no-one has a real place" (NTR 87). In this respect "Judaism" resonates with the "Socratic message"—leave the countryside—which accordingly begins to appear somewhat less than "Greek." The rationalization of the universe signals simultaneously the risk of "blowing up the planet" and the promise of life "beyond any horizon," where the "opportunity" arises to "let the human face shine in all its nudity" (DL 302; DF 233). "Wo…Gefahr ist, wachst das Rettende auch…"

"I have always asked myself if holiness… can exist in a world that has not been desacralized" (SS 89; NTR 141). "Judaism" is thus (contra Hegel, Freud, et al.), "decidedly, a religion of adults" (NTR 15). To endure the radical implications of the "death of God" (which is to confront, Levinas insists, the matter of his "life" as such), "a singularly mature infancy" (AE 121; OB 95)—Nietzschean *Mündigkeit*—is required. In its "marvelous precocity" (DL 163; DF 122), Judaism "feels very close to the West," that is, to the secular pursuit of "intellectual excellence"—"by which I mean philosophy" (DL 30; DF 15). This is no rational theology whereby a bereft humanity substitutes, for a reified divinity, a fetishized Being or Man or Nature—the heaven-on-earth exposed by Nietzsche—or, "as some young men do in Israel, …the Jewish People or the Working Class" (NTR 14). Nor is the maturational model ("maieutic awakening of a common reason" [TeI 194; TaI 219]) pertinent. "Teaching," an incessant "content overflowing the container" (TeI 179; TaI 204), neither assumes the immanent teleology of *Bildung* nor accomplishes the autonomous interiority of self-conscious thought.

"Radical youth" (HAH 43; CP 92)—briefly, "heteronomy" (DVI 152)—thus characterizes the "generous impulse," despite or because of the "sobriety" (SS 7; NTR 91) of its iconoclastic claims. The opposition between faith and enlightenment (already exposed by Hegel as the sacred cow of "the" Enlightenment) is displaced by a chiasmus announcing the "prosaic" rationality (TeI 177; TaI 203) of a "faith purged of myths" (TeI 50; TaI 77). "Religion" thus veers away from both the "royal road of traditional piety" (MT 360; CP 33) and the "sacred delirium" (AE 194; OB 152) of cult. Both prolong the fantasy of homogeneity, whether as the redemptive harmony of forgiveness (see MT 360; CP 33) or as the animistic fusion evoked in "incomparable springtimes" (AE 230; OB 182) promising renewal with every breath. Behind the "ecstatic" appeal to transcendence, Levinas detects the "theater machinery" of an immanence all the more coercive for being obscured— "reflections of our own looks, mirages of our needs, echoes of our prayers" (ibid.) —the projective identifications of a consciousness seeking self-confirmation in what it finds. The promise of parousia simply sanctions the persistence of what is there. Only "metaphysical atheism" meets the demands of a "monotheism" released from the "violence of the sacred" (TeI 50; TaI 77), negotiating an "absolute orientation" (HAH 46; CP 94) beyond the parochialism of site. In its "extraordinary everydayness" the subject is "flushed out" of the "'mysterious' nucleus of 'inwardness,'" placed "under a leaden sun without protective shadows" (AE 179-85; OB 141-45).

Such a "cathartic" movement of desacralization (SS 10; NTR 92) marks the uneasy transition from ethics to politics, simultaneously subtends and (therefore) undermines the very primacy of ethics as "first philosophy," thus tracing the "limit" (AE 200; OB 157)—if not the "limitation" (AE 203; OB 159)—of responsibility: the point where responsibility "is troubled and becomes a problem." Thus is announced "the birth of the question" regarding justice (AE 200; OB 157). If not a "degradation" or "degeneration" of anarchic responsibility (AE 203; OB 159), justice nonetheless effects the latter's perpetual "betrayal" (AE 201; OB 158) in introducing measure—the synchronic "calculus" of intelligibility (AE 202; OB 159)—whereby the ethical relation is interrupted but thereby sustained. For if with the entry of *le tiers* (the third), "the whole of humanity" (a totality) looks at me in the face of the Other (TeI 188; TaI 213), the Other as such becomes "contemporaneous" (AE 200) and accordingly interchangeable with all the others—"both the neighbor and the face of faces," representative in its singularity, "both visage and visible" (AE 204; OB 160)—in short, both face and faceless member of the crowd. Thus follows the "reversion of the incomparable subject into a member of society" (AE 202; OB 158).

In this "original equality" (MT 371; CP 44) the face is disfigured in being "looked at" or "stared down" by all the others, whose gaze effects an "incessant cor-rection"—an establishment of rectitude, rights, reciprocities—a cor-rection contemporaneous with (and therefore logically prior to) the very asymmetry that is to be "corrected": "*le visage se dé-visage*" (AE 201; OB 158). Both self and Other enter a transparent order in which "there is no distinction between those close and those far off"—a society characterized by homogeneity, nonproximity, hence complete effacement—and yet in which there "also" (the logic of this contiguity needs elucidation) remains "the impossibility of passing by the closest" (AE 203; OB 159).

A similar commensurability between me and the Other now obtains. In "service" to the third (to whom it is simultaneously equal, hence obviously not in service), the Other "joins me" (*se joint à moi*) or (note the symmetrical syntax) "joins me with him" (*me joint à lui*) precisely in *enjoining me* to joint responsibility (TeI

188; TaI 213). The presence of the third converts the Other's command into a recursive "command to command him who commands me" (MT 371; CP 43), rendering me, in the face of the Master, another master. A reciprocity follows whose dialectical dimensions cannot go unremarked. The Other becomes my *confrère*, fellow member of a collectivity—the one "with whom" (not "to whom," Levinas insists) one "renders justice" (MT 371; CP 43).

Such an intrusion of the third is not a contingency occasioned by the factual presence of other people, but a structural presupposition of every encounter, the original "doubling" (TeI 188; TaI 213) whereby the ethical dyad divests itself of its "imaginary" (in Lacan's sense) exclusivity and temptation to narcissism. It is the "permanent" intervention of the third (AE 201; OB 158) that prevents the ethical from congealing into the coziness of a tête-à-tête encounter—the "closed society" (MT 360; CP 32) of lovers, "forgetful of the universe," always on the verge of lapsing into "laughter and cooing" (TeI 187-88; TaI 213). The third protects the ethical relation by "correcting" it, sustains asymmetry by "betraying" it. Without such a corrective the ethical bond would in any case betray itself (by lapsing into hierarchy, egology, conciliatory specularity), but without the means to elaborate such self-betrayal as both necessary and insufficient.

Levinas locates this "third" in various positions (again a Lacanian reading is tempting). At times the third looks at me "in the eyes of the Other" (TeI 188; TaI 213); at times he is the "wounded" outsider (MT 360; CP 32), blinded to the inequality between me and the Other, at times the "unimpeachable and severe witness inserting himself" within the *entre nous* of our "private clandestinity," which he loudly publicizes and in so doing preempts. Sometimes I find myself positioned as a "third"-party witness to a face-to-face that evidently excludes me, posing the question (not without its prurient overtones), "What are the other and the third party to each other?" (AE 200; OB 157). For although both the Other and the third are said to be "my neighbors," the third is a neighbor to my neighbor somewhat differently than he is to me. "The other stands in a relationship with the third party, for whom [or for which] I cannot entirely answer.... The other and the third party, my neighbors, contemporaries of one another, put distance between me, on the one hand, and the other and the third party, on the other."[4]

Thus the gap simultaneously widens and narrows between me and the Other. The latter's "contemporaneity" with the others not only "puts distance" (AE 200; OB 157) between me and them but equally "joins" me with the Other—thereby inserting a corresponding distance between the two of us and "all the others"— precisely in our common "obsession" for "humanity" as a whole (AE 200-1; OB 158-59). But such a chiasmus of distanciation and approximation signals the reemergence of "proximity" at a higher level—the approach to an approach that recedes precisely where it comes closest.

Such triangulated proximity relates to the (non)appearance of the ultimate "third person," the Illeity, which in withdrawing as my interlocutor traces the retreat of every interlocutor, signaling the ultimate impossibility of every face-to-face. Such a "profile" (DE 199; TO 44) simultaneously sustains and undermines the possibility of frontal encounter, introduces "obliqueness" into the "uprightness" (*droiture*) (HAH 63; CP 106) of every symmetrical *tutoiement* or intimacy, inscribes "he in the depth of the you" (DP 116; CP 165). Illeity—"let us say the word, this divinity" (HAH 61; CP 105)—triangulates the "ethical bond" in referring it to what is "other than the other, other otherwise" (DP 117; CP 165-66); conversely, "a you is inserted between the I and the absolute He" (DE 215-16; CP 72-73). Desire is thus determined as an "intrigue à trois"—a "plot" disrupting the "bipolar game" of disclosure and dissimulation, a "third way" (HAH 59; CP 103-4) beyond the "cache-cache" (DE 214; CP 71) of cognition. Illeity is structurally oriented toward the third, sustains ethics by tracing its "limit." But this nontheological theology is precisely *politics*. Levinas writes: "to go toward Him is to go toward the Others"—plural—"who are in the trace" (DE 202; TO 46).

Part Four

This means history: the responsibility of responsibility to enter "a historical world, ...simultaneous in a book" (AE 207; OB 162). What is at stake is obviously not (at least not obviously) *Heilsgeschichte, Weltgerichte*, the history of the victors (DL 223; DF 170), which in its "virile" cruelty (TeI 221; TaI 243) "efface[s] the trace of blood and tears" (DE 207; CP 64). Or not only. That history (the only sort Levinas recognizes) aestheticizes existence as a "salvation drama" (TeI 52; TaI 79) that in its haste to reach the "last act" (TeI x; TaI 22) is "enacted in spite of me and make[s] game of me" (TeI 52; TaI 79), reducing me to a "theatrical role" (AE 173; OB 136)—masked, stripped of ethical singularity.

The entry of the third both prolongs and disrupts this conciliatory drama. In its concern with economic equality, justice "interrupts" the "march of history" (MT 373; CP 45), breaks the "vicious circle" of a violence augmenting through every reparation. The "quantification of man" both effaces singularity and arrests the violence of such effacement, presenting a "superior form of economy" whereby "a justice of redemption" might be envisaged. The opposition of totality and infinity would be subverted. Simultaneity (violence) assumes "metaphysical" proportions. The "silhouette" of a face "petrified" within a "universe of mediations" (DE 207; CP 65) becomes inseparable from the "profile" (DE 199; TO 44) of the *au-delà*.

Benjamin identifies such an "apocalyptic" *éclatement* (AE 113; OB 89) of the continuum as the rupture induced by "historical materialism," as what breaks the consoling "chain" or "rosary"—Levinas's "cordon of totality" (AE 121; OB 95)— "gliding smoothly as a thread between the historian's hands" (I.3.1233). Where Levinas speaks of "cutting the threads of the context" (DE 207; CP 65), Benjamin reminds us that the *coupure* more resembles a tangle than a clean break.

For in "cutting through" historicism (I.2.695; ILL 255), "historical materialism" obviously *intersects* with, and hence risks prolonging, the conciliatory vision of *begriffne Geschichte*. It enunciates a radical synchronicity, *Stillstellung*, without which thought lapses into an empiricism sanctifying the given thus functioning as idealism's obverse. It grasps history as an intensive totality or "monad" (the idealist resonances are crucial), that is, from the standpoint of a final judgment without which the just demand for a radical egalitarianism—the classless society—could not be posed. To see history as a whole is precisely to shatter the continuum by recognizing the "incessant" force of victimization as a danger no less pressing for having already occurred.

In this sense Benjamin describes history itself as a "face," but one stripped of all spiritual inwardness so as to assume the radical exposure of a corpse: *facies hippocratica*. "Everything about history that, from the very beginning, has been untimely, sorrowful, unsuccessful, is expressed in a face—no, in a skull" (I.1.343; OGT 166). The dead body—signifying not my "heroic" (DVI 256) being-toward-death or the Other's being-toward-death but the already dead Other—expresses the irreparability marking simultaneously the utter futility of the ethical prohibition ("thou shalt not commit murder") and (therefore) the extreme urgency of its claim. It is as a *dead face* that history presents itself to those alive. The face of history is "defeated," decomposed by an immemorial past. It exhorts the living to an "absolute assignation" (AE 178; OB 140), to what Benjamin designates as a "secret agreement" with the dead (I.2.694; ILL 254). Such an alliance is marked by the belated urgency of a radical anachronism (too early and too late for contact): the "arrhythmia" (AE 211; OB 166) or "irregular rhythm" (I.1.373; OGT 197) puncturing the continuum of time.

This nonencounter attests not only to the failure of resuscitation—the mask speaks the impossibility of the dead regaining voice, breath, *spiritus*—but equally to a failure to have securely died. "*Even the dead* will not be safe from the enemy if he wins" (I.2.695; ILL 255). "Profond jadis, jadis jamais assez…." The apparition of the face as death mask, resisting all idealization, means, for the survivors, an incessant wake. Perhaps "attention." Perhaps insomnia. Such is the response to a "state of emergency" that is "not the exception but the rule" (I.2.697; ILL 257), to the revolutionary sobriety of a disenchanted world.

That might require, Benjamin concludes his essay on surrealism, the act of exchanging, "to a man, the play of human features for the face of an alarm clock, that in each minute rings for sixty seconds" (II.1.30; R 192).

Notes

1. Walter Benjamin, *Gesammelte Schriften* (Frankfurt: Suhrkamp, 1980-89), I.2.479; *Illuminations*, trans. Harry Zohn (New York: Schocken, 1969), 222-23 (henceforth ILL). References to the German edition will be indicated simply by volume, part, and page number. Other English translations will be abbreviated thus: CB: *Charles Baudelaire: A Lyric Poet in the Era of High Capitalism*,

trans. Harry Zohn (London: Verso, 1983); OGT: *The Origin of German Tragic Drama*, trans. John Osborne (London: Verso, 1977); OWS: *One-Way Street*, trans. Edmund Jephcott (London: Verso, 1985); R: *Reflections*, trans. Edmund Jephcott (New York: Harcourt, Brace, Jovanovich, 1978). For all citations, I will use the existing translations, modifying them where appropriate.

2. The identical opposition occurs in both Levinas and Benjamin. "Truth is not an unveiling [*Enthüllung*] that destroys the mystery, but rather a revelation [*Offenbarung*] that does it justice" (I.1.211; OGT 31). "The absolute experience is not disclosure [*dévoilement*] but revelation [*révélation*]" (TeI 37; TaI 65-66).

3. Bertold Brecht, Die Massnahme, "Die Auslöschung," in *Werke*, Bd. 3, Berliner und Frankfurter Ausgabe, Stücke, 3 (Frankfurt: Suhrkamp, 1988), 78.

4. AE 200; OB 157, translation modified. The syntax is ambiguous: "L'autre se tient dans une relation avec le tiers–dont je ne peux répondre entièrement même si je réponds–avant toute question–de mon prochain tout seul."

Contributors

CATHERINE CHALIER is Agrégée de philosophie and Docteur d'Etat. Her publications include *Judaïsme et altérité* (1982); *Figures du féminin* (1982); *Les matriarches* (1985); *La persévérance du mal* (1987); *L'alliance avec la nature* (1989); *L'histoire promise* (1992); *Pensées de l'éternité* (1993); *Levinas, l'utopie de l'humain* (1993); and *Sagesse des sens* (1995).

ROBERT GIBBS is the author of *Correlations in Rosenzweig and Levinas* (1992) and of various essays in modern Jewish thought. He is currently finishing a book entitled *Why Ethics: Signs of Responsibilities*, which examines a set of thinkers including Levinas, Derrida, Habermas, Peirce, Royce, Benjamin, Rosenzweig, and others in order to re-orient ethics by focusing on how using signs implicates us in responsibilities for what other people do.

CHARLES E. SCOTT is Edwin Erle Sparks Professor of Philosophy at The Pennsylvania State University, University Park. His most recent books are *The Question of Ethics* and *The Language of Difference*.

BERNHARD WALDENFELS is Professor of Philosophy at the Ruhr-University Bochum. He studied with Merleau-Ponty and Ricoeur in Paris. He has been teaching as visiting professor at the New School, and is working in the field of phenomenology and contemporary French philosophy. His recent publications include *Ordnung im Zwielicht* (1987); *Der Stachel des Fremden* (1990); and

Antwortregister (1994). He is also the co-editor of books on Schütz and Gurwitsch, Merleau-Ponty, and Foucault.

HUGH MILLER is Assistant Professor of Philosophy at Loyola University Chicago. He received his doctorate in philosophy from the University of Toronto in 1993 with a dissertation on the idea of God in Hegel and Levinas. He is presently working on a book on Levinas and the philosophy of religion.

PATRICIA H. WERHANE, formerly Wirtenberger Professor of Business Ethics at Loyola University Chicago, is Ruffin Professor of Business Ethics at the University of Virginia. Her works include *Ethical Issues in Business*, edited with Tom Donaldson (4 editions); *Persons, Rights, and Corporations; Adam Smith and his Legacy for Modern Capitalism;* and *Skepticism, Rules, and Private Languages*.

ELISABETH WEBER is Associate Professor at the University of California, Santa Barbara. She is the author of a book on "persecution" and "trauma" in Levinas's oeuvre (*Trauma und Verfolgung*, 1990). She has edited a collection of interviews on "Jewish thought in France today" (*Jüdisches Denken in Frankreich*, 1994, with E. Levinas, J. Derrida, J.-F. Lyotard, P. Vidal-Naquet, and others) and *Points...* by Jacques Derrida (1995).

ROBERT BERNASCONI is Moss Professor of Philosophy at the University of Memphis. He is the author of *The Question of Language in Heidegger; History of Being;* and *Heidegger in Question*. He has co-edited two books on Levinas: *The Provocation of Levinas* with David Wood and *Rereading Levinas* with Simon Critchley. He is currently working on issues in continental philosophy, Hegel, and social and political philosophy.

FABIO CIARAMELLI teaches philosophy at the University of Naples Federico II. He is the author of *Ethique et transcendance: Essai sur Levinas* (1989). He has also published several articles in Italian and in French on ethics, political theory, and the relationship between Heidegger and Freud.

PAUL DAVIES teaches philosophy at the University of Sussex, having previously taught at Loyola University of Chicago and De Paul University of Chicago. He is the author of several articles on Levinas, Blanchot, and related topics. A book, *Experience and Distance*, is forthcoming. He is currently working on material for a book on philosophy and the idea of a literary project.

ANDREW TALLON is Professor of Philosophy at Marquette University. He received his doctorate From Louvain University in 1969. In 1975 he spent six weeks with Professor Levinas in Paris. Some of his other publications on Levinas' philosophy have appeared in *Philosophy Today, Man and World,* and *Philosophy & Theology*.

CONTRIBUTORS / 237

WILLIAM J. RICHARDSON is the author of *Heidegger: Through Phenomenology to Thought* (Preface by Martin Heidegger) and co-author (with John P. Muller) of *Lacan and Language. Reader's Guide to the Écrits* and *The Purloined Poe: Lacan, Derrida and Psychoanalytic Reading*. A graduate of the William Alanson White Psychoanalytic Institute (New York City), he was formerly Director of Research at the Austen Riggs Center (Stockbridge, Mass.). He is now Professor of Philosophy at Boston College and engaged in the private practice of psychoanalysis (Newton, Mass.).

EDITH WYSCHOGROD is J. Newton Rayzor Professor of Philosophy and Religious Thought at Rice University. Her recent books include *Saints and Postmodernism: Revisioning Moral Philosophy* and *Spirit in Ashes: Hegel Heidegger and Man-Made Mass Death*. She is now working on the questions of memory, history, and community.

MEROLD WESTPHAL is Professor of Philosophy at Fordham University. He is the author of *History and Truth in Hegel's Phenomenology; God, Guilt and Death; Kierkegaard's Critique of Reason and Society; Hegel, Freedom, and Modernity; Suspicion and Faith;* and recent essays on postmodernism and the philosophy of religion.

THEO DE BOER was Professor of Philosophical Anthropology at the University of Amsterdam from 1968 until 1992. Since 1992 he has been Professor of Systematic Philosophy at the Free University of Amsterdam. His publications include *Between Philosophy and Prophecy; On the philosophy of Emmanuel Levinas* (Dutch, 1976); *The Development of Husserl's Thought* (1978); *Foundations of a Critical Psychology* (1982); *The God of the Philosopher and the God of Pascal* (Dutch, 1989); and *On Subjectivity* (Dutch, 1993).

JILL ROBBINS is Associate Professor of Comparative Literature and English at the State University of New York at Buffalo. She is the author of *Prodigal Son / Elder Brother: Interpretation and Alterity in Augustine, Petrarch, Kafka, Levinas* (1991), and is currently completing a book entitled *Reading the Ethical: Levinas and Literature*. She is also the editor of a collection of Levinas's interviews, forthcoming from Stanford University Press.

ADRIAAN PEPERZAK is Arthur J. Schmitt Professor of Philosophy at Loyola University Chicago. Previously he taught philosophy in Utrecht, Nijmegen, and Amsterdam and at several universities in the United States, France, Italy, Spain, and Indonesia. Among his books are *System and History in Philosophy* (1986) and *To the Other: An Introduction to the Philosophy of Emmanuel Levinas* (1993). He has also published five books on Hegel and studies in thematic philosophy.

DAVID TRACY is Andrew Thomas Greeley and Grace McNichols Greeley Distinguished Service Professor of Theology at the Divinity School, University of Chicago, where he has taught since 1969. He is also a member of the Committe on the Analysis of Ideas and Methods. Among his recent works are *Plurality and Ambiguity: Hermeneutics, Religion and Hope* (1987); *Dialogue with the Other* (1990); and *Naming the Present* (1995).

JOHN LLEWELYN has been Reader in Philosophy at the University of Edinburgh and Visiting Professor at Loyola University Chicago and Memphis State University. His publications include *Beyond Metaphysics?*; *Derrida on the Threshold of Sense*; *The Middle Voice of Ecological Conscience*; and *Emmanuel Levinas: The Genealogy of Ethics*.

HENT DE VRIES is Professor of Philosophy at the University of Amsterdam. He is the author of *Theologie im pianissimo* and *Zwischen Rationalität und Dekonstruktion. Die Aktualität der Denkfiguren Adornos und Levinas'* (1989, translation forthcoming) and the co-editor, together with Harry Kunneman, of *Die Aktualität der Dialektik der Aufklärung. Zwischen Moderne und Postmoderne* (1989) and of *Enlightenments. Encounters between Critical Theory and Recent French Thought* (1993). He is currently completing a booklength study entitled *ADIEU* and co-editing with Samuel Weber a collective volume of essays on *Violence, Identity and Self-determination*.

REBECCA COMAY teaches philosophy and literary studies at the University of Toronto and writes on nineteenth- and twentieth-century Continental philosophy. She is the author of a forthcoming book on Hegel and Heidegger, *On the Line: Reflections on the Bad Infinite* and is currently working on a book on Walter Benjamin.

Index

Abandon, 57
Abraham, 174, 212, 218
Absence, 56, 57, 80, 97, 144, 173, 177, 218
   corporeal, 43
Absolute, 155, 191, 214, 215, 218
Absolution, 191
Abstraction, 98
Accusation, 47-48
Accusative, 45, 48, 53, 55, 56
Accused, 78
Address, 218
À-Dieu, 205, 211
Adriaanse, H. J., 171n1
Advent, 117n1
Aesthetics, 137-147
   vs. the religious, 138-139
Affectivity, 98, 118n1, 190
   nonintentional, 107-117, 118n6, 119n7
Affirmation
   pre-originary, 101
Alien, 46
Alienation, 44-45
Allergy, 117n1, 152, 174

Alterity, 28, 43, 78, 80, 139, 141, 144, 175, 202
Altruism, 111
"Always already," 190
"Amen", 199, 207-208
Amor fati, 48
Ambiguity, 102, 206
Anachronism, 88, 177
Anachrony, 26, 54, 190
Analogy
   of being, 111
Anamnesis, 74-75, 187
Anarchy, 26-27, 32, 45, 48, 51n13, 56, 71, 88, 93, 101, 166, 206, 214, 230
Annihilation (*Vernichtung*), 201
Anonymity, 192
Anscombe, G.E.M., 67n7, 67n10
Anspruch, 42
Anterior
   posteriority of the, 88
Anti-semitism, 82, 126
Apel, Karl-Otto, 137, 163, 171n4
Appearing, 87
Appetites, 108

Apology, 71, 79
Approach, 97, 101, 175, 176, 231
A priori, 49, 80
Archaeology, 112
Archè, 46, 51n13, 88, 93
Arche-trace, 178, 181
Archetype, 108, 110, 201
Aristophanes, 151
Aristotle, 40, 125, 153, 157, 162, 165, 186, 188, 196, 214
Art, 137-147, 214, 225
Assimilation, 188
Asymmetry, 99, 104, 230
  double, 191
Atheism, 22, 164, 168, 200, 207, 230
  of the will
Au-delà, 204, 214, 232
Aufhebung, 41, 153
Aught (*Icht*), 200
Aura, 224-226
Auschwitz, 48, 70
Austin, John, 205, 209n7
Authority, 111
Autonomy 43, 56, 153, 190. *See also* Freedom
  vs. heteronomy, 6-7
Autosignification, 176

Barth, Karl, 152
Bataille, Georges, 144, 146
Baudelaire, Charles, 226-227, 233n1
Being, 45, 62, 80, 162, 185, 188, 205, 213. *See also Il y a* and *There is*
  and non-being, 206
  beyond, 98, 206
  essence of, 189
  finite, 164
  manifestation of, 87
  modalities of, 206
  otherwise than, 32
  perseverance of beings in, 213, 214
  phenomenology of, 189
  understanding of, 165
  vs. image, 138
Being-at-home-with-oneself (*Beisichselbstsein*), 187
Being-for-one-another, 45
Being-in-the-world, 188, 207

Being-there, 156
Being towards one's own death, 207, 233
Belief, 139-140
Benevolence, 44, 48
Benjamin, Walter, 223-228, 232-233, 233n1, 234n2
Bergson, Henri, 127, 166
Betrayal, 75, 230
Beyond
  not (*pas au-delà*), 96
Bible, 19. *See also* Torah.
Bifurcation (*bifurs*), 142-143
Blanchot, Maurice, xiii, 41, 50n3, 50n4, 50n5, 85n1, 95-96, 138, 143-147, 175, 176, 209n11
Bloch, Ernst, 223, 227
Blondel, Charles, 127
Bloom, Harold, 181
Boehme, Jakob, 201
Bonaventure, 185, 195, 196
Boredom, 187
Brecht, Bertold, 227, 228, 234n4
Breton, André, 138
Brunschvicg, Léon, 208
Buber, Martin, 59, 139, 223
Burning (*brûlure*), 213, 214, 215

Calculation, 49
Care (*Sorge*), 43, 206, 213
Caress, 46
Caring. *See Fürsorge*
Casey, Edward, 182n2
Catastrophe, the. *See* Holocaust
Categorical imperative, 52n17, 157
Categories, 72
Cathexis, 141
Celan, Paul, 73, 78
Childs, Brevard, 179, 182n9, 182n10, 182n11
Chomsky, Noam, 61
Chouchani, Mordechai, 3
Christendom, 159
Christianity
  encounter with God in, 155
  encounter with Greek philosophy, 162
Chronology, 70, 71
Coexistence, 167
Cogito, 62, 127

INDEX / 241

Cognition, 141, 143. 232. *See also* Knowledge
Cohen, Hermann, 17, 19, 21, 23, 23n2
Commandment, 12, 55, 231
Community, 42, 60, 61, 62, 65, 215
Compassion, 44
Complex, 114, 121n16
Comprehension, 63, 166, 169
Compulsion, 44
Conatus essendi, 189, 213, 214
Concept, 164
Concreteness, signifying (*déformalisation*), 88
Cone, James, 195
Concupiscence, 189
Confrontation, 66
Connaturality
    affective, 109
Consciousness, 25, 27, 29, 31, 33-34, 48, 54, 56, 79, 116, 157, 190
    cognitive, 107
    doubling of, 140
    kerygmatic function of, 128
Contact, 80
Contamination, 33
Contemporaneity, 231
Contestation, 79
Context, 176, 187
    signification out of, 175-176
Contract
    social, 163
Conventionalism, 61
Conversion, 33, 45
Co-responsibility, 44
Corporeality, 191
Covenant, 34
Creation, 108
Critchley, Simon, 63, 67n11, 182n7
Critique, 101
Cut, 32, 70, 232

Dative, 47
Death, 70, 113, 214, 233
    killing of, 73
de Beauvoir, Simone, xiii
Debt, 45, 49
Decision, 201
Deconstruction, 178
    of essence, 200
Demand (*Mitanspruch*), 49
Demonic, 215, 218
Deontology, 43
Derrida, Jacques, xiv, 100, 104, 104n1, 143, 151, 156, 157, 159n1, 178, 179, 181, 182n5, 182n7, 205, 209n6, 215-218, 219n4, 220n6
Desacralization, 230
Désastre, 143
Descartes, 168, 174, 201
Description
    phenomenological, 83
Desire, 90, 98, 187, 194, 225, 232
    metaphysical, 112, 186
    vs. need, 153, 154, 188, 189-192, 198
Destitution, 77
Destructuration, 88
Deus absconditus, 180
de Waehlens, Alphonse, 83-84, 86n6, 99, 104, 165-166
de Wind, E., 75n4, 76n11
Diachrony, 46, 57, 71, 83, 88, 108, 110, 113, 118n1, 190, 206
Dialectic, 40, 46, 65, 114, 213
Dialogue, 40, 45, 167
    Platonic, 40
Difference, 33, 46, 71, 91, 177
Differend, 70
Dilthey, Wilhelm, 162, 164, 166
Direction (*sens*), 129
Disaster (*désastre*), 143-144, 208
Disclosure, 153, 176, 226
Disconnection (*Ausschaltung*), 169
Discontinuity, 17
Discourse, 71, 176
    philosophical, 72
Disinterestedness (*désintéressement*), 10, 144, 213
Dispossession, 47
Disquietude (*Besorgnis*), 206
Dissimulation, 176
Disturbance, 176, 177, 178-179
Divergency (*écart*), 87
Divinity, *See* God
Dostoyevski, 55, 58n3
Double bind, 181, 215, 217
Doubt
    Cartesian, 168

Doxa. *See* Belief
Drama, 41
Drash, 202
Dualism, 62-63
Duns Scotus, 162
Duration, 217
Duty, 55
Dwelling, 153, 164, 188

Echo, 46
Eckhart, Meister, 201
Economy, 167, 178, 187-189, 194, 225
Ecstasy (*Ekstasis*), 44, 55
Edelmann, Marek, 52n15
Ego, 45, 62, 71, 72, 116. *See also* Self *and* I
    as a form defecting from consciousness, 80
    murderousness of, 77
    wounded, 74
Egocentrism, 60
Egoism, 154, 216
    psychological, 60
    ethical, 60
    rational, 60
Egology, 60, 64, 231
Ehyeh asher ehyeh, 180
Election, 10, 229
Eliade, Mircea, 157, 197
Elsewhere (*ailleurs*), 187
Embodiment, 108
Emotion, 110
Empathy, 44
Empiricism, 79, 100, 227, 232
En deçà, 204, 214
Enigma, 49, 51n14, 57, 78, 82-83, 87, 99, 102, 176, 181, 217, 226
Enjoyment (*jouissance*), 46, 113, 153, 164, 188
Enlightenment, 151, 157, 162, 170, 226
Entscheidung, 201
Epic, 41, 80
Epiphany, 117n1, 154, 191
Epoché, 169
Equality, 90, 91, 230
    economic, 232
Equipment. *See* Zuhandenes
Erasure (*biffures*), 142-143
Ereignis, 144

Erotic, 224
Eschatology, 161
Es gibt, 126, 144, 189, 218. *See also* There is, *Il y a*
Essence, 10, 29, 30, 61, 80, 96, 118n6, 164, 194, 200, 227
    as *essance*, 189
    deportation, dissolution of (*Entwesung*), 201
    intuition of, 162
Eternal, 88
Ethics, xv, 13-14, 33, 49, 97, 137, 173, 178
    and the immoral or amoral, 214
    as first philosophy, xv, 59, 62, 65, 66, 87, 205, 230
    as universal, 139, 212
    communicative, 39-40, 42, 53, 217
    decriptive, 59, 62, 65
    naturalistic, 217
    normative, 59, 62, 65
    responsive, 39, 49
Eudaimonia, 188
Everyday, the, 228
Evil, 156
Exaltation, 167
Exception
Excess, 27, 33, 175
Exile, 27, 30, 99
Existence, 118n6
    positing of, 168
    sabbatical, 228-229
Exodus, 187
Experience, 79
    ethics does not proceed from a special, 97, 99
    heteronomous, 174
    moral, 103
    nonintentional, 207
    nonphilosophical, 84, 99-101, 165
    religious, 170
    saturated, 84
    thematized, 79
Expiation, 55, 165
Exposure, 44, 62, 64, 167, 233
Expression, 128, 166, 176, 227
    facial, 175
    pain of, 71-72
Exteriority, 62, 121n15, 147, 187
    vs. interiority, 113

Face, 48, 57, 72, 78, 97, 108, 112, 137, 154, 157, 167, 175, 207, 216-217, 224, 226-228, 230
  dereliction of the, 80
  undoing of (*se dé-visage*), 230
Face-to-face, xv, 62, 63, 65, 77, 88, 90, 92, 109, 117, 121n14, 128, 231
Facticity, 63, 166
Faith, 33, 167, 211, 213
  and knowledge, 162
  knight of, 218, 219
Father. *See* Paternity
Fault, 47
Fear, 166
Fecundity, 78
Feeling, 30-31, 46, 109, 120n9
Feuerbach, Ludwig, 152
Fichte, 48
Finite
  absolutization of, 227
Forgetting, 75
Form, 137
Foucault, Michel, 42, 151
Francis of Assisi, 195
Fraternity
Freedom, 6-8, 12, 33, 46, 63, 117, 120n8, 190. *See also* Autonomy
Freud, Sigmund, 116, 126, 127, 131, 156, 159, 160n5, 229
Future, 41-42, 50, 71, 121n14, 175

Gasché, Rodolphe, 182n6, 183n18
Generosity, 174, 189
Genocide, 51n15
Gentleness, 77
Genus, 80
Gerundive, 41
Gesture, 27, 46-47, 88, 227
Gibbs, Robert, 202, 209n4
Gift, 144, 174, 189
Gilson, Etienne, 195
Ginzberg, Louis, 183n15
Giving, 46-47, 50n5
Glance, 224-225
Glory, 170, 179, 192
Glotz, Peter, 51n15

God, xiii, 17-23, 25-26, 27-35, 50n1, 57, 117, 147, 152, 155, 156, 158, 159n4, 178, 188, 191, 194, 199-203, 205-208, 214, 215, 218, 232
  and being, 161
  and the political, 92-93
  as Absolute Other, 194, 195, 197, 215, 217
  as *causa sui*, 169, 181
  as *ipsum esse subsistens*, 169, 195
  as Supreme Being, 164, 168-170
  attributes of, 157, 180
  death of, 28, 170, 207, 229
  effacement of the name of, 207-208
  essence of, 202, 206
  experience of, 206
  going toward (*à Dieu*) or away from (*adieu*), 217-219
  hidden, 57, 180
  image of, 108, 109, 111-112, 114
  knowledge of, 152, 156, 180
  name of, 192, 194, 195, 207, 215
  not mediator between persons, 155
  of Judaism, 18
  proof of the existence of, 57, 164
  proximity of, 179, 181, 191
  revealed, 173
  speaking of and to, 217
  trace of, 179-182
  works of, 180
Gods, 188, 200
Good, 49, 52n17, 185, 190, 192, 194, 216
  beyond being, 174, 185, 195, 196
Goodness, 35, 174, 189
Grammar, 27, 46, 61, 78
  of assent, 200
Gratuity, 44
Greek, 3
  and Hebrew, 4, 25-26, 34-35, 82, 84, 167, 229
Greisch, Jean, 148n1
Guardian (*Vormund*), 43
Gutierrez, Gustavo, 195
Guilt, 49, 75

Haar, Michel, 85n1, 118n4
Habermas, Jürgen, 60-61, 67n5, 137
Habit, 110

Happiness, 90
Hatred, 78, 82
He (*Il*), 155, 192, 20, 232. *See also* Illeity
Hegel G.W.F., 21, 28, 83, 84, 157, 158, 200, 201, 203, 213, 216, 217, 227, 229
Heidegger, Martin, 11, 18, 43, 81, 84, 111, 113, 123-124, 128, 138, 144, 152, 153, 165, 166, 186, 188, 200, 204, 206, 213
   and Dilthey, 162, 166
   and Nazism, 126
Height (*hauteur*), 14-16, 20-23, 79, 155, 157, 169, 190, 191
Heisenberg, Werner, 61, 63
Hereby, 203
Here I am. *See Me voici*
Hermeneutic circle, 42
Hermeneutics, 85, 159, 164, 166, 187
Heterogeneity, 104
Heteronomy, 7, 40, 174. *See also* Autonomy
Hildebrand, Dietrich von, 108
Hinneni. *See Me voici*
Hinterwelt, 186
History, 232-233
Hobbes, Thomas, 60, 66n1
Holiness, 6, 12
Holocaust, 3, 52, 65, 72
Home, 79
Horizon, 20, 54, 156, 165, 185
Hospitality, 79, 170
Hostage, 44, 47, 55, 96, 100, 108, 115, 167, 190
Humanism, 228
   of the other human being, 207
Humility, 15, 90
Hunger, 77, 189, 225
Husserl, Edmund, xiii, 26, 43, 44, 45, 51n11, 51n12, 54, 58n1, 76n10, 87, 124, 128, 153, 162, 163, 168, 169, 171, 171n2, 188, 207
Hyperbole, 17-18, 22, 72, 100, 108, 205

I, 155, 164. *See also* Ego
   speaking (*je de l'énonciation*), 130
   spoken (*je de l'énoncé*), 130
Icon
   vs. idol, 197
Idealism, 28, 213, 227, 232

Idel, Moshe, 197
Identification, self-, 213
Identity, 30, 34-35
   logic of, 78, 81, 82
   to be without, 78
Idolatry, 190, 225, 227
Illeity, 56-57, 206, 218, 231-232
Il y a (there is), 95-96, 117, 189, 214, 218, 219
Image, 138, 226
   plastic, 175
Immanence, 173, 176, 200, 230
Immediacy
   of ethical responsibility, 88
Immemorial, 43, 53
Immortality, 175
Imperative, 41. *See also* Categorical imperative
Imputation, 40-41
Incarnation, 214-215
Incognito, 140, 181, 227
Incommensurability
   of the other and consciousness, 27, 32
   of God and Israel, 27
Indeterminacy, 61
Indexicals, 62
Indicative, 41
Indiscretion, 144
Individual, 72
Individuation, 61
Ineffability, 144-145, 164
Infinite, 17-18, 32-33, 56, 80, 88, 98, 155, 170, 173, 194, 197, 202, 206, 215
   bad, 21
   idea of the, 108, 111, 114, 137, 147, 174
   "in-" of, 97
   verbal, 204
Infinition, 17, 56
Ingratitude
   of the other, 174
Inhuman, the, 82
Insanity, 72
Insomnia, 233
Inspiration, 217
Instant, 89
Institution
   political, 90
Instruction. *See* Teaching

Intention
  empty (*Leermeinung*), 43
Intentionality, 31, 45, 108, 117, 153, 157, 167
  affective, 107-114
  double, 112
  of nonrepresentational consciousness, 107
  of representational consciousness, 107, 119n7, 119n8
Inter-essence, 189, 194
Interiority, 62, 64, 113, 167, 212, 213
Interlocutor, 54, 63, 155, 231
Internalization, 71
Interpassion, 47
Interpellation, 176
Interpretation, 164
Interruption, 10, 26, 28-29, 31-32, 48, 72, 88, 103, 178-179
  as intermediary event, 44
Intersubjectivity, 191
Intimacy (*tutoiement*), 232
Intrigue, 87, 232
  of language, 101
  of one-for-the-other, 168
Inversion, 45, 206
Invisible, 191
Inwardness, 79, 233
Ipseity, 27, 56, 80
Israel, 26
  of fact, 82
  as Universal, 82
Iteration, 167

Joyce, James, 209n10
Judaism
  and philosophy, 3-5
  a religion of adults, 229
  and ethics, 22
  as responsibility for the entire universe, 81
  as persecuted, 81
  destiny of, 81-82, 83
  encounter with God in, 155, 158
  non-ontotheological theology of, 181
  particularism of, 82, 83, 170
  universality of, 82, 170, 229
Judge, 49, 78

Judgment
  last, 40
Jung, C. G., 110, 114-116
Justice, 13, 48, 56, 60, 62, 65, 88, 91, 92, 96, 139, 196, 230-231
  corrective, 42
  distributive, 42, 167
Justification, 40

Kafka, Franz, 147, 227, 228
Kant, Immanuel, 22, 44, 49, 61, 157, 158, 163, 214, 217, 228
$\kappa\alpha\theta'$ $\alpha\vartheta\tau o$, 160n8, 176
Kierkegaard, Søren, 138-140, 147, 153, 158, 159, 159n2, 160n6, 211-213, 215-217, 219, 219n1, 220n5, 220n7
Klages, Ludwig, 166
Knowledge, 97, 153. *See also* Cognition
  and belief, 139-140
  and interest, 153
Kraus, Karl, 224, 228

Labarrière, Pierre-Jean, 182n7
Labor, 154
Lacan, Jacques, 42, 126, 231
Language, 29, 61, 62, 71, 79, 128, 144, 208
  as "giving withholding," 144
  ethical, 95-104, 137
  ontological, 79, 81
  possibility of ethical, 96
  private, 61
  religious, 141
Law, 11-12, 40, 43, 49, 90, 92, 174, 187, 216
Leap, primordial, 89
Lefort, Claude, 91, 94n5, 94n6, 94n7
Legitimation, 49
Leiris, Michel, 141-143, 148n2, 148n3
Lessing, G. E., 170
Levinas, Emmanuel
  life of, xiii-xiv, 123-125, 126
  works of, xiii-xiv
Lévi-Strauss, Claude, 126
Libertson, Joseph, 146, 148n6
Life, 166
  love of
Lifeline, 70

Limit, 47, 230, 232
Lingis, Alphonso, 67n13
Liturgy, 175, 191
Logic, 78, 103
Lonergan, Bernard, 118n5
Logos, 4, 25, 28, 41, 71, 72, 79, 82, 128, 151, 153, 157, 204
Lyotard, Jean-François, 70, 73, 75n5, 76n16, 151

Maimonides, Moses, 10, 152
Manifestation
 horizon of, 89
 religions of, 197
Marcel, Gabriel, xiii, 107
Marion, Jean-Luc, 197, 209n8
Mark, 177
Marten, Rainer, 76n18
Materialism
 historical, 232
Marx, Karl, 84, 156, 159, 160n6, 186, 226
Meaning, 29, 31, 61, 87, 108, 111, 128, 129, 142, 145
Me voici (Here I am), 45, 129, 130, 179, 215, 225
Mediation, 72, 89, 176
Memory, 71, 177. *See also* Remembrance
Merleau-Ponty, Maurice, xiii, 107
Messianism, 161
Metaethics, 59, 65
Metaphor, 72, 73, 83, 114, 153, 190
Metaphysician, 84
Metaphysics, 152, 167, 178
 and ontology, 163
 traditional, 143
Methodology
Midrash, 28
Monologue, 41
Monotheism, 34, 230
Morality, 49, 59, 65. *See also* Ethics
Mortality, 74
Moses, 174, 179
Most-High, 16, 19-21, 189
Mourning, 205
 possibility of, 74
Murder, 73, 217
 commandment not to, 78, 111, 233
 mass, 73

Mysticism, 153, 157, 197, 200, 215
Myth, 48, 157

Naïveté
 philosophical, 100
Nancy, Jean-Luc, 217, 219n3
Narrative, 80
Nationalism, 31
Nature
 uniformity of, 163
Nazism (National Socialism), 30, 51n15, 70, 72, 73, 82, 126-127, 211
Nearness. *See* Proximity
Necessity, 46
Need, 153. *See also* Desire
Negation, 41, 137, 143, 146
 of negation, 200
Negativity, 96, 130
Neighbor, 17, 26-27, 31, 32, 54, 55, 71, 78-79, 80, 97, 117, 167, 198, 218, 231
 stranger in the, 153
Neuter, 96, 154
Niederland, William G., 69, 75, 75n2, 75n3, 76n6, 76n7, 76n8, 76n9, 76n12, 76n13, 76n14, 76n17
Nietzsche, 27, 33, 48, 52n18, 159, 166, 186, 196, 198, 199, 200, 201, 203, 204, 209n2, 211, 214, 216, 229
"No", 200-203
Noesis
 and noema, 147
Nominative, 42, 45, 47, 55, 56
Non-indifference, 71, 170
Nothing
 of God, 200-201, 203
Nought (*Nicht*), 200
Noumenon, 225, 228
Nourishment, 188
Nozick, Robert, 67n12
Nudity, 154
Numen, 225
Nyssa, Gregory of, 195
Objectification
Objectivity, 154, 194
Obligation, 55, 99, 144, 215
 feeling or sense of, 163
Obliqueness, 232
Obsession, 27, 28, 30, 33, 48, 54, 55, 56,

70-71, 80, 96, 108, 116, 167, 231
O'Connor, Noreen, 118n4
Odysseus, 174
One, 26
One-for-the-Other (*l'un pour l'autre*),
  31, 44, 56, 75, 96, 144, 168
Onto-theology, 22, 181, 200
Ontology, 144, 167, 185, 205
  and the ontic, 166
  and theology, 52n17
  "breaking" of, 163
  categories of, 48, 80
  fundamental, 87
  language of, 33
  originarity of, 87
  phenomenological, 188
Openness, 167
Opinion, 162, 167, 170. *See also* Belief *and* Doxa
Oppressor, 77-85
Optative, 41
Origin, 88, 206
  as paradoxical duality, 89
  deconstruction of, 88-93
Other, *passim*
  and the Others, 49
  as *Autrui*, 50n3, 178, 189, 191, 208, 218
  as God. *See* God
  as stranger, 80
  general (*Autre*), 178
  in the self (*l'autre dans le même*), 45, 56
  misery and poverty of, 81
  other than the, 218-219, 232
  pain and fault of, 80
  solidarity with the, 109, 116
Ought, *vs.* is, 42, 59
Ousia, 186
Outside (*au dehors*), 44
Overprinting (*sur-impression*), 177

Paganism, 197
Paradox, 89, 96-97, 102, 166, 185-186
Parmenides, 152, 162, 214
Parousia, 181, 230
Participation, 157, 164
Pascal, 58n2, 113, 189
Passion, 47-48, 213

Passive, 47-48
Passivity, 28, 30, 45, 48, 56, 129, 190
  passivity of, 56, 72, 97, 167
Past, 50n1, 87, 111, 177
Past, immemorial, 56, 57, 87, 91, 111, 173, 177, 190. *See also* Immemorial
Paternity, 120n10
Patience, 47, 174-175
Peirce, C.S., 227
Peperzak, Adriaan, 219n2
Persecuted
  solidarity with the, 82, 86n4
Persecution, 27-28, 30, 32, 48, 69-75, 77-85, 108, 115
Persons
  as multiple modes of transcendence, 84
Peut-être, 205-206
Pharisees, 158
Phenomenology, 28, 87, 88, 96, 100, 166, 167, 186
  French, 107
Phenomenon, 87, 89, 100, 226, 228
  vs. noumenon, 127, 228
Philo, 195
Philosophy, 41, 50n4, 60, 62, 100, 163, 166, 186
  and religion, 151, 152
  failure of, 102
  moral, 60
  history of, 84
  of life, 162, 164, 166
  pluralism in, 84-85
  positive, 207
  social, 163
  universality of, 84-85
  rooted in a specific kind of experience, 84-85
Photography, 226
Physis, 186, 201
Place, 55
  and non-place, 44, 47, 72
  "my p. in the sun", 113
Plato, xv, 21, 23n5, 48, 49, 52n17, 56, 59, 60, 110, 138, 157, 165, 165, 174, 186, 187, 188, 194, 195, 196, 226
Platonism, 21, 196, 198
  Christian, 195
Play, 46, 54
Plotinus, 185, 195

Pluralism, 63, 130
Plurality
　human or social, 89
Poetry, 137, 147
Poiesis, 84
Politics, 27, 35, 230
　and theology, 224, 232
　differing from tyranny of totality, 90
　incapable of finding a general criterion outside of itself for deducing its rules, 91
　institutional dimension of, 92
　non-political limit of, 90
　originarity of, 88
　symbolic character of, 92
Possession, 116, 153
Pour-soi, 60
Power, 205
　raising to a, 72
Pre-beginning, 45-46, 56
Pre-original, pre-originary, 87-93, 129, 163-164, 190, 208
Presence, 97, 108
　metaphysics of, 178
　ontological, 159n4
Present, 50n1, 178
　presence of the, 87
Presentation, 112
Priest, ascetic, 33
Primary
　primacy of the, 87
Procreation. *See* Fecundity
Prod-esse, 44
Profile, 231, 232
Project, 112
Projection, 111, 114-115
Proper, 46
Property, 226-227
Prophecy, 30, 161, 167, 170, 217-218
Protention, 54-55
Proust, Marcel, 138, 140-141
Provocation, 98
Proximity, 16-23, 26, 28, 31, 32-33, 49, 55, 56, 71, 88, 97, 98, 108, 167, 189, 224, 225, 231
Pseudo-Dionysius, 185, 195
Psyche, 75
　objective, 111, 115
Psychoanalysis, 70, 127
　Jungian analytical, 114-116
Psychosis, 71, 96
Punctuality, 178

Rachi, 77
Rawls, John, 56, 60-61, 67n4, 67n6
Rationality
　contemplative, 154
　instrumental, 154
　responsible, 154
Reality, 61, 126
　as rational, 84
　objective, 61, 66
Reason, 41
　enlarged (*élargie*), 43
Reciprocity, 64, 174, 231
　lack of, 43, 65
Recognition, 29, 90, 174, 177
Rectitude, 230
Recurrence, 32, 42, 46-47, 56
Reduction, 167
　Freudian, 111
　phenomenological, 128
　transcendental, 168
Reference, 177
Reflection, 141
Regress, 103
Reimarus, 162
Relation, metaphysical, 90
Religion, 48, 90-91, 229
　as adrift, 151, 156, 158-159
　degeneration of, 156-157
　dialectical character of, 197
　philosophy of, 161-152, 167, 169-171
　relation to ethics, 152-156
　r. of disruptive prophetic proclamation, 197
　r. of manifestation, 197
　tyrannical, 156
Repetition, 72, 103, 145-146
Representation, 57, 72, 80, 83, 119n7
Republic, 11-12. *See also* State
Resemblance, 80, 138
Resignation
　infinite, 217
Responding
　before or to (*répondre devant* or *à*), 49, 78

for (*répondre de*), 49, 50n3, 78
    for oneself (*se répondre*), 48, 56
Response, 31, 39-52, 54, 110
Responsibility, 7-11, 17, 26, 28-29, 33-34, 39-52, 77, 96, 164, 165, 170, 179, 204, 206, 215, 219, 230, 232
    as excessive, 99
    as relation to the trace, 173-182
    for others, 49, 53, 64, 97, 190, 212
    for the other, *vs.* self-responsibility, 43-46, 49
    for the responsibility of others, 47, 55
    limit of, 230
Responsivity, 116
Ressentiment, 198
Retention, 54-55
Re-tracing (*re-trait*), 177
Revelation, 176, 180, 191, 206, 226
Reversal, 44
Rhetoric, 167
Ricoeur, Paul, 50n1, 50n2, 109, 111, 114, 120n11, 120n13, 170, 171n8, 197
Rickert, Heinrich, 164
Riddle. *See* Enigma
Righteousness, 158
Rimbaud, Arthur, 114, 187, 192n2
Rosenzweig, Franz, 7, 18-19, 20, 21, 23n1, 23n6, 195, 199, 200-204, 206, 207, 209n1, 209n3, 209n3, 223, 229

Sache selbst, 154
Sacred, 158, 197, 230
    vs. holy, 156
Sacrifice, 90, 217
Sacrilege, 218
Said (*Dit*), 30, 40
    ontological, 87
Sages (*Tannaim*), 20, 22
Same (*le Même*), 63, 146, 164, 178, 213, 215
    vs. the Other, 118n6, 177, 189
    eternal return of the, 56
Sandel, Michael, 67n3
Sartre, Jean-Paul, xiii, 60, 107, 111, 120n12, 171
Saussure, Fernand de, 202-203, 209n5
Saying (*Dire*), 10-11, 44, 62, 65, 130
    sincerity of, 101
    vs. Said, 4, 42, 46, 62, 64, 66, 104, 111, 118n6, 128, 144-145, 204
    vs. Unsayable, 144-145
Scheler, Max, 107
Schelling, F.W.J., 201, 204, 207
Schneider, Monique, 118n4
Scholem, Gershom, 197
Schopenhauer, Artur, 110
Science, 66, 128, 162, 171
    as *episteme* or *Wissenschaft*, 154, 162
    opposed to opinion (*doxa*), 162, 167
Self (*le soi*), 45-46, 62, 167, 175, 178
    and Ego, 112
    concern for, 49
    consummation of, 215
    giving up of, 219
    identification, 213
Self-consciousness, 190
Selfhood, 47
Self-interest, 60
Selflessness, 165
Self-responsibility, 39-41, 43
    enlarged (*élargie*), 43
    for the other (*sich verantworten*), 45, 53
Semiotics, 154
Sensation, 137
Sense (*Sinn*)
    and non-sense, 96, 215, 219
Sensibility, 80, 190
Sentence, 202-204
    frames, 202
Separation, 14-15, 22, 56, 78, 91, 168, 191
Shekhinah, 9
Shoah, the. *See* Holocaust
Sign, 128, 129, 138, 146-147, 154, 173, 177
Signature, 203
Signification, 54, 56, 57, 62, 87, 96, 173
Signifier
    and signified, 128, 154, 155, 177
Simultaneity, 177
Singularity, 225
Site, 79, 230
Sittlichkeit, 158, 217
Skepticism, 101, 206
Socialism, 141
Sociality, 64, 65
Society, 88, 91
    exteriority of with respect to itself, 91
    ontological principle of, 88
Socrates, 48

Solicitude, 81
Solipsism, 62-63
Solitude, 141
Soul, 75, 162
Space, 13-15
    curvature of, 15
Speech, 54, 128
    breaking of, 74
    constative acts of, 205
    denotative acts of, 176, 205
    ideal situation of, 61, 65
    illocutary acts of, 203
    locutary acts of, 203
    performative, 176
    vs. writing, 64
Speaking, 46, 164
    possibility of, 213
Spinoza, 153, 189, 213
Spontaneity, 28, 32
State, 90, 168, 214
Stoicism, 48
Stranger, 79, 164
    in the neighbor, 153
Structuralism
    and poststructuralism, 154
Subject, 42, 51n6, 60, 167
    decentering of, 155
Subjection, 42, 97
Subjectivity, 28, 31, 42, 72, 97, 103, 153, 167, 185, 213
    passive, 98-99, 200
Substitution, 43-45, 47-48, 50, 51n10, 53, 56, 64, 78, 80, 96, 110, 112, 115, 144, 165, 167, 189, 190, 219
Suffering, 47-48, 69, 155, 158, 187, 204, 214, 215
    suffering of the, 72
Superlative, 72
Supplement, 154
Surplus, 90, 175, 215, 219
Survivor syndrome, 69, 75
Suspicion
    hermeneutic of, 111
    of ideologies, 170
Symbol, 108, 110, 111, 114-116, 126
Synchronicity, 232
Synchrony, 110, 113, 118n1
Syntax, 31
System, 72

Talmud, 9, 152, 155, 183n16
Teaching, 15, 62
Technology, 229
Teleological suspension, 153
    of the ethical, 219
    of the religious, 154-159
Teleology, 42, 45, 112
Tenderness, 72
Tephillin (phylacteries)
    of God, 180
Text
    textuality of the, 103
Thematization, 48, 56, 57, 71, 164, 167, 206
    as generalization, 164-165
    inversion of, 166
Theology, 152, 173, 179, 205, 232
    and the political, 224, 232
    crisis of, 155
    liberation, 155, 195-196
    natural, 164, 168, 170
    natural *vs.* revealed or supernatural, 157, 162, 170
    negative, 137, 180, 200
    not a science, 161
    philosophical, 157-158, 169, 185
    positive, 199, 200, 207
Theophany, 179-181
Theoria, 84
Theosophy, 157
Thereby, 203
"There is", 214. *See Il y a* and *Es gibt*
Thinking
    grammatical, 200
Third, 40-41, 42, 43, 46, 48, 49, 88, 90, 91, 92, 128, 155, 167, 191, 196, 218, 230-231
Thomas Aquinas, 186, 195
Thou, 116
Thought, 174
    heterological, 100
    thinking more than it thinks, 98
Time, 13
    break-up of, 71, 72
    clock, 71
    closure of, 70
    of the other, 41, 175

quasi-, 190
sense of, 69
Torah, 8-9, 10
Totalitarianism, 213
Totality, 13, 89, 157, 163, 164, 225, 232
   breakup of, 164
Totalization, 90, 147
Touch, 72
Trace, 17, 46, 56-57, 72, 74, 83, 110, 112, 113, 116, 142, 154, 159n4, 173, 176, 177, 179, 218, 227, 232
   erasure of, 181
   sign-trace, 180
   trace of the, 178
Tracing-erasure, 178
Tradition, 29-30, 156
Transascendence, 186
Transcendence, 5, 13-15, 21, 22, 27, 79, 84, 92, 98, 137, 142-143, 147, 153, 169-170, 174, 176, 179, 181, 185, 193, 194, 200, 207, 218, 219, 227, 230
Transcendent, 64, 79
Transcendental, 27, 28, 65, 78, 163
   method or philosophy, 163, 167, 168
Transdecendence, 214
Transference, 111
Transgression, 186, 211
Trauma, 48, 70, 74, 96, 115, 126, 214
   immemorial, 74
Tribal, 30, 33-34
Truth, 80, 163
   and untruth, 128, 130
   persecuted, 213
   religious *vs.* propositional, 140
   triumphant *vs.* persecuted, 139
   vs. opinion, 162
Tyranny, 12, 90

Unconscious, 70, 71, 110, 112, 127, 128
Undecidability, 29, 103
Understanding , 166
Universality, 164
   despotism over individuals, 90
   political, 90
Universalization, 30-31
Univocity, 206

Unsaid, 30
Unsaying (*dédire*). *See* Saying
Unveiling, 176
Uprightness (*droiture*), 232. *See also* Rectitude
Utilitarianism, 188
Utopia, 50

Value, 109, 188
Verlaine, Paul, 187
Victimization, 49, 233
Violence, 48, 49, 69, 72, 78, 115, 137, 139, 186, 187, 214, 216, 230
   being subject to, 78
Vision, 153, 224
Voice
   second, 72
Vulnerability, 71, 74, 108, 129, 167

Wahl, Jean, xiii, 84, 86n9
Western philosophy, 78, 87, 165, 174
Will, 68-69, 110
   rôle in reduction, 168
Windelband, Wilhelm, 164
Withdrawal, 32, 176, 215
Witness, 33, 74, 231
Wittgenstein, Ludwig, 61-62, 63, 67n7, 67n8, 67n9
Work, 174. *See also* Labor
World, 175
   and earth, 187
   destruction, as phenomenological thought experiment, 214
Wound, 74, 115, 231

"Yes", 199-203, 206, 208
Yessence, 201
Yochanan, Rabbi, 77
You, 155, 191
Yugoslavia, 52n15, 126

Zwischenereignis, 44